3/15

Nancy,

Writing this book provided a route to greater peace. May your blessings be abundant.

Lovingly,
E. Marie Oberle

Outhouse to Penthouse

E. Marie Oberle, Ed.D.

Copyright © 2014 by E. Marie Oberle, Ed.D.

All rights reserved. No part of this book may be reproduced, scanned, or distributed in any printed or electronic form without permission.

First Edition: December 2014

Printed in the United States of America

ISBN: 9781939237-34-7

Published by Suncoast Digital Press, Inc.

Sarasota, Florida, USA

Table of Contents

Dedication and Acknowledgments	v
Foreword: By Chaplain Shane Dresen	vii
Introduction	1
Chapter 1: Early Childhood	5
Chapter 2: Looking For Greener Pastures	13
Chapter 3: Discovering Courage Within	19
Chapter 4: My Knight	31
Chapter 5: Early Years of Marriage	41
Chapter 6: Open to Opportunities	53
Chapter 7: Putting Down Roots	61
Chapter 8: Family in Transition	75
Chapter 9: Turning Points	87
Chapter 10: Unexpected Career Opportunities	103
Chapter 11: A Life to Savor	115
Chapter 12: A Test of Faith/A Family Affair	137
Chapter 13: Grief… A Necessary Process	147
Chapter 14: My Authentic Self	159
APPENDIX A: FAMILY TREE	171
APPENDIX B: ODE TO DADDY "O"	173
APPENDIX C: GEORGE'S MEMORIAL SERVICE	177
APPENDIX D: MARIE'S GEMS OF WISDOM	181
APPENDIX E: LETTERS FROM RICHMOND	183

Notes from the Author/Disclaimer

I have tried to recreate events, locales and conversations from my memories of them. In order to maintain their anonymity in some instances, I have changed the names of individuals and places. If you are mentioned by name and my account does not match your recollection, there was no offense intended.

—Marie Oberle

Dedication and Acknowledgments

This book is dedicated to my mother. It is:

    A celebration of my life

    A love letter to my family

    A legacy to my family

    A salute to strong women

My first great thanks go to our God, my silent partner. He directed me to tell my story and has contributed in unique and surprising ways. Now I need His direction and how best to use my story.

Next, my loving family was in total support throughout the process… suggesting ideas for the title, book cover, and anything I asked of them. The writing started as therapy.

The most directly involved and always available to me for advice, confirmation and coaching was Barbara Dee. With five chapters of my book done, the project was put on hold because of my dear husband, George's illness. Finally, two years after he died, I revisited the project and only felt lukewarm about its completion. I needed a professional opinion of what I had written. Knowing that George's hospice chaplain, Shane Dresen, had an editor he respected I contacted her. It was Barbara Dee's words of encouragement that got me back on track.

The end product is much more comprehensive than either of us perceived in the beginning. The book seemed to take on a life of its own as creative ideas were forthcoming. For example, I am a very private person and could easily write facts, but was not comfortable sharing my feelings. Little Emily became my crutch. Thus began the "organic process" (Barbara Dee's words). Whenever Barbara observed that I needed another resource, she made it happen. For example, she put me in touch with a writing coach, Chloe Rachel Galloway, for a few lessons in adding emotion and creating "scenes" in my narrative. This professional help was the icing on the cake; the book evolved into a product I feel proud to publish.

Every contact with my publisher, Suncoast Digital Press, Inc., has been helpful. In addition to Barbara, Martin Steele contributed valuable editing, and Ben Doherty somehow managed my too-many-to count photographs I just had to include for sentimental reasons. A huge thank you to my book team—Barbara Dee, of whom I have complete confidence, "had my back"; Chaplain Shane reacted to ideas, leaving the final word to Barbara Dee; and Chloe helped me write with more feeling. This team was there with encouragement and praise through the entire process. They have become dear friends.

Posthumous acknowledgment goes to my husband and soul mate. Much of this book reflects his imprint on my life. Writing this book has helped to fill the hole in my heart.

—Marie

Foreword
By Chaplain Shane Dresen

I would not have written some of the things in this book. I don't have that kind of raw courage.

I know Marie through her husband, George Oberle. At the end of his life, I had the privilege of being his hospice chaplain. In this very personal relationship, as one can imagine, I got to know the family quite well. I was glad I could be there for Marie, though her faith in God was what carried her through.

We had often barefooted the sandy beaches of Sarasota comparing life notes. Brief, well-crafted sketches were shared, testing if each other could handle the heavy freight coming. As I began to read the early drafts of this book, I was initially shocked. "Why didn't you tell me?" Tears running down her tired face, "I was too ashamed."

I assured her there was nothing to be ashamed of, that she had not done anything wrong. At the same time, I was impressed that she had the guts to tell the truth about her life; she wrote the book she told me God had encouraged her to write. To be so vulnerable, sharing such intimate issues of personal family life, almost feels like betrayal. Isn't it better to just keep the past in the past? Why not just put on that pretty face? Isn't it easier for us to continue masking the gut-wrenching events that shaped us, coping as best we can? But the inner turmoil takes a toll, forcing action.

And so Marie began to write the story of her life: the shattering of childhood; the anguish of horror dressing up in shame pretending all is well; the drive to be somebody, to rise to the top as a powerful and beautiful woman shattering the glass ceiling, confronting "this is a man's game."

Driven to succeed, she climbed higher, and yet the longings persisted. The mask was drawn ever tighter. She battled through the confusion of "who am I?" Like a professional actor who plays each part so well they lose their own identity, Marie finally faced her greatest challenge. Who am I? What have I become…is there a real me?

This book is the journey of that search, of struggle and heartache, of victory and defeat, but getting up and entering back into the game. I am reminded of words of Theodore Roosevelt:

It is not the critic who counts; not the man who points out how the strong man stumbles, or where the doer of deeds could have done them better. The credit belongs to the man who is actually in the arena, whose face is marred by dust and sweat and blood; who strives valiantly; who errs, who comes short again and again… who spends himself in a worthy cause; who at the best knows in the end the triumph of high achievement, and who at the worst, if he fails, at least fails while daring greatly, so that his place shall never be with those cold and timid souls who neither know victory nor defeat.

This is Marie's story—with all the wisdom of the above quote from a woman's point of view, in a different place and a different time. What a story it is!!

There is something about writing down one's own life experiences. I've heard that "by writing our old story, we find ourselves in the midst of a new story, one in which we have the freedom to be our true selves."

Marie's memoir, *Outhouse to Penthouse,* might just do that…help each of us find our true selves in our own story—and discovering courage within. Thank you, Marie.

—Shane Dresen, Hospice Chaplain and Author

Introduction

You can accept or reject the way you are treated by other people, but until you heal the wounds of your past, you will continue to bleed. You can bandage the bleeding with food, with alcohol, with drugs, with work, with cigarettes, with sex, but eventually, it will all ooze through and stain your life. You must find the strengths to open the wounds, stick your hands inside, pull out the core of the pain that is holding you in your past, the memories, and make peace with them.

—Lyanla Vanzant, *Yesterday, I Cried.*

Little, wide-eyed Emily, in your feed sack dress and Mona Lisa smile, since coming across your picture… your eyes have haunted me by the secrets they hold. I've tried a lifetime to bury you, along with my painful past, without succeeding.

When I intellectualized my life, I saw no reason why I could not move forward. However, I found that the truth has a way of catching up with you. I went through the motions of achieving success after success, but my inner voice kept telling me I would never be good at anything. I would fail at being a daughter, friend, lover, wife and mother. *Little Emily, I plead for your help… I need to know who I was, who I am.*

For over five decades, I felt poisoned by guilt for my perceived part in my mother's death, and ashamed for not taking ownership of my past. Even though I spent a lifetime trying with all my strength to repress my past, it continued to plague me at the most unexpected times. The unresolved grief for the loss of my mother has been a heavy burden to bear. Believing I could escape my torment by denying it, I chose to act as if I was like everyone else, though my impoverished childhood, broken family, and dead mother comprised a unique and tragic life script. My cover-up attempts have done more damage to my psyche than any other actions in my life.

Little Emily, I want to tell you where I am now in my life, so that you can understand why I continually tell myself, "Why go back to the pain of the past? Just continue to go forward." After all, I want my legacy defined by what I have accomplished, not by the past. Yet, I'm surprised by how much of my layered past life defines who I am. I guess I've been afraid to expose parts of my past for fear of being ridiculed, diminished or seen as flawed. I was in constant fear of being found out as unworthy, worried about not being accepted, and terrified of disconnection.

Not long ago, I was participating in a Bible study focusing on prayer. I felt a strong need for more purpose in my life, and was searching and praying for God to use me in a way that would help me give back to the many people who had contributed to my beautiful life.

Until November 2011, I lived with George, my husband and soul-mate, enjoying our retirement and our amazing family. I continue to live in our penthouse with an expansive balcony view of the Gulf of Mexico and the intra-coastal waterway. I am a woman who has had it all—but not at the same time. Based on outside appearances, my life may be envied by many. I have acquired a façade of confidence.

My day usually starts with appreciating the glorious and ever-changing sky. At times, the clouds look like the continuation of the sea, azure, grayish blue; other times, they look like balls of floating cotton. Today, they are mostly like white cotton candy in all shapes and sizes, but some are tinted pink by the sun shining above them. This view is visible from every room in our condo.

My routine is to quickly dress in comfortable yoga attire, plus walking shoes. After washing and creaming my face, I add a little coral lipstick, put on a straw hat so that I don't have to comb my short, warm-brown hair which I color to cover the gray. (When George was alive, I always brought in the newspaper from the hallway, so that he could leisurely read it in bed.)

With a cup of coffee in hand, I head for the beach, just across the street from my condo. I descend from the 10th floor to the lobby via the elevator and walk from my driveway across the street and through to the beach. According to coastal experts and trip advisors, Siesta Key has literally one of the most gorgeous beaches in the world. The sand is soft and as white as snow, 99.9% quartz crystal. It glistens in the sun and feels like walking in sugar. The Gulf of Mexico shoreline is never the same; it runs the gamut from being tranquil to being angry. The shades of blue and aqua flicker with the reflecting early sun. *Little Emily, can you comprehend such a place?*

An early morning walk is a Blessing for the whole day.

—Henry David Thoreau

My walk on the beach is a Blessing—God's presence and Nature's beauty fill my senses. As I walk down the wooden boardwalk, I see the waves rushing toward me, like a lover's arms welcoming; each individual has his or her own relationship with the gulf…I have a love affair.

I feel so free and open to the wonders of nature. In a dreamy way, my mind often wanders: *Will I see dolphins jumping playfully in their natural habitat? Will I see seagulls in their usual groups facing the sun? Will the little sanderlings be scampering at the edge of the water, looking for food? Will I see any loggerhead turtle tracks made while locating a spot in the sand to lay their eggs? What shells washed up overnight? How many fishing boats will be anchored in my view? Will the sand sculptures from yesterday remain, or have they been demolished? Will I see my usual people walking?*

My mind feels free and welcoming. *You see, little Emily, this is a major highlight of my day.* I've even stopped women, to whom I have said "good morning" many times, to become better acquainted. I wonder how I am perceived by other walkers? I'm a 120 pound, 5'3", older retired woman, but not matronly looking. I actually work at staying fit and attempt to defy the aging process. I am a curious person, especially when it comes to people. It is during my daily walk that I count my blessings and plan my day.

On one bright sunny morning, April 4, 2008, I nearly took my sensuous surroundings for granted and treated my walk as a chore to complete. Instead of feeling the light warm breeze caressing my skin, smelling the freshness of the salty ocean air and my usual feeling of gratitude and awe, I walked at a fast pace, swinging my arms and making a mental list of must-do tasks before leaving that day for a six-week stay in our Oklahoma home. As I came to the place a considerable way down the beach called Point of Rocks, I hurriedly turned around to return.

What occurred was profound! I had an awesome feeling of mental alertness, like my mind was being controlled by someone else. I was oblivious to my surroundings and in complete compliance as my spirit seemed to be joined by the spirit of a higher power. *Was God finally answering my prayers?* This possessed feeling was like nothing I ever experienced; it was something like being hypnotized. I felt someone was present but not visible to me.

"Marie, it's time to write your book," the presence said to me.

I don't even like to write, I thought. *How can this be? I've been praying for ways to serve others. How will this help others?* I continued my walk as if in a daze while chapter titles were revealed to me. I wondered, *does this mean including the good, the bad, and ugly?* Well, I didn't really want to remember the ugly, the struggle of essentially being on my own at age 13, the pain, the shame and the guilt. I questioned, *does God think I need to heal before I can adequately give back? Or is he telling me the book will accomplish both?*

I thought I had done just fine building a good and joy-filled life without ever dredging up the past that I so desperately tried to forget. I had buried it so deeply that I could usually pretend it didn't even exist. Yet, I knew that with God's help, I would tell my story. Through God, all things are possible; this notion sunk slowly into my body. My mind no longer racing, I knew with absolutely clarity that I would write a book!

God even gave me a title: *Celebration of Life*. I thought, *Yes, I do have a life to celebrate, but I only want to celebrate part of it. Don't hate me, Little Emily… but I don't want to remember you. I can't identify with the one little school picture I have of you. That's poor little Emily. I'm Marie.* (Yet I have this photo enlarged and displayed in my bedroom.) *I've been studying your eight-year-old face. Your eyes say so much. I wish I could look out from those eyes—to be you, looking out—but I cannot.*

The book, my memoir, started to take shape in my mind. To begin, I needed to chronicle what happened in my life from 1932 to 1943, when my angel (my mother) rescued me. I have tears in my eyes as I search for answers to my many questions. *What are you thinking; what are you feeling? Are you happy; are you sad; are you hungry; are you cold? Do you have dreams of your mother? Do you have goals? Are you just trying to survive?*.

In trying to make sense of my life, I've come to think of it as a giant puzzle. As a child, there were few pieces to fit together. To survive and grow, we all need to fulfill basic needs —food, shelter, love, and cuddling and diapering to feel safe and secure. This is the base of Maslow's (1943) hierarchy of needs. Contacts are limited mostly to family. If we have these, all the pieces fit to make our life puzzle complete—a baby thrives in that environment.

Little Emily, you are missing some of those puzzle pieces—something's missing in your life to help you feel secure. I feel that you are searching—you missed the love, cuddling and comfort needed to make you feel good about life, and about yourself. Sometimes, you went to bed hungry. Sometimes, you were fearful, and no one comforted you. You don't even have the pieces necessary to form the foundation needed to continue up the hierarchy of needs. Toddlers are usually given simple puzzles which they quickly learn to put together to see the full picture. You never had the necessary puzzle pieces, nor did you ever have a puzzle.

Maslow's theory is that people are motivated to achieve certain needs. When one need is fulfilled, a person seeks to fulfill the next, and so on. Maslow states, "The need to fulfill such needs will become stronger the longer the duration they are denied." *Little Emily, you are already behind on Maslow's ladder with basic needs being first, followed by safety, social needs, esteem, and lastly, self-actualization.*

I acknowledge that I need to recall my painful past. I'm asking God to give me the courage to relive the pain, guilt and insecurity of my childhood—and to complete the mission He has for me. While reading a daily devotional, I was led to read 2 Corinthians 3:1-11. I did, and writing my memoir made more sense. I was reminded that we are Christ's "letters of recommendation" to all who read about our lives. I closed my Bible and took a deep breath, and I answered the whisper within by exhaling all my resistance. I thanked God for helping me understand. He would help me triumph over the complexities of my circumstances.

Psychologists say that once you confront what haunts you, it no longer has power over you. This thought is comforting; it could lead to freedom and even peace of mind. I thought, for my memoir to be authentic, the title should be *Outhouse to Penthouse*. My life evolved from being a "field hand" to living in a penthouse. *So you see, Little Emily, this is where you come in... I'm asking for your help in remembering those early years, when just surviving was the constant focus and indoor plumbing was beyond our means. I need you to help me remember who I used to be, and together, we will explore how I got to where I am.*

Our Oklahoma home turned out to be the perfect environment to develop the game plan for my book. It was a new, ranch-style, brick, open floor plan, nestled between large pecan trees, and built on the Floistad's three-acre lot. Our daughter and family live only a "stone's throw" away. Here, we celebrated my 77th birthday, gained the family's insight and support for my book and set my completion date for April 7, 2012, my 80th birthday. I thought, *this is God's plan for me; I hope he knows that he will have to take the lead. I only know how to record research, not write a book.*

Outhouse to Penthouse is the story of my life as I remember it—what I've been told and what I discovered in my research. Uncovering repressed memories is a bit scary—and for the most part, torture. My intention was not only to revisit and heal my past, but also to tell my story of a girl growing up during the Great Depression, yet finding her way along the path to the American Dream. It has been documented many times that the era in which we are born contributes to who we are as a person. Thus, I include highlights of world events in each of the decades included in my book, as well as the changing role of women. These add new pieces to fit into my life's puzzle.

Even the best of plans often need adjusting. I completed the first five chapters of *Outhouse to Penthouse* before my dear husband became seriously ill in 2008. The remainder of this book was written after my George's death in 2011. Completing it without the help and support of my soul-mate was more difficult than I could ever have imagined. It seems like all of my memories are bittersweet, but I feel that God wants me to finish my journey. He keeps putting encouragement in front of me in interesting and unusual ways. He is guiding and giving me the courage to get out of my comfort zone, take risks, relive and record my therapeutic journey from <u>my outhouse to my penthouse</u>.

Little Emily, this will be a self-exploration to discover the necessary pieces to complete our life puzzle, and then we will be one and the same. I feel so grateful to be shown this means to that end. "Inspired" is a word which comes from Latin roots meaning "God-breathed." *Now I look to you, Emily, for inspiration to complete this daunting task and write the story of my life.* Perhaps others will be inspired to move through their pain, guilt, or shame, and evolve and grow through their experience.

Chapter 1

Early Childhood

I did not lose myself all at once. I rubbed out my face over the years, washing away my pain, the same way carvings on stone are worn down by water.

— Amy Tan

Yes, life batters us, whether we are rich or poor, public or private. My wound is like a slow, silent hemorrhage of the soul. On the outside, I look as if I've got my act together, but I encounter those dark, stormy days when I feel very small, very fragile, and very frightened, as if I might shatter into a thousand pieces and break into heartrending sobs at something as simple as a "How are you?" This is my life.

I came into the world on April 7, 1932 in rural Kentucky during the darkest, most desperate times in American history. This was three years into the Great Depression. History reminds us that farmers were struggling with low prices for their products, going bankrupt and losing their farms. The weather was even against them—the "Dirty '30s" were known for dust storms, insects, summer heat and winter cold. The national unemployment rate was 25%. From 1920 through 1932, there was a 50% drop in household income nationwide. Farmers, especially young people, were losing hope and moving away because of the "grinding poverty and shattered family relations." Schools were shortening their days or closing their doors. By 1935, of 10 million high-school-age Americans, four million were out of school. Twenty-five thousand teenagers, boys and girls, were "riding the rails", a term describing the desperate and dangerous practice of hopping aboard freight trains to leave the family farm in search of a paying job. "It was a terrible way to live," recalled a 15-year old who rode the rails for three years. "It was rough and dangerous, but there was also a mystical quality, not knowing what tomorrow would bring."

"I have moments of real terror when I think we may be losing this generation," said First Lady Eleanor Roosevelt, who made that era's youth problem her personal crusade.

Another way teenagers and young adults were getting away from home was by taking the gamble to start their own families, even when they were not able to support themselves. Such was the case of my parents. I have been told that at age 20, my father, Dillard Whittymore—a muscular, dark-haired lad with sad brown eyes and an olive complexion—was working his parents' farm when he was charmed by a flirty, petite, hard-working neighbor girl, 15-year-old Margaret "Maggie" Ledger. Today, they would be considered children themselves. However, in that era, and in their circumstances, they were surely more mature than people their age in later generations. They were married April 1, 1929 in Clay County, Kentucky. I wonder what hopes and dreams they could have had at that dark time in our history. It must have been a universal thought that "life cannot get any worse." I want to believe there was good chemistry between mother and dad, and that they were in love.

I am told that I was named after my paternal great grandmother, Emily Marie Whittymore, whom I never knew. There are many things and people I maybe knew, or should remember, but do not. In fact, only disjointed pieces of those painful years as a farmer's small child exist in my memory. Trying to re-inhabit my childhood seems impossible. I've moved through so many decades, all the time trying to block past memories. There is one image that, by Divine Providence, is wholly preserved and is with me today, even after over seven decades of neglect: the second-grade photograph of Little Emily you see on the cover of this book. Her clear eyes have not faded and seem to be urging me to sharpen my memories for her sake. Discovering Little Emily has motivated me to find answers to questions I should have asked in my childhood. Emily serves as a crutch… learning about someone else… not me. But we are one and the same. Those were such unhappy, anguishing times; it is no wonder my psyche remembers so little. I've often referred to my situation as being hatched. I was born and learned to survive, even to excel.

And yet I know those survival skills have served me all my life, including today, and I shall forever be grateful. My faith assures me that the right circumstances and the right people are already here and will show up with what I need for my journey. I have a strong need to look back at my parents' actions, as well as my own, with more empathy and compassion. I need to be able to understand experiences in the context in which they happened and to do all of this without judgment. My memoir may be laced with sadness, even bitterness—but the overriding theme is gratitude.

According to the 1930 census, my parents lived in Jackson County, Kentucky, and they were caring for four children, ages one, two, four, and six. When Mother became pregnant, the children were temporarily dispersed to other family members. This wasn't unusual in those times; without access to medical doctors, antibiotics, child welfare and so forth, lives were cut short by tuberculosis, cholera, childbirth, accidents, various infections, economic disasters and environmental threats. Families made their own rules as they adapted to early deaths.

The 1930s were truly hard times with multiple hardships to endure. My family was only one of many families going through unbearable times. *Little Emily, I've tried to imagine what it was like, during the Great Depression, to have so much responsibility with little education and very limited opportunities.*

My older sister, Helen, was born in 1930, when our mother was only 16 years old; our younger sister, Rhoda, was born in 1934. Parents of all ages focused on survival for themselves and for their families. Children were often taken out of school to work the farm. My parents' early years of marriage appeared to consist of farming and having children. Without birth control and little or no money to spend on entertainment, sex was likely a cheap way to find distraction, diversion and pleasure. Also, I've read that in agrarian times, large families were the norm as they provided much-needed workers for the farm. I wonder if Dad was disappointed that his first three children were girls. *Little Emily, I so want to believe that my mother and dad had some happy times.*

In late 1934, when Rhoda was only a few months old, my mother took her to Cincinnati, Ohio, to visit her sister, Dovie (Ledger) Hicks, and did not return. I have been told that Dad bullied Mother into returning Rhoda to the farm. Perhaps he expected Mother to also stay. However, she returned Rhoda to Dad, but had other plans for herself; they did not include living on the farm. I'm told her goal was to find the means to a better life for herself and her girls. *Little Emily, how frightening this must have been for her to take this enormous step.* It must have also been overwhelming being a single father with a baby, a two-year-old and a four-year-old. Fortunately, Dad had some family in the area. Aunt Drucy (the aunt who raised Mother), whom I don't remember, assisted in our care.

Little Emily, do you remember being left alone much of the time? The first memory of my childhood is a scene where my sisters and I are huddled in a corner, crying. *Our house was on fire!* Dad was out in the fields planting tobacco. I don't remember how we girls got out of the house, but I recall seeing household items being tossed out the second floor windows. For years, I had nightmares and would wake up coughing and feeling strangled from inhaling the smoke. Repeatedly, I would see our house totally engulfed in flames. Those nightmares are so embedded in my psyche that, decades later, I shared this with an interpreter of dreams. His interpretation was: "You were not ready for the changes in your life and were fighting against them. Alternatively, it could be highlighting passion and love for those around you."

Little Emily, as I look back, I've tried to put myself in Dad's shoes and imagine the helplessness he must have felt...yes, I know—you never once saw him smile. He was likely asking himself, "Where do we go from here?" I pray that his faith was a resource for comfort. Some times were in fact peaceful, all beings consumed in the rhythm of farm work, but there was little joy experienced by anyone. It wasn't unique to our family; thousands of other families were in the same boat. This was a time for striking out on a new path, if the old one turned up short. John and Drucy Ledger must have taken us into their home after the fire.

My second memory of my childhood was of a major change in the household. I gained a stepmother, Polly, a stepsister, Ruby (eight years old, like my sister, Helen), and a stepbrother, Harold, who was six years old, like me. This was in March 1938. I don't remember a wedding, but I assume they were married by a justice of the peace. A wedding would have required more financial resources than they had. Polly, a small, stern-looking woman with short, curly, light brown hair, was two years older than Dad and had been widowed for five years. Her husband had died of tuberculosis. We four Whittymores moved into her house. All the houses we lived in looked much the same: frame two-story, peeling paint, broken windows, small porches with broken boards, two chimneys (one to carry smoke from the wood burning stove in the kitchen and one to carry smoke from the potbellied iron stove in the living room) overgrown weeds, and broken-down farm equipment in the yard.

I don't remember much about the integration of the families, except no one appeared very happy—especially my older sister, Helen. She felt that Ruby, Polly's daughter, was treated more favorably than she. Ruby didn't like Helen, and the feeling was mutual. Ruby was able to work inside the house, while Helen worked in the fields and was treated poorly and punished often. It seemed to me to be without reason. I can hear Polly say to Helen in her high, shrill voice, "Go fetch me a switch and make it a big one." Polly left large welts on Helen's legs by repeatedly hitting her with the switch. I felt like defending my sister and attacking Polly, but I was helpless and hoped that Dad would stop her. He remained silent with a sad look on his face. As young faces stared daggers through Polly, she would say, "You other young'uns will get the same thing if you interfere." Rhoda and I also experienced the switches, but not as frequently as Helen.

Generally, it was work as usual but with more mouths to feed and hands to do the chores and the farm work: feed the livestock, gather the eggs, milk the cows, work in the garden and the fields, carry water into the house from the pump, help with laundry, et cetera. I can remember how I hated my least favorite job, milking the cows. The udder was always dirty with manure, which I had to clean off, and then I had trouble squeezing hard enough to get any milk.

Though they undoubtedly figured their partnership could bring at least some improvement to their struggling lives, Dad and Polly's early years of marriage were plagued by hardships and poverty. However, neither had known any other way of life. Winters were particularly challenging without running water and electricity. All four girls slept in one bed. This wasn't all bad in the winter; it helped us stay warm. *Little Emily, I tried to visualize four giggling girls in one bed sharing stories, but I can't.* Everyone must have been too exhausted, and they wouldn't have had anything to laugh about.

Light came from kerosene lamps. We had some heat from the wood burning stove in the living room and the cook stove in the kitchen. Without a telephone, radio, newspapers or neighbors nearby, there was almost no communication with the outside world. What a bleak existence!

A major change during that first year of marriage was the first schooling for Helen and Ruby. They were both eight years of age. I wondered why Harold and I, both six years old, didn't attend. I can only assume we were needed for chores. Fortunately, Polly owned a treadle sewing machine and could make school clothes. At that time, feed for the cattle came in colorful sacks—Polly used these sacks to make dresses and bloomers for the girls and shirts for Harold. We children took turns kneeling on the floor and manually moving the treadle of the sewing machine so that Polly would not tire so readily with long hours of sewing. There was little variety in our wardrobes, as the style of the dresses usually looked the same, but the feed sacks came in many colors.

Harold and I started school the following year at age seven. Rhoda started school the next year at the traditional age of six. We all walked barefooted to a one-room school with one teacher for 12 grades. Attendance at school was sporadic, since chores came first. An added chore, a pleasant one, was the care of a new half-brother, Dillard Junior, who was born in 1940.

Our diet depended on what was raised on the farm. I have fond memories of "butchering day!" Whether it was pork or beef, the smell of fresh cooked meat was tantalizing! Even today, I remember the delicious smell and taste. Of course, at the time, I had no grocery-store-bought meat for comparison, but now I can say it just doesn't compare in flavor. The only fleeting sense of having "enough" was when we had that abundance of meat at butchering time. What we couldn't eat fresh was smoked or dried. The butchering itself made me nauseous—all that blood—and I felt sorry for the poor animals. I don't recall how the animals were killed, but I hope it was humane. The attitude regarding killing an animal for food seem to be that providing food for the table was their role in life. The animals were part of the farmer's economics, as were the Whittymore sisters.

I remember using the skirt of my feed sack dress to wipe the dirt off fresh vegetables and eat them in the garden. I especially liked the tender peas, juicy ripe tomatoes, carrots, and radishes. Also, we had fruit trees—apples and peaches. Of course, without refrigeration, it was necessary to can most of our fruits and vegetables. We did have a deep, covered hole in the ground that was called a cellar. This kept fruits and vegetables cooler, so they would last longer. The worst stomach ache I can remember was from eating too many green apples. (I knew better, but I was *hungry* and they tasted so good.) I was always hungry when I walked home from school, but we had to immediately get to our chores. It had also been a bad day at school, so I needed something for comfort. I could not expect human comfort, a kind word or a hug… so I ate green apples. Perhaps my subconscious thought I would get some attention; no such thing.

Little Emily, you're missing so many of your puzzle pieces—things that make you feel secure. I feel you searching. You missed the love, cuddling, nurturing and comfort needed to make you feel good about your life and about yourself. You so wanted love and a feeling of belonging. How else could you feel whole?

Food often became scarce between harvesting crops and butchering. Wild game, such as squirrels and rabbits, were a big part of our diet. If we didn't eat what was served on our plates, we went hungry. In time, I learned to eat almost everything. I even liked dandelion greens, but I didn't like gathering them. Certainly, everything on the farm that was edible was efficiently used. Farms in that era were largely self-sustaining. Nothing was thrown away; it was recycled.

I've described the house, but not the surroundings. To the right of the house was the cellar, then a dirt road driveway with a dilapidated pickup truck. Beyond that was a large garden. Behind the house was the outhouse, and beyond that was a fairly dilapidated barn with two stalls for cows and one for the work horse. To the left of that were some chicken coops with fields beyond.

There was a tremendous amount of work to be done on the farm, from early morning until late at night, to provide for the needs of our big family as well as to raise crops for sale. I remember the back-breaking job, in the sweltering heat, working in the tobacco fields and having to remove worms from the plants. Each of the many, many worms was long, green, fat and ugly. We had to squash them with rocks or sticks or anything lying around—and they were filled with awful looking brownish-green fluid. UGH! But, tobacco was the crop that Dad could depend on to sell in order to have money for seed, plants, and food for the animals to sustain the farm.

In addition to farming, Dad worked briefly in a coal mine in Harlem County, Kentucky. I can still see him returning home with his clothes and skin covered with coal soot and dirt. He wore a helmet-like cap with a carbide lamp attached. A miner's light was essential to his labor, but catastrophic if it ignited the methane gas present in the dark, dangerous environment. Mining was (and continues to be) very dangerous. Miners faced death from collapsing mines, oxygen deprivation, accidents and lung disease. Most of the time, Dad returned home tired and angry. To vent his anger, he commonly threw any item near him. Any of us children in sight would run and hide. We feared being disciplined with his belt. His punishment was harsh. As I look back, I feel it is amazing that conditions at home were not worse. It was a time of widespread economic struggle, and actually, we were fortunate to grow up on a farm during the Great Depression. I knew hunger, but most of the time we had food, while thousands ate in soup kitchens, or went without food.

It has helped me better understand my early life by reviewing what was going on in our country during my childhood. In James Condo Rains' book, *A Child of the Depression*, he writes: "The 1930s were the toughest and the darkest 10 years of the American 20th century. It was the decade of the 1930s that tempered and toughened the children of the Depression who later became the World War II generation." Tom Brocroft, in his book, *The Greatest Generation*, states: "One was expected to be tough ... there was no tolerance for weakness." I was so very wrong in suppressing my childhood memories just because they were painful. More recently, I have read extensively about the Great Depression and this has made a tremendous difference in my thinking. I now have great admiration for Dad, Polly and Mother for finding the means to survive during such difficult times! Many did not have their courage.

Studs Terkel, in his book, *Hard Times,* reminds us that the coal and lumber industries were hit hard prior to 1929 when banking and big businesses suffered. "People had nothing to live on, and children fainted in school from hunger long before the stock market crash," he states. On Wall Street, stocks dropped from as high as $115 a share to a mere worth of $2 each. People were devastated and felt hopeless to the extreme. It wasn't unusual for stockbrokers to jump out of their Wall Street office windows, thinking they were saving their family the shame. Other men killed their families and then themselves because they couldn't see any future. Some people who used to drive a Cadillac found themselves humbled and grateful to at least have shoes, since walking was now their only means of getting around.

It is hard to imagine how desperate people felt, and that it only went from bad to worse. Once a job was lost due to a company's severe financial woes, there were no other jobs to be found. It was usual for a thousand men to wait in line all day for three or four job openings. Normally law-abiding, honest people were driven to desperate measures: People were stealing clothes off others' clotheslines, milk from back porches, and chickens from a neighbor's barn just to survive. "This was the time of crushed hopes and shattered dreams," Terkel states. The most consistent feeling described by the historians and authors was **fear**. Families were forced to give up idealism, and even their core values, in order to deal with the reality of having to do whatever it took to stay alive.

Little Emily, in my life, I have learned that in all catastrophes, there is the potential for benefit. I found it enlightening, reading about all that was going on in the world while my family, in our isolation, remained oblivious. The following are examples of the indomitable creative spirit in those times:

1930

Brother Can You Spare a Dime is written by E. W. Harbor; it went on to be viewed as an anthem of the shattered dreams of the era.

1932

Pearl S. Buck wins the Pulitzer Prize for *The Good Earth.*

Tobacco Road by Erskine Caldwell is published.

The "Three Musketeers" candy bar, Frito-Lay Corn Chips, and Skippy Peanut Butter all had their debut.

Revlon is founded.

Tabu perfume is created by Jean Carles and launched by Dana.

Olan Mills, Inc. portrait photography studios are founded.

Tarzan the Ape Man, starring Maureen O'Sullivan and Johnny Weissmuller, premieres.

Destiny Rides Again, starring Tom Mix, premieres.

A Farewell to Arms, *Grand Hotel*, *The Mummy*, and *Murders on Rue Morgue* debut.

Toastmasters International, Inc., is founded in California.

Esquire, Family Circle Magazine debuts.

1933

The Lone Ranger debuts on the radio.

Popeye the Sailor cartoon shorts produced for Paramount Pictures.

1935

Fibber McGee and Molly radio show debuts.

Little House on the Prairie by Laura Ingalls Wilder is published.

Movie-goers see first appearance of "Porky Pig" in Looney Tunes cartoons.

Parker Brothers introduces and markets "Monopoly."

Toll House Tried and True Recipes by Ruth Wakefield is published.

1936

Boulder Dam (now known as Hoover Dam) is completed.

Gone with the Wind by Margaret Mitchell is published.

Look Magazine and *Newsweek* launched.

Little Emily, you knew nothing of these—your world was one of daily survival. Since moving out of my isolated environment, through the years I have experienced, in one way or another, everything on the above list. I've listened to countless songs and radio programs, read the books and magazines, eaten the candy bars, prepared and eaten the chocolate chip cookies, spent endless hours playing Monopoly, had family pictures taken by Olan Mills, tried Tabu perfume (though I found the fragrance too heavy), wore Revlon lipstick and nail polish, visited Hoover Dam, and participated in Toastmasters. It's as though a world (unknown to me) was being created parallel to mine…only later did I see and participate in it.

In 1939, John Steinbeck wrote *The Grapes of Wrath*, which won awards and became famous for its realistic depiction of a poor family of tenant farmers struggling to survive the Great Depression. Unlike my family, who stuck it out in Kentucky, the family in this classic story leaves Oklahoma (along with thousands of other "Okies") to head for California, seeking jobs, land, dignity and a future. This book (and later, movie) gives people who are too young to remember that era as close-to-reality a story as I've ever seen—times really were that tough.

Counting on our land and our own hard labor to survive was all we knew. Certainly, habits of hard work, survival, ambition, and drive were ingrained in me. It shames me to think that as I grew older, I was embarrassed to talk about my childhood. Now, I feel blessed to have learned to survive! To grow up really poor was not so exceptional during the 1930s. I believe the era in which you were born contributes to your concept of self. Volumes have been written about the characteristics of each generation. These only offer a starting point for further exploration.

Herbert Hoover served as president from 1929 to 1933. He was a popular World War I hero who promised more prosperity and more bonuses to big businesses. It didn't happen! Even after the stock market crash, Hoover stated, "Prosperity is just around the corner." Perhaps this provided a momentary glimmer of hope, but this is when the situation went from bad to worse.

The voters, being very disillusioned, elected Franklin D. Roosevelt into office in 1933. His platform focused on relief, recovery and reform. He is probably best known for his "New Deal," a comprehensive plan to combat the nation's economic troubles. In his first 100 days in office, Roosevelt implemented many government-regulated programs that helped ease the Depression. Among the new programs were: the Agriculture Adjustment Act (AAA), the Emergency Banking Relief Act, the Federal Deposit Insurance Corporation (FDIC), the Civilian Conservation Corps (CCC), and the Public Works Administration (PWA). The CCC was one of the most popular New Deal programs. This program put three million young men between the ages of 18 to 24 to work providing unskilled labor related to the conservation and development of natural resources during the height of the Great Depression.

These programs did help for a few years. However, in 1937, President Roosevelt, believing the worst of the Depression was over and that recovery was well on its way, scaled back on deficit spending. This resulted in what was called the Roosevelt Recession. In reality, the Depression was far from over, and the economy was not ready to stand on its own. Without federal support, the economy crashed again and put millions out on the streets once more. This was the end of the New Deal handouts. Both Polly and Dad benefited from the PWA. Because Polly had her own sewing machine, she was given a job at $21 a month making items determined by the government. As a matter of pride, many families would not take public money. These proud families also believed most people were relying too much on the government to save the country. Therefore, they would do anything rather than take a handout. Doctors even worked as janitors. Some of this pride continues today; *but not nearly enough.*

Chapter 2

Looking For Greener Pastures

No pressure, no diamonds. No pressure, no pearl. No pain, no gain. No Cocoon, no beautiful butterfly. It's in the uncertain and dark and unclear and broken times that we learn who we really are and what we are capable of.

—Kenny Nola

Looking for greener pastures, my family made the decision in February 1941, to move from Kentucky to Indiana—Polly's parents lived on a farm in Scottsburg, Indiana. I was eight at the time. A neighbor with an open-bed truck drove us with our limited belongings to Scottsburg. In the front seat was the truck driver, Polly, Rhoda and Dillard Junior (still just a baby). Dad and the rest of us children were in the back, squeezed in around the furniture, clothes and other belongings. Yes, it really was like a scene from *The Grapes of Wrath*. I have never been so cold in my life! To this day, I can't stand to be cold! The only pleasant memory of that move was a kind lady giving us hot chocolate when we stopped for fuel.

Little Emily, I think at this time maybe your life seemed a little easier, and at least provided relief from tobacco worms! In fact, life in Indiana was a little easier for everyone. Dad and Polly had decided that farming would not be their only livelihood. Dad took a job in a canning factory in Austin, Indiana, near where we lived. Also, on the positive side, I remember having plenty of family and neighbors around. Dad's half-brother, Hub, as he was called, and his family also moved to the area. New relatives, neighbors and my school experiences were all new puzzle pieces to fit into my life.

Our "new" house wasn't much different from our houses in Kentucky. *Little Emily, through you I see your house, as viewed from the narrow dirt road. As I look through your eyes I see it is two stories tall, neglected in appearance, and framed with peeling paint. There is a window on each side of the front door, two windows on the second level, two chimneys appearing through the reverse-V-shaped roof to carry the smoke from the pot-bellied iron stove in the living room and the wood burning stove in the kitchen, a dilapidated outhouse, and a frame barn missing nearly a fourth of its boards. There is a vegetable garden to the right of the narrow dirt driveway where an aging farm truck is parked, overgrown weeds and grass surrounding the house, rolling farmland on either side and the back of the house, and below the hill at the back of a house is a well with a pump to provide the water needed for the family. There is also a steep hill across the road that is your shortcut to your one-room school. On both the right and the left, your neighbors are within viewing distance. Your house doesn't have a front porch (like most of the houses built in that era).*

The front door leads directly to a small entry containing the coat closet. The small living room is to the left and the master bedroom is to the right. The kitchen off the living room is just large enough for an old, scratched, rectangular wooden table, the cooking stove, and a small table with four drawers for silverware and cooking utensils, as well as open shelves above for dishes.

Little Emily, even with your help, I cannot see our family seated around the table. Did this ever happen? I want to see joy somewhere in my childhood.

A pantry to the right of the cabinet contained the large cooking pots and pans, and food items that were purchased in large quantities. Attached to the back of the kitchen was an enclosed back porch with a laundry tub (also used for bathing), a washboard for scrubbing the clothes, and a hand-turned wringer to remove some of the water before hanging them on the clothesline.

The interior of the house, sparsely furnished, felt cold and unwelcoming without rugs on the scratched, worn wooden floors, and with no curtains on the windows or pictures on the floral wallpapered walls. With that many children, one would expect to see books or toys, but none were there. Unstable wooden stairs led to a small landing and two bedrooms with small closets, but the few clothes we had were stored in wooden vegetable crates. There was a rusty iron bed in each room covered with handmade colorful quilts.

Little Emily, as I think of you there, I get a hollow sick feeling in my stomach, and my heart aches knowing that you are experiencing abandonment by your mother and that you yearn for her arms around you.

This kind of existence makes one feel worthless, flawed and insignificant. There is very little to look forward to—just more chores and farm work. Like everyone else in the family, I was trying to survive without hearing expressions of affection or encouragement—just commands.

Yes, Little Emily, your best times were in your daydreams of your mother while hoeing in the fields or garden, or before going to sleep; you thought of her and what it would be like when she came to take you off the farm to live with her—wherever that was.

At this house, the chore I disliked most was carrying water from under the hill to the kitchen for drinking, cooking, laundry and the occasional laundry tub bath. In the winter, it was necessary to prime the frozen pump to make it work. This required carrying water from the house to pour over the pump to thaw. Water was heated on the kitchen stove for laundry and for baths. I don't remember bathing very frequently, especially in the winter. When we did, the oldest would be first in the laundry tub, placed in the living room, with limited privacy. We all used the same water and towels. Ugh!

It was not until the United States entered World War II in December 1941 that industry began to recover and the economy began to turn around. One school of thought was that FDR led us into World War II to improve the economy. When the war started, domestic programs were swept under the rug. Men were pleased to go to war, where they would have uniforms, food and money. With men at war, women were relied on to work in the factories. Publishers did themed stories such as, "The more women work, the sooner we will win the war." The media created "Rosie the Riveter," a cultural icon representing the American female factory worker. The slogan was: "We can do it" and it served to encourage women into non-traditional jobs.

Recently, in 2014, Ellen DeGeneres (host of a television talk show) interviewed a 93-year-old woman (still active and working) who started working on the assembly line as a riveter at age 22. "I would get up at 4 AM to be at work by 5 AM… now I have more choice of my hours," she said.

The 1940s decade was dominated by World War II. Here are a few additional events of that era:

1940

Franklin D. Roosevelt elected to an unprecedented third term as US President.

Nylon stockings introduced to the market.

The first McDonald's restaurant opens.

1941

Jeep invented.

M&M's candy created.

The Germans created the first programmable computer.

Japanese, on December 7, attacked Pearl Harbor, in Hawaii.

Mount Rushmore completed.

1942

The beginning of the Holocaust in Europe in which over 11 million died.

1944

Bretton Woods created the World Bank and International Monetary Fund.

D-Day offensive took place on June 6.

1945

Microwave oven invented.

"Rosie" memorabilia; Veterans' Day display in Sarasota (2014)

My father did not go to war. Shortly after Dillard Junior was born in 1940, Dad was drafted into the Navy and went for basic training; after this, he was discharged. I have been unable to find out the reason for his discharge. It could have been because of health reasons, age, or family responsibilities (considering that he had six children). Jobs were more plentiful with so many men going in the service. By this time, there were five of us children in school. It was a one-room, rundown school within eyesight of our house, with an outhouse at the rear of the building. Barefooted, we took a shortcut down one hill and up another.

Little Emily, you remember how school was such a refuge. Herbert Weir was the teacher for all 12 grades. I didn't like to miss even one day, even though it was there that I experienced one of my most embarrassing moments. I procrastinated too long to go out to the freezing cold outhouse, and wet my bloomers while sitting at the desk. I sat there as if nothing was wrong until school was out. I waited until almost everyone had left and ran out as fast as I could, trying to avoid being seen. I was so mortified, and so cold with my clothes being wet. While at school, I didn't have to do chores, but I knew they would be waiting when I returned home. The feeding and milking we did before school. As soon as we returned home from school, Polly was there to give us our orders for the afterschool chores.

There were only about 30 students in this one-room schoolhouse. Since children the same age varied in their years of schooling, groups were combined by levels of schooling, not age. We shared books, and I don't recall ever having handouts or supplementary resources. The chalkboard was the primary teaching tool. I don't remember having either art or music. Playing games at recess was our physical education. At the beginning of school each day, we would stand and give the Pledge of Allegiance to our American flag. *Little Emily, I so regret this is no longer the practice.* Older students were often assigned to work with the younger grades. I think I benefited from eavesdropping on other classes. It became clear to me when we attended the large junior high school in Richmond that we missed a lot of grammar, punctuating, and writing skills. My report card showed lower grades in that area.

Playtime was rare. During recess at school, we played "Ring-Around-the-Rosie" or "Annie Over" outside the one-room school. At home in the summer, we caught June bugs and tied them to the clothesline to watch their buzzing. With Dad's pocket knife, we played "Mumbly Peg" which involved placing the tip of the knife blade on part of your body and flipping it so that it would stick upright in the ground. Each player performs in turn until they miss. Yes, the knife sometimes landed on bare feet! "Skin the Cat" also was a game of skill. This type of exercise is currently used in gymnastics or in fitness programs, using bars or gym rings. We would grip a tree limb or barn rafter and begin with "a dead position" with hands turned out, arms and legs straight, toes pointed, and raise the legs up, continuing the movement until the feet passed up through the arms and overhead into the pike inverted hand position, and continue to pass the feet around and down toward the ground. This was fun, and you could do it alone. You just needed a tree limb or anything over your head and strong enough to sustain your weight. Yes, limbs did break… falls were frequent. Later in life, X-rays revealed my old fractures. But I don't remember any injuries keeping me from being sent out to pick tomatoes or worm tobacco plants.

Our government, in 1942, introduced the rationing of practically all consumer everyday goods. No longer could you just walk into a shop and buy as much sugar, butter, or meat as you wanted; nor could you fill up your car with gasoline any time you liked, even if you could afford it. It was all about sacrificing at home for the war efforts. Rationing was one way to make sure everyone got their fair share. War ration books and tokens were issued to every family, dictating how much of each item any one person could buy. This program was administered through the US Office of Price Administration (OPA). It took eight thousand rationing boards to administer the program.

Life magazine, April 20, 1942, reported: "Uncle Sam last week assumed the role of fashion designer. Sweeping restrictions aim to save 15% of the yardage now used on women's and girl's clothes apparel through such measures as restricting hem and belts to two inches, and eliminating cuffs on sleeves." There were heart-tugging reminders and other publications urging participation in the war effort for those still on the home front. The buying of war bonds and making of victory gardens were encouraged. The national maximum Victory speed was 35 miles an hour, a practice to save the use of gasoline.

This government program had little effect on our family. We were already living on what we could raise ourselves and were accustomed to doing without.

Periodically, we attended church. All of us children rode to the service in the back of the pickup truck. I recall being frightened by the emotionalism. The preacher spoke loudly about the fiery hell you would endure if you didn't repent your sins and be baptized. People would shout, some asking for forgiveness, some crying. I remember wanting to run and hide, just as I did with my father's anger outbursts. The only thing I liked was the songs. That is the only time I remember hearing music.

An occasional treat after church was Dad buying a brick of ice cream and sharing it in the town square before returning home. With his grimy pocket knife, he would cut the ice cream into small chunks that we could hold in our hands to eat. In that era, most small towns had their businesses arranged in a square with a little park area in the middle. Also, I remember a few times that on pay day, Dad would bring home a couple of candy bars that he cut into small pieces so that we each could have a taste. It isn't surprising that I'm not very fond of sweets, as they were rarely available (in hindsight, that was a good thing). Obviously, Polly didn't have much time for baking.

Dad enjoyed auctions and trading farm items. Maybe this helped the restlessness I sensed in him. He never seemed contented. Sometimes, he would let one of us children accompany him. This was a treat. I remember having a feeling of freedom as I walked around exploring the items for sale and watching the people. There are other children there, but I was too shy to talk with them. They were dressed similarly to me in their feed sack clothes and barefooted.

Polly was a small, deceptively frail looking woman, but she ruled with an iron fist. My sisters and I remember her as being really mean and bossy. Gail Sheehy writes that gender roles were strictly differentiated in that era. "Women were defined by their womb and housewifely skills," she states. "The man ruled his household. Some states designated a man's wife and children as part of his property, like his horse." I don't think this was true in our household. The older children were expected to take care of the younger ones. I remember attending a funeral for my stillborn half-brother and was forced to kiss him. That was scary! In June, 1943, another half-brother, Bill, was born. Our family now consisted of three of *his*, two of *hers* and two of *theirs* for a total of seven children. Later, I was told that Polly actually had 11 pregnancies… five lived—the others were miscarriages, stillborn, or died shortly after birth. She was a really strong woman! She lived to be 101 years old. She died in 2009 in the home of my half-brother, Dillard Jr., and his wife, Jalynn. *Little Emily, think what could life have been like with Mother living to that age, instead of dying in 1947, 62 years earlier.*

I recently read an article that took me back to the 1920s and 1930s. "That time has yet to be replicated on such a grand scale," it read. "The 25% unemployment rate was a reality back then. But corners were cut, ends were met, and the generation that lived through it still stand as a testament to getting past the rough times." People who survived that decade understood courage. The Whittymore children were not the only children of that era who completely missed what it was like to have a childhood.

Chapter 3
Discovering Courage Within

I'm a firm believer that the path of discomfort offers us so much more than comfort ever has. Discomfort may very well be the most powerful change agent we have in our arsenal for becoming all that we can be—- and achieving the kind of success in life that we want.

—Marc Schoen, PH.D, *Your Survival Instinct is Killing You* (2013)

As hard as I tried to conjure up an image of Mother's face, I could not. Of course, I did not have a photograph of her. I don't think there was a single photo in our house of anyone. The first time I ever saw a camera was when my school picture, the very one on the cover of this book, was taken. Yet I could conjure up the feeling of being with her, the feeling I longed for day and night. In my dreams, she was beautiful, generous and, most of all, loving. The anticipation of eventually being with mother was the only light in my dark world. What I had consistently prayed, dreamed and wished came true in the summer of 1943. Mother came to the farm to take me and my sisters to live with her in Richmond, Indiana.

When I saw her and realized why she had come back, my heart was bursting with both joy and fear; fear that my father would not let us go with her. I don't know the dialogue that transpired between Dad and Mother, but I remember Dad saying, "Who is going to pick tomatoes?" We were seasoned farm workers—Rhoda was 9, I was 11 and Helen was 13. It would have made me feel better to know that we would be missed for other reasons, but at least we did, after all, get to leave with our mother, our life-saving angel. We were three bruised and angry children, desperate to feel cared for and loved. *Is this the way you remember that awesome day, Little Emily?*

The change for me was like moving from a decade of darkness into a bright, beautiful new world. Yes, Mother was all I had dreamed of and more! She was amazingly caring, loving and talented, and more liberated and independent than most women in her era. In the 1940s, single women didn't have much freedom of opportunity. For example, they couldn't obtain loans in their own name. Somehow, she owned a plain, white, moderate-sized frame house at 400 S. 10th Street in Richmond, Indiana. She lived in the front part of the house and used the small apartment at the rear for her sewing business. Here we experienced our first indoor plumbing and electricity.

Mother's bedroom and the kitchen were upstairs. Downstairs were two bedrooms, a bathroom and a living room. My older sister Helen occupied one bedroom while Rhoda and I shared a room. The home was so welcoming! This is the first time I had seen window treatments, upholstered furniture, and carpeting. It felt like a palace.

Mother building her greenhouse in Richmond (c.1940)

When she had left the farm in 1934, the Depression was far from over. I wonder how she survived when she went to Cincinnati. We were told it had been her goal in leaving Dad—to give us an opportunity for a better life than she had. I don't know much about her life prior to when we joined her, except she really had to have worked like a slave to achieve so much, being a single woman with little education. It wasn't until the US entered World War II in December 1941 that industry began to recover and the economy began to turn around. There were likely more opportunities then for Mother.

It was September 2, 1945, when President Truman declared it to be V-J Day ("Victory over Japan"). It was about that time that the Whittymore girls had a door open to opportunity (going to Richmond). A huge, 25-foot statue "Unconditional Surrender" was later created based on the WWII photo of "George the sailor" kissing a nurse in Times Square, taken by photographer Alfred Eisenstaedt on August 4, 1945. A replica of this famous sculpture is located in Sarasota in front of a marina as a reminder of the victory for our country. I often pass by it and have a double dose of gratitude, for it also reminds me to thank God for the victorious day my sisters and I were liberated from the farm.

I regret that I waited too long to interview anyone about Mother. I was unable to locate any of her family. However, I learned recently from my one and only still-living Richmond friend and classmate that I have kept in touch with, Becky Lester Wuertemberger, more information about Mother's life. Becky enjoys genealogy, and so did some research on the Ledger family.

"Unconditional Surrender" sculpture, Sarasota, FL

She discovered that Mother was the youngest of three sisters. Her mother died when she was an infant. The sisters were separated, and at age one, her Aunt Drucy took her to raise. This was the same aunt that later helped raise me and my sisters. I can imagine how much my mother must have missed her sisters. I am grateful she tried so hard to keep her three girls together.

Maggie Whittymore and sister, Rebecca Wise (1940)

Mother was extremely talented and skilled when doing any kind of work with her hands. She could design, sew, knit, and crochet. She even built a greenhouse to start plants for her garden, which encompassed the entire backyard, except for a cherry tree and flowers. Mother loved flowers. She spaded the entire area by hand and religiously tended to her flower beds and garden. She worked full-time at the Belden Manufacturing Company during the day and was a seamstress at night and on weekends. She specialized in window treatments and furniture upholstery. To me and my sisters, our home was a haven of love. We so yearned to be loved.

Richmond is located in east central Indiana, bordering Ohio. Its population was approximately 25,000, and it featured a municipal airport, one high school and Glenn Miller Park. The community was proud of these features, as well as being called the "City of Roses," because Hill Roses was located there. Today, Highway 41 runs through the middle of Richmond. This highway goes north and south from Miami, Florida to the upper peninsula of Michigan. There was some industry, but it was and still remains primarily a peaceful residential Midwestern community.

It wasn't surprising that, in this small-town setting, I felt (and I'm sure I looked) like a "duck out of water." This is the way my mother must have also felt when she left the farm. I'm sure I looked and acted like a hick or country bumpkin. My skin that wasn't covered by a feed-sack dress was sun-colored, almost black, from working the fields in the blazing sun. It was a bizarre tan. Also, I was self-conscious about the way I talked, as I could tell that I sounded different. My vocabulary was poor—there were so many words I didn't know. I was uncomfortable everywhere but home.

Mother immediately took on the daunting task of civilizing and socializing us. I wanted to fit in and to learn more about what everyone else seemed to already know. I never minded her corrections or table manner instructions; I felt cared about for the first time. We had our first medical and dental checkups. Previously, if a tooth ached, it was pulled. Our medical staples on the farm consisted of Vicks salve, mercurochrome, and cod liver oil.

We started attending the First Christian Church, which was within walking distance. Mother purchased our first store-bought lingerie, and other clothes. Also, we got our first swimming suits so that we could start swimming lessons at the YWCA.

Rhoda, Marie, Helen and Mother, Richmond home (1946)

I remember the other children giggling at our strange tans when they saw us in our bathing suits. Mother didn't have a car, so she walked, biked or took the bus. She probably never had the opportunity to drive. The Wise family—Rebecca (Mother's half-sister), Henry, and their three children—were her only family in Richmond. I'm sure they were helpful and supportive, but I barely remember them.

My, what a shock and adjustment fall brought! Whereas before, we went to a one-room school, we now started attending a large junior high school, Hibbard. *I felt so ill prepared.* I had never been in such a crowd of other children. For starters, I watched them to figure out how to do what they already knew to do, like how to go from one room to another when a bell rang, and how to learn each subject from a different teacher. Life was spinning in a whole new orbit.

Mother was sensitive to our insecurity—even fear—and insisted our school work came before chores. She often said, "My life is about helping my girls have a better life than I had. *Education* is primary." I remember being so very proud when she came to school events. When she was dressed up in her well-coordinated ensembles, she would turn heads. She was slender, about 5'4", with light brown, permed hair, parted in the middle to make her narrow face appear broader. She had hazel loving eyes, and she wore very little makeup. She walked straight and proud. *She didn't learn this on the farm*, I thought. To me, she was beautiful.

Her wardrobe was different than I had seen. The war, causing a shortage of materials, influenced fashion. Geometric patterns and shapes were in style, as well as patriotic nautical themes, and dark green and khaki dominated the color palettes. Trousers and wedges were replacing the dress and more traditional heels, respectively, due to the shortages. Women on the farm only wore modest dresses. Mother did work usually thought of as work done by men and wore more utilitarian clothing. Her wardrobe included pants in addition to her beautiful dresses and hats. I loved the hats she designed and made. I wanted so very much to please Mother, as well as my teachers and other students. I felt out of place and *yearned to* be accepted.

As challenging my new life was for me, what a drastic change this had to have been for Mother. I'm sure she must have felt overwhelmed with the responsibility of three girls. At times, I felt overcome with the need to ask her questions. I don't know why I didn't. I guess I didn't want to "rock the boat." Life had never been so good. A male friend would visit occasionally, but mostly, her life was her daughters and her work. I loved the four of us being together. Oh, how I had dreamed of this. Financial resources must have been very scarce. I'm sure I wasn't as appreciative as I should have been of the sacrifices mother was making for us. She was so generous with her love. It seemed she was trying to make up for the nine long years without her girls. I wonder if being separated from her sisters made her more determined to keep us together.

Gradually, I felt more comfortable in this new life and worked at erasing the past experiences from my memory. I became more precise in my enunciation of words—I so wanted to talk correctly. At school, I tried to win over the teachers by volunteering to erase the blackboard, or anything to gain favor. Teachers responded by helping me be successful in my studies. They reinforced positive results. Even though my sisters and I were two years apart in age, there was only one school year difference because of the age we started to school. This was unusual, and it gained some recognition by our teachers. Our music teacher attempted to start a sisters' musical group, but I, for one, couldn't carry a tune, and still can't. It was surprising I did so well in school—an old report card I found shows A's in all subjects except English, Music and Art which were B's. The second semester I earned all A's…I so wanted to please Mother. Eventually, I started making some friends other than my sisters.

Church became a big part of my life. I missed Mother attending with us, but she usually chose to stay home and catch up on her sewing projects. Her extra sewing work was needed for money to make ends meet. When I look back, I don't recall her ever doing anything to just relax or pamper herself. What a heavy load for her to carry alone. She never complained to us. When we returned from church, a nice brunch was always waiting. Cooking wasn't a big thing with Mother because of time constraints. She used the vegetables and fruits she canned, and supplemented with inexpensive cuts of meat she purchased. She cut corners whenever possible. For example, Mother used baloney to grind up for ham salad. Our meals were never elaborate (she had no choice but to be frugal) but they were nourishing, and made with love. What more could I want? Following our meal, we would do chores together. There was usually gardening, lawn and housework to be done on weekends. Occasionally, we would have a social afternoon with Mother's half-sister and family. Life was good. However, it was short-lived.

SUNDAY, DECEMBER 25, 1947, life for us Whittymore sisters completely and utterly collapsed. The four of us had enjoyed Christmas Eve together, which included the rare treat of a movie, and then opened our presents. Mother had made red felt hats and purses for each of us. There wasn't much money to be spent on gifts, but I was content, because being with Mother was my special gift.

On Christmas morning, my sisters and I dressed for church, wearing our red felt hats and carrying our matching purses, feeling a little self-conscious as this was not what teenagers were wearing. We were being as quiet as possible so that Mother could sleep in. We knew she had been working late at night making our Christmas gifts.

Our walk home was very fast-paced because of the chilly weather. Our house was only about five blocks away, through a small park, past small frame homes, past The Friendship House, to our little white, frame house. We were always eager to enjoy brunch with mother. This being Christmas, it would be even more special.

Helen was the first to enter our house. She went through the living room, our bedroom and up the stairs to the kitchen. Rhoda and I heard her scream. "MOTHER!" Then—"We need help!" I ran next door, frightened and sobbing. I didn't know what was wrong, but I knew it must be something terrible. My throat felt constricted and when I tried to call out for help, I couldn't. Still, our neighbors followed me.

We ran up the stairs, two steps at a time; my distraught sisters were hovering over mother as she lay on the floor. She was pale and lifeless beside her bed, looking like a fallen angel. Soon there were lots of adults around that I didn't know. My pain was gut-wrenching. My sisters and I were crying and holding on to Mother, pleading, "Don't leave us…don't leave us!"

She was taken away and I was in a dark place. Terrible thoughts kept racing through my mind, one after the other. *Why did God let this happen? What will happen to my sisters and me? We're abandoned. I'm such a bad child… It's my fault. I didn't deserve her love. I don't want to live without her; the person I loved most in this world. How insensitive we were not to see this coming.* I felt guilt, fear, sadness, and loneliness. Then I felt numb.

I don't even remember where we stayed that Christmas night, nor do I recall much of the day or the next few weeks. I don't even remember the funeral. I later learned she was laid to rest in the Earlham Cemetery. After the numbness wore off, all I was aware of was a painful, gaping hole in my heart. Life for us Whittymore sisters completely and utterly collapsed. We didn't even have a chance to tell her goodbye… No note… No explanation. How can we ever understand? Our lives will forever be changed. Did she possibly think we would be better off? I felt alone with my guilt, a terrible sense of abandonment and rejection. I just wanted our beautiful, caring, loving mother back. I guess nothing lasts. That's why we need to make every moment special.

She was only 33 years old. I feel such pain when I think of the joyless life she had. To me she will always be young and beautiful and loving. I've read that child's memories are mostly sensate. They're not equipped with the analytical skills to make sense of what they see. I guess that is why I remember her clean fragrance, the feel of her arms around me, the kindness in her voice and how safe I felt in her presence. The 18 months with Mother had been such a beautiful gift and had made so many positive changes in my life. For me, it had been the beginning of opportunities, but it was the end of any opportunities for mother. When told that Mother had taken her own life by drinking rat poison, I felt tremendous guilt, thinking the responsibility of three young girls was too overwhelming for her to deal with. She must have felt she couldn't go on living the way she was living. She must've been in a very dark place, with her mind in turmoil. Research tells us that most people are in deep depression when they commit this act, and that more suicides occur at the Christmas season than any other time of the year. We should have observed some signs, but we didn't. We can only live with our regrets.

As perfect as she seemed to me, I have often wondered if she had made God a larger part of her life would she have ended it in such a way. To end her life…my thought is, it must have been a last-minute decision. She grabbed the only poison available. Perhaps she was disappointed in us? If she had left us with Dad, would she still be alive? It is said that "the people we love most are always mysteries." What did I know about my mother, her goals, her dreams, her pain, regrets, guilt… any joys?

As I look back, I remember reading that, "people who think dying is the worst thing, don't know a thing about life." To Mother, death must have appeared easier than living at the moment she chose to take her own life. *Only God knows the answer.* Over the years, I've thought of dozens of permutations of behavior that, in my mind, could have saved my mother's life. I have tormented myself with "alternate endings." I have imagined countless explanations, trying to understand the unfathomable truth that my mother committed suicide. *Little Emily, I wish I could hug you tightly and help you through that soul-shocking time. Sometimes I wonder how you were so strong through it all.*

Ultimately, I realized that there are no answers. At least, not ones we can understand in our imperfect human state. As I have matured in my spiritual life, I better understand. I also realize something else—God doesn't call us to understand. Instead, he calls us to forgive. "With men it is impossible, but not with God; for with God all things are possible." (Mark 10:27) As a child, the only way I could justify my loss was by taking a Pollyanna attitude, "everything happens for a reason." Still, this did not reduce my guilt.

Much later, Dad came from Salem, Indiana, where he lived, to Richmond, Indiana to return us to the farm. He had not been a part of our lives since the summer of 1943 when Mother took us to live with her. I can only assume that Mother's half-sister made the decision to keep Dad away from us as I did not know until I was told much later that he had come for us. As much as I detested him in some ways, it might have been comforting to know he remembered we existed, and had made that effort.

We three sisters were placed with a local family, Ed and Louise Ross. Louise was our English teacher at Hibbard Junior High School and Ed was the Sanitation Engineer for Richmond. We were in the eighth, ninth and tenth grades. The City Courts, our church, and school must have worked together for what they believed to be in our best interest. The Court appointed a lady from our church, LaDonna Hockenberry, as our agent and the Bank as our guardian. The bank agreed we could live in the house and not pay mortgage payments until the youngest graduated from high school. Then, the bank would own the house. Certainly, such arrangements would be unheard of as I write this in 2010.

Life moved on, but I don't know how. As I reflect, so many years later, the good Lord was looking after the Whittymore girls. He must have put a shell of protection around us. Mother opened the doors of opportunity while other caring people influenced our lives in so many extraordinary ways. Not once did I feel angry or blame Mother for what she did. It just hurt so much to try to visualize what her state of mind must have been. How could her daughters have been so unaware? Had I been unappreciative? Could I have helped more than I did to ease Mother's heavy load? I am not sure which overwhelmed me more, sadness or guilt. *My heart breaks for you, Little Emily.*

The Rosses were caring and supportive. Ed, a large jolly-looking man with a friendly smile and laughing eyes, was especially warm and comforting. I remember long evenings of Ed playing Monopoly with us. Louise, with light-brown permed hair and a kind face, was matronly looking in appearance and was by nature more reserved, very cultured, independent, and an excellent role model. They were middle-aged and did not have children. We lived with the Rosses for the remainder of that school year, then returned to our little house on 10th Street.

An older couple rented mother's sewing apartment in the rear of the house, helping to provide us with a meager income. Under these conditions we were allowed to live by ourselves with Mrs. Hockingberry checking on us once a week. She and her husband, Ivor, did not have children. She was petite, attractive and very "prim and proper"… always perfectly coiffed and corseted. (Well-dressed women wore girdles or corsets, according to my home economics teacher.) She was not the warm and nurturing type—I think she felt the need to distance herself from becoming emotionally involved. We dreaded her "white glove" inspections but knew that if we stepped out of line, other arrangements would be made and we might be separated. The three of us would do anything to be able to stay together at that time…one can only imagine the bond that our shared tragedy had forged.

Somehow, God gave us enough courage to continue school. But I felt different. I was still in a dark place obsessed about mother's death. Yet, none of my classmates mentioned it; neither did my teachers. I don't have a memory of anyone saying, "Do you want to talk about it?" In my fits of despair, I even considered suicide as a way to get close to mother. Buried deep was the feeling that I was wearing a "scarlet letter." This feeling was intensified when I would overhear whispering and speculation about the reason for mother's actions: "She must've had an incurable disease", or, "She must have been pregnant", or, "She must've been crazy." This didn't help my relenting sadness and guilt.

My sisters and I lived on bare subsistence, surviving on Social Security, rent from the apartment, and the little money we could earn. Helen, being the oldest, felt responsible for her younger sisters. The managing of the household fell on her shoulders—what a heavy burden she must have felt. Until I was 16 and eligible for a Social Security Card, I worked at a soda fountain in the Wayne Dairy store.

The owner's son was a classmate and escorted me to my first high school dance. (This was the era of the swing dances.) His dad was kind enough to employ me without a Social Security Card. I remember being thrilled and surprised when one customer gave me a fifty-cent tip—that was quite generous since I was making only twenty-five cents an hour. From age 16 until I graduated from high school, I worked as a nurse's aide at Reid Memorial Hospital. It was, and still remains the only hospital in Richmond. My work there provided a little money to contribute to the household budget.

Reflecting on the challenging years following Mother's death, I can only feel gratitude for all the wonderful people who touched our lives in so many positive ways. It could have turned out so differently. In today's world, I don't believe it would have been possible for three young girls to live alone. Personally, I felt responsible to our church, our school, and the whole community, and always tried to live up to their expectations. As I look back, needing to feel accepted and worthy, guilt and shame forced me to put so much value on what other people think…I may have lost myself in the process of trying to meet everyone else's expectations. I believe this led me to striving for perfectionism in all aspects of my life—trying to feel worthy. My sisters also feared that if we failed to meet everyone's approval, we would be separated.

We survived our own cooking, such as it was. We made the few clothes we wore and worked hard at school. That didn't leave much time to sleep. Teachers went out of their way to see that we were exposed to some cultural activities. For example, my homeroom teacher, stately, white-haired, caring Emily Murphy, invited me to a violin concert. When Miss Murphy asked me why I didn't use my first name (Emily), I thoughtlessly said, *I don't like it.* I felt embarrassed about my statement, as well as my difficulty staying awake during the concert. It had nothing to do with the concert, but my lack of sleep.

In spite of our responsibilities outside of school, and feeling inferior and insecure because of our circumstances, we all took leadership roles in school. I remember jumping for joy the year I defeated Jim Brown, our star basketball player, by one vote to become the president of our class. This was just my second year off the farm—I must have changed a lot in that time! Dear Ed Ross, Sanitation Engineer, said, "You won because I campaigned for you through the sewer lines." He always had something nice or funny to say and was so easy to love. In addition to participating in other clubs specific to our interests, each of us served in the Y-teen Cabinet which meant that we had our own Y-teen Group. This was a broad-based YMCA service and social club. During our senior years, I was elected Queen of Hearts and Rhoda was elected Prom Queen. Brave Helen, paved the way and was an impressive act to follow in the way she successfully demonstrated her leadership qualities.

Little Emily, life puzzle pieces continued to show up in all shapes and sizes. Then, I didn't have the insight or take the time to analyze their impact on my life. I do know that with each successful experience, I was less fearful and was gradually building my inner courage. I've learned that courage is a "heart" word. The dictionary states that, in its earliest form, it meant, "to speak one's mind by telling what is in one's heart." Over time, the definition changed and today we typically associate courage with heroes and brave deeds. But to me, this definition fails to recognize the inner strength and level of commitment required for us to actually speak honestly about who we are and about our experiences, good and bad. I've come to think of speaking from our hearts as "ordinary courage." Nelson Mandela wrote, "I learned that courage was not the absence of fear, but the triumph over it. The brave man is not he who does not feel afraid, but he who conquers that fear." Writing this book is helping me understand that future happiness depends on how we resolve and integrate where we have been. *You are helping me to do this, little Emily*

The end of the war meant the end of rationing, and the rest of the world seemed to be in what was called "post-war prosperity." However, prosperity clearly escaped us. My sisters and I were still struggling to survive day by day. I remember being envious of the girls who could afford matching sweater sets and other beautiful store-bought clothes. That must have had an impact on me—I now own at least four sweater sets (they are not currently in style) and a wardrobe full of fashionable clothes.

Her Majesty, Queen Marie Whittymore (1951)

At our high school, it was a tradition that seniors wore yellow corduroy pants or skirts. The Whittymore girls made their own skirts. I don't think we ever washed the skirts because the fad was to have classmates sign your skirt and you wouldn't want to wash off any of the precious signatures.

Television was introduced about this time and research was being done to provide it in color. We didn't even own a radio…but I don't think I envied material things that other teenagers had as much as I envied them having loving parents. It wasn't the TV I wish for, it was my fantasy of a family watching it together.

Holidays were especially lonely times; Christmas unbearable. *Little Emily, how sad that when others were making merry, you dreaded Christmas and felt no joy at all.* I continued to feel that my sisters and I were different. I felt more pity from others than acceptance. As I look back, I wonder if this was more in my mind than in actuality.

What was going on in the outside world didn't seem to be relevant in our small world, as historically significant as they were. World highlights include:

1945

V-J Day (Victory over Japan) declared.

WWII ends, but the events of that year include the Battle of Iwo Jima, the liberation by US troops of Nazi concentration camps, and atomic bombs being used on Japan.

1946

ENIAC, the first general-purpose computer, was unveiled at the University of PA. It took up 1800 square feet of space and weighed nearly 30 tons. It was acclaimed, in part, because it could hold a ten-digit decimal number in its memory bank.

It's a Wonderful Life, featuring James Stewart and Donna Reed, is released.

1947

The first "instant camera", the Polaroid, introduced in New York.

Death of a Salesman by Arthur Miller published; Helen was in the local play production.

Secretary of State, George Marshall, outlines the Marshall Plan for American reconstruction and relief aid to Europe.

1948

Harry S. Truman (incumbent) defeated Thomas E Dewey for US president (greatest election upset in American history).

United States recognizes Israel as a country.

1949

First nonstop flight around the world, captained by James Gallagher, lands in Texas.

Hopalong Cassidy, television's first western, premieres.

North Atlantic Treaty Organization (NATO) established.

I had almost no thoughts of world events, and certainly no fantasies of world travel or adventure. After-school activities were difficult enough to fit in, because I worked then and also on weekends at the hospital. My first trip outside of Richmond was to attend Girl State on the campus of Ball State University in Muncie, IN. The Daughters of the American Revolution (DAR) sponsored this annual event for a high school boy and girl selected by the faculty to learn more about the workings of our Government. Mixed with my life challenges, I did have some fortunate opportunities for which I am grateful.

There wasn't much time for dating. We did appreciate boys that could drive—I'm not proud of this because it was a selfish means of transportation. Since we sisters were so close in age, it wasn't unusual for a young man to visit and invite whichever sister was home to go out to the movies or whatever. (We didn't have a telephone.) Not surprisingly, this sometimes resulted in conflict between sisters, but most of the time, this was not a problem as we had so many of the same friends. I did make a personal decision to not date anyone that also dated either of my sisters.

During my senior year I dated a boy from a nearby town who was three years older than me. To me, he was a good friend. My mistake was to accept an engagement ring prior to his going into the navy. It didn't take me long to acknowledge that feeling sorry for someone is a poor basis to build a lasting relationship! Also, his family wanted too much of my time. He probably asked them to take care of me. I saw my future differently than they did: their vision for my future was that I would start planning a home and they would help. His mother said, "Women don't need a college education to be a wife and mother." I soon returned his ring. This freed me to focus on other opportunities that might be available.

I remember being motivated by wanting to make my mother proud. Her rules to live by, and a strong legacy for her daughters were:

Soap is cheap; you may be poor, but there isn't any excuse to be dirty.

Never take welfare; it decreases your value.

Work ethic and education will enrich your life.

I wondered if mother had had my opportunities… what would she have done with her life? To me, she was a miracle worker; she put her daughters in an environment to succeed (her reason for leaving Dad). I also wonder what my life would have been if I stayed on the farm? (My stepsister married at age fifteen.)

I wanted to think that mother was with God, and together they were watching over us, but I wasn't sure, because I had heard that taking one's own life or anyone else's is a sin. *Little Emily, oh, how these thoughts tortured you. There was no way for you to make sense of things, to understand the puzzle of your life with so many pieces missing.*

Later in life, an amazing and comforting thing happened. Mother must have been on my mind while sitting in church. I started aimlessly paging through the Bible, and all at once the words of St. Paul of the Ephesians seem to jump off the page at me: " Be kind to one another, and also God in Christ has generously forgiven you." I knew then my mother was in heaven. Now, I believe that Mother is my guardian angel and this makes me feel more secure. At that time in my life, I was angry with God for taking her away, but more angry with myself for not being more sensitive to her needs. Now I pray to understand His plan. I believe he has a plan for each of his children and we need to be open to his directions. My life has taken so many turns—it makes me dizzy to think of the frequent changes or new puzzle pieces I struggled to put in place. Of course, I've made mistakes, but for the most part, I think God directed me on the right path.

Following high school graduation, the Whittymore sisters had to face career choices. In the 1950s, a woman's role was generally viewed as a wife and mother. Following WWII was a time of greater prosperity and the "baby boom." Now, men needed the jobs and women who had held them during the war returned to the home to care for their families. Girls furthering their education usually took a secretarial course or attended college to prepare for teaching or nursing. Helen, with the poise and looks of Jacqueline Kennedy, felt responsible for her younger sisters, including financially. She took a secretarial course and then worked full time doing office work.

Another door of opportunity opened for me. I received a full scholarship for the nursing program at Reid Memorial Hospital where I was already working. I feel the award was based more on need than scholastics as I was a good student, but not at the top of my class. This was an inexpensive way to further my education as I clearly did not have the financial resources to make other choices. Living expenses were kept at a minimum: I lived in the dormitory, wore uniforms, and ate my meals at the hospital. However, I did obtain a loan of $500 from the Bank to use for spending money. I lived very frugally, as I have most of my life.

In reflecting on the six years following Mother's death, now that I have the luxury of doing so, I'm able to see the truth in the quote by Marc Schoen in the beginning of this chapter. My path of discomfort may have been the powerful change agent that pushed me into a "new normal." I came to accept that life for me would never be the same, and I struggled to find a new path, still holding on to the exhausting emotional burden of guilt and shame. I hadn't accepted that my guilt wasn't realistic, considering my age at the time of Mother's death. Also, prognosis for mother's condition was far more condemning than a medical one would be decades later. This reduced my guilt a little but not the pain. I continued my Pollyanna means of survival, telling myself there is some good in every painful crisis.

How we survived, I don't know—I give God the credit—He gave us the courage and he didn't give up on us. I've heard that in Chinese, the symbol for "crisis" is comprised of two parts: "change" and "opportunity." Family therapists concur that a crisis in a family provides an opportunity for new patterns of behavior to develop. *Little Emily, this gave me encouragement since we had no established, healthy family patterns to meet our needs for balance, love and acceptance.*

With help, I'm learning how important, yet painful, it is to work through my grief instead of repressing it. If we don't, it can be as insidious as cancer. We grew up in an era when surviving was tough…there wasn't time for grieving or feeling sorry for yourself. Examples showed us that no matter what challenges are put in your path, you sweep them under the rug and move on. My sisters and I didn't even talk about our loss, but dealt with it in our own way, but not always the wisest way. There is great tenacity in the human spirit!

Chapter 4
My Knight

"And most important, have the courage to follow your heart and intuition. They somehow already know what you truly want to become. Everything else is secondary."
—Steve Job, Stanford commencement speech, June 2005

Little Emily, my life surely seemed to be on the fast track. Without a break following high school graduation, I entered nurses training. There, I had little free time between my classes at Earlham College as well as classes at Reid Memorial School of Nursing. The student nurses were used widely to staff the hospital, therefore, we had long clinical hours. New pieces were still being added to my life puzzle, faster than I could put them in place. I didn't see my sisters very often and I really loved and missed them! We had been inseparable for so many years. *We only had each other.*

It was at this time, a very special young man, George Oberle, came into my life in a most unusual way. It was the last semester of his senior year at Earlham College and the second semester of my freshman year. In the Student Union, he observed me defeating a few of his fellow athletes in ping-pong. (I was surprised at this because my only introduction to ping-pong had been during physical education class in high school.) Appearing somewhat cocky, more a sense of confidence than arrogance, George approached the table, looked me right in the eye and said, "I can beat you." I proceeded to win, and it seems then I must have become a challenge in more ways than just as a ping-pong opponent.

I saw him occasionally around campus. Then, I learned that George was my sister's escort to her senior prom. Rhoda and George met when he was student-teaching at her high school.

(L-R) Pat Dotson, Becky Lester, Marie Whittymore, Homer Henry (Richmond, IN, 1951)

George with first car (yellow Chevy) and brother David (1952)

Since we were the only family that Rhoda had, Helen and I were proud guests at the prom and we all celebrated our dear Rhoda being crowned Prom Queen. To me, Rhoda looked the most like our mother in facial features with her narrow face, olive complexion, and expressive eyes; her hair was darker and her eyes were brown where Mother's were hazel, and Rhoda was taller with a curvier figure and more flashy taste in clothes. Helen and I looked more like mother in stature and hair color, and preferred more a subdued style of dress.

Shortly after the prom, George phoned and asked, "Do you have time this week to see me? I would like your input on a concern that my friend has." We set a time that he could stop by my dormitory. It seemed that his friend had dated a young lady, but really wanted to date her friend. He asked, "What do you think this would do to the girl's friendship?" I quickly commented, "I personally feel it might endanger the relationship between the girls." We then enjoyed an outing at Glenn Miller Park —swinging and acting like kids. Yes, I was attracted to him. He had not fooled me...I could easily see that *he* was the friend in his story. I dismissed the idea of dating him as I wouldn't do anything that I felt could hurt either of my sisters.

Soon after my conversation with George regarding his problem, Rhoda called me to explain her relationship with him. She did feel special being escorted to her prom by a popular college athlete, but to her, he was just a friend. George had told her of his interest in me and, knowing that we sisters were extremely close, he wasn't taking any chances. She encouraged George to see me and me to see George. This I did.

However, George was not the tall, dark handsome man of my dreams. He was about 5'10", slim, but muscular, blonde, had a winning smile and a very healthy-looking tan (he had recently returned from spring break in Florida). George was often told that he looked like Kirk Douglas, the actor, even though he didn't have a cliff in his chin like Kirk. George played three varsity sports in college—baseball, basketball and football—and planned a career in coaching athletics.

Following Rhoda's graduation from high school, our house was now owned by the bank. Helen and Rhoda moved into an apartment. Rhoda used the little money in our bank account to attend Ball State University which meant she would be moving to live about three hours away, though with no car, visits between us were rare. My classmates became my extended family and occasionally I would spend a weekend with a fellow student. I especially appreciated the family interaction and unity. What a treat! Pat Dotson from a large family in Manchester, Indiana, was my roommate. Also, I babysat for some of the physicians' children and got to know their wives who were encouraging of my education efforts and very supportive, even offering to loan me clothes for special occasions.

My "knight" was still in the picture. Even though I had craved love all of my life, I was fearful and thus reluctant to be receptive to George's attentions. My early perception was that we were too opposite in personality and backgrounds to consider a long-term relationship. He was extremely outgoing, and exuded confidence. He appeared to know himself and have direction for his life. In contrast, I was embarrassed by my past, unsure of what I wanted in life, and just moving forward by taking advantage of opportunities as they presented themselves. For example, I was pursuing a career that chose me by means of a scholarship. I was just trying to survive. I even attempted to arrange a date between George and my roommate, thinking they had more in common, especially their love of sports. (I had not been exposed to the world of sports.) The result was that George arranged a date between my roommate and his friend, and continued to pursue me.

Since George only had only a few weeks until he graduated, I agreed to go with him to a bonfire party. As I learned more about George's reputation for playing the field, I almost cancelled the date. I had not had a lot of dating experience in my convoluted life. As it turned out, I had nothing to worry about as his friends kept a flashlight on us the entire evening. I soon learned that they were repaying George for doing the same to them. (Throughout his life he was a jokester.)

George H. Oberle, Earlham College graduation, 1952

At George's college graduation, I had the pleasure of meeting his warm, accepting family. He was the oldest of four children: Jackie, his sister, was one year younger than me, and Jerry, his brother, was five years younger than George, and David, a baby brother, was born when George was a sophomore in college. His parents were hard-working, middle-class midwesterners and had sacrificed to send George to a private college. It was very expensive even though he received scholarships and work-study opportunities.

The manner in which I was immediately embraced by his family made me more comfortable in my relationship with George. As I said, I lived with a constant sense of embarrassment and shame—I had not come to terms with my dirt-poor early years, my mother and father's break-up, my lack of sophistication, and, of course, the stigma of my mother's suicide. I questioned, do I have the courage to reveal my past…even the dark side of me? I was fearful of rejection. I experienced many sleepless nights because I had mixed feelings about our relationship. For the first time in my life, I was physically and emotionally drawn to someone of the opposite sex, and I did not want to let my fears dictate my destiny. Yet, the timing was not good. I was feeling disorganized with not enough time to study, work … adding a complex relationship to my jam-packed life made me feel like there were not enough hours in the day.

Little Emily, you understand how much I was wishing I could turn to Mother for advice. After all, love and romance were puzzle pieces I had never had. I was confused about what was actually happening. These were new emotions as I found myself just wanting to be with George. I knew that sharing my past would be a painful and risky step; but how could I expect George to let me into his heart if he thought I didn't trust him enough to be honest? Little by little, I opened up about my past, and opened my heart. What a relief to discover that neither George nor his family cared about my past, that they liked me for me. This feeling of being cared about and accepted gave me a start to some important healing, and also the courage to let myself fall in love.

Following graduation, George returned to his home in Indianapolis, about 70 miles from Richmond. He accepted his first coaching job at Mooresville High School to begin in the fall of the year. We saw each other on weekends during that summer. This arrangement worked for me as I was in summer school and did not have much free time. *I continued to miss my sisters*! Rhoda was working at a dress shop saving money for college, and Helen continued in her office job. Since the bus was our only means of transportation, it wasn't easy to get together. Neither of us had a car and taxis were too expensive.

The year that George taught in Mooresville, I occasionally spent weekends in his parent's home. When I accompanied him in chaperoning his school's senior prom, I felt daggers in my back from girls that likely had a crush on him. He was becoming an increasingly important person in my life. Just thinking of him would send a flutter of electricity through my body. There appeared to be a special chemistry between us and I had not felt this before—such a powerful, wonderful, confusing and euphoric feeling! He was loving, caring and understanding. At times I was frightened by the intensity of my feelings for George; he claimed love at first sight. I was beginning to think that *maybe* with his love and support I could become the person he was looking for, even though I felt I had a long way to go. I thought I must be falling in love. *Can he possibly be that special person I want to spend my life with?*

We became engaged the summer of 1952 in a rather humorous way. A group of Earlhamites were having a picnic in the Indianapolis area. To save George the trip to Richmond (70 miles) to pick me up, I rode with our friend, John Sauffer, and joined George at the picnic. Following the picnic, George looked at me in a mischievous way and asked, "Will you take a walk with me? I don't think we'll be missed." I smiled as he took my hand. We were walking on a baseball field near the picnic area and catching up on each other's lives. Then he said in his confident manner, "I have a reason for this walk." We stopped walking and faced each other on third base. As I look back, it wasn't even pretty—it was the end of summer and the grass was brown—and there wasn't any shade. I was getting a little nervous and I asked him the reason. He said, "I needed some time alone with you." He didn't get down on his knee, nor did he appear nervous; he just pulled me into his arms, gave me a long kiss and confidently stated, "I love you, Marie, and I know, without doubt, that I want you for my wife." I felt shaky and was getting that giddy feeling in my stomach. He didn't appear nervous as he pulled the ring out of his pocket. "Will you marry me?" My mind went into a spin. I did want to say yes— but, I thought, *this is too soon—what about my education? I don't know anything about being a wife and mother. Does he know what he's getting into?* My doubts remained swirling in my mind as I said *yes*, and he put the ring on my finger. Again, I had that euphoric feeling and knew that this must be love. (It was completely different than when I had accepted a ring while in high school.)

Back at the picnic, the group of college friends didn't appear surprised and celebrated with us. We all laughed about the symbolism of George proposing on third base; baseball was his favorite sport. Adding to the humor, I returned to Richmond that evening with another of George's male friends. Ha! This shows our practical side. He was in graduate school at Butler University and we both had class the next day. I was thrilled that someone—someone so special—had asked me to share his life, but frightened that I could not live up to his expectations. He was a person I respected, could continue to grow with, and the chemistry was there from the very first touch. Oh, how I wished that I had greater confidence that I could be a good wife.

Fortunately for both of us, George soon returned to his alma mater, Earlham College, to teach, coach, and serve as head resident of a boy's dormitory. However, this move did have two downsides. First, I would become a faculty wife. The prospects of this were overwhelming! To me, the faculty wives at this Quaker college were mature, highly educated and pioneering types. I had such feelings of inadequacy! I knew there was so much more learning and maturing for me to do. Second, I didn't feel very positive about making a home in Richmond. *It was the past that I wanted to forget.*

My sisters celebrated our engagement, as they were both fond of George. About this time, Rhoda withdrew from Ball State University to accept a management position in a dress shop in Crawfordsville, Indiana. Dear, persevering Helen was following her own dream to attend college. She had explored her options for scholarships, work study, and so forth, and enrolled at Indiana University in the fall of 1953.

A large part of my senior year consisted of internships in specialty areas of nursing. Two were out of state. The first was in pediatrics at Children's Hospital in Cincinnati, Ohio. George transported me there and back in his flashy yellow hard-top convertible. He also visited regularly. I have wonderful memories of dancing with him under the stars at Moonlight Gardens in Cincinnati. I wasn't a good dancer and had not had much practice, but George was and it was easy to follow his lead. *Little Emily, you could not imagine such a strong and positive relationship, full of new and exciting experiences, and building trust, but you had what it took to grow into those wonderful experiences.*

The 1940s-style crooners like Frank Sinatra and Dean Martin vied with a new generation of big-voiced singers like Perry Como, Johnny Ray, Frankie Lane, Patti Page, Rosemary Clooney, Dinah Shore, Doris Day, Eddie Fisher and others. This was the era of the "Big Band" sound and Glen Miller was our favorite big band; his theme song was Moonlight Serenade. Even today, I can feel the powerful chemistry between us as George held me close and we danced to these great bands playing romantic songs like "Tenderly," "Unforgettable," "Too Young," "Love is a Many Splendor Thing," and "Love Me Tender." We also enjoyed the big bands of Tommy Dorsey, Benny Goodman, Woody Herman, Duke Ellington, Harry James, and others. The song, "Tenderly," was *our song* throughout our life time together. Those evenings were magical!

As I look back on the era of my nurse's training, there were two major world crises that made a lasting impression on me. I was at a vulnerable age and soon learned that my deep sympathy for people in pain, mentally or physically, did not make for an objective and effective caregiver.

First was the polio epidemic in the late 1940s and early 1950s. While in high school and working in the hospital as an aide, I was exposed to this paralyzing disease. The polio virus attacks nerves in the central nervous system that control muscle action. Polio doesn't discriminate between gender, race or age. Many of the stricken had to spend long periods in an Iron Lung, a cylindrical metal unit in which only their heads were visible. It made it possible for polio patients whose breathing muscles were paralyzed to breath. In 1952, statistics reported 57,000 people in the US had been struck with polio. People born after 1955, the year of the polio vaccine, have no idea of the fear this illness engendered. My clinical instructors continually cautioned me about empathizing too strongly with the patients. Of course, they were right. It was emotionally draining but I couldn't seem to change.

I still remember the first patient that died under my care. He was an elderly man who had become very childlike and was confined to bed. His family ignored him. At that time, it wasn't unusual for such patients to spend their final months in the hospital. I supplied him with small trucks and other toys to play with in bed and spent some of my free time with him. I learned to love that old man and grieved when he died. Death was such a mystery to me; so much I didn't understand. My strongest feeling about death was fear…likely a residual effect from my mother's suicide. As long as I was associated with Reid Memorial Hospital, I avoided that room.

The second nursing experience that became an indelible memory occurred during my second out-of-state internship. This was in the psychiatric hospital at the Great Lakes Naval base. Unfortunately for me, it was in December, January and February. *I thought I would freeze to death!* The cold icy winds off the lake chilled me to the bone! My wardrobe certainly wasn't adequate for the frigid temperatures, but thankfully my knight presented me with a warm coat. (He told me later that his mother thought the gift too personal.) I constantly battled colds and tonsillitis which lowered my enthusiasm for the internship.

The psychiatric patients we cared for were casualties of World War II. These were young sensitive men who would likely have lived normal lives if they had not experienced the trauma of military war-time service. For various reasons, they could no longer deal with whatever experiences they were facing while fighting for their country. These men escaped reality by retreating into psychotic conditions. Some were treated with medications and counseling, while lobotomies were performed on the more seriously disturbed veterans. Lobotomies were successful in relief of mental disturbances, but this drastic brain surgery also greatly reduced their ability to function. *I really hurt for those young veterans, who were only a few years older than me.* They would be severely limited mentally, the rest of their lives, as a result of serving their country. It didn't seem fair—though no part of war is fair. Our service men and women are asked to live the worst horrors that man can perpetrate on man. Again, I found that I could not simply go to work and think of caring for these soldiers as simply a nursing job. Having visits from George to look forward to helped me get through those trying and depressing days.

There were advantages of being in the Chicago area. It was the largest city I had ever visited and I marveled at the elegant-looking shops and skyscraper buildings. Actually, Indianapolis was the only other large city I had visited. I learned to use and appreciated the mass transit capabilities and even ventured downtown just to see the sights. The huge department stores were staggering in their consumer offerings. I remember visiting Marshall Field during the Christmas season and asking the question, "Where did they grow the large Christmas tree that was displayed?" I was embarrassed by my naïveté when I was told how many trees were combined to make such a huge tree; my 'hayseed' was showing again.

Life in the 1950s, often described as a time of conformity and marked by conservative values, is a decade that many look back on as a "golden era" when times seemed ideal. But it was not a decade free of fear or violence, with the Cold War on one side and the Korean War on the other. After the depression of World War II, however, Americans relished those relatively peaceful years. The following are a few major highlights of that era:

1950

First modern credit card introduced.

First organ transplant.

"Peanuts" cartoon strip is first published.

N. Korean troops invade S. Korea and President Truman orders US to S. Korea's defense.

1951

Color television introduced.

Walt Disney's 13th animated film, *Alice in Wonderland*, premiered.

1952

Car seat belts introduced.

Polio vaccine created.

A nuclear bomb test was held in the Nevada desert.

1953

DNA discovered.

First *Playboy* magazine published.

1954

First atomic submarine launched.

Report came out saying cigarettes cause cancer.

Segregation ruled illegal in America.

I was happy to return to Richmond that cold winter of 1953-54. Certainly, Richmond was not as cold as Chicago. We resumed wedding plans for that summer. As of June, my classes would be over, however, I would still have six months of clinical work to complete at the hospital prior to a December, 1954, graduation.. My attitude about marriage plans was one of uncertainty; I felt that I was too young, too busy, and woefully ill-prepared. I was terribly anxious about wanting to please George while lacking confidence in my ability to be the kind of wife he wanted. I had taken to heart what I learned in psychology class: "If you are a product of a broken home, you're more likely to also have an unsuccessful marriage." *This was scary!* I knew so little about running a house, cooking, etc. Also, when I graduated, I would have a school debt. In spite of my apprehensions, we set the wedding date for August 1, 1954…George was always very persuasive.

George, coming from what was considered a traditional family in that era, expected the same for himself. I wanted his love but also wanted a career—and in time, a family. As I stated earlier, I believe that we are greatly influenced by what is going on in the era in which we were born. This was the time in our country when books were emerging with radical ideas, especially ones about rethinking feminism. In the late 1940s to the early 1960s, as families enjoyed postwar prosperity, they became more materialistic. Television advertising was new, and very effective. Middle-class families couldn't afford items advertised on television, so often the television became the babysitter and women returned to the workforce. No longer just housewives, they began to expect more domestic help from their husbands. Records show that there was a direct correlation between this phenomenon and the increased divorce rate.

The book by Betty Friedman, *The Feminine Mystique*, questioned the role of middle-class women as wives and mothers. She saw women's oppression as a result of society itself rather than unjust laws. About this time, means of contraception became more easily available and this had a significant impact on women—for the first time, they could plan their lives. Certainly, my mother had been ill-prepared to be a single parent. I rationalized that I would at least have a career to fall back on if necessary. *I knew in my heart that I would do everything possible to prove that I could have a successful marriage, in spite of coming from a broken home.*

With the wedding date set, it was necessary to obtain permission from the Hospital Board to move out of the dormitory prior to graduation. I was the first student to make this request. This being successful, we continued with wedding plans. Since I didn't have anyone to give me a wedding nor did I have the money, I preferred to just include our families and have a small affair. However, I swallowed my pride, and we prepared for a church wedding with my knight footing the bill even though he was not rolling in money. (He was making $3,000 a year plus his housing in the boy's dormitory and meals in the cafeteria.) Being accustomed to living frugally, it was easy to be that way as I prepared for the wedding.

I made my own dress and George's wonderful, talented sister, Jackie, made my "going away suit." (Such a suit was traditional, along with white gloves.) A dear friend, Louise Miller, helped my sisters make the attendants' dresses, their hats, and my veil. Louise Ross, the generous teacher we girls lived with right after mother's death, treated us to a bridesmaid's luncheon. The wedding and reception were held at The First Christian Church, my childhood church.

Today, I look back and find humor in a number of situations regarding our wedding. I didn't see the humor at the time. Here are a few:

I had come down with a bad case of shingles and an unsightly fever blister, likely stress related, and felt miserable.

George was late to the rehearsal which was in Richmond—he was in Indianapolis waiting with his family for the delivery of his sister's baby, his parent's first grandchild, Stan Dorrell.

Following rehearsal, I had to return to the dormitory and sew tiny covered buttons down the back of my wedding dress and press it. *You could say that I wasn't very prepared.*

George arranged for us to rent a unit in Vet Village on the Earlham campus. He furnished it from the used furniture ads in the newspaper. Prior to George going to the church, he had to deal with an overflowing toilet—his aunt Naomi had spent the night there and had to wade out of a flooding bathroom in her wedding attire.

Corky Cordell, the county Sheriff, had a nifty little horse trailer and tractor appropriately decorated, parked in front of the church. His plan was to handcuff us and take us in the trailer to the jail for overnight. Thankfully, this plan did not succeed. Jerry, George's brother and best man, was "Johnny-on-the-spot" and tackled Corky as he was trying to handcuff me. The sheriff was a big man—I didn't realize Jerry was so strong. Fortunately, Corky was not injured and remained our friend. This prank afforded us a lifetime of laughs.

Sherriff Corky Cordell (in trailer) with Ed Ross (1954)

Nevertheless, on that extremely hot August day, without air conditioning, we were married!

Whenever the subject of our honeymoon comes up, George always said, "I've spent a lifetime making up for our honeymoon." (And he did successfully do that.) After the wedding day, we only had a week before George would have to report to the Army Reserve Summer camp. Hearing of the availability of an inexpensive, modern cabin on Indiana Beach, George made reservations and that is where we headed for our first night as man and wife.

(From back left) John Sauffer, Louis Robbins, Jim Sedgwick, Pat Dotson, Helen Whittymore, Rhoda Whittymore, Marie Oberle, George Oberle, Gerald Oberle, Rick Kendall, Becky Wise, David Oberle (1954)

It was late in the evening when we arrived. I immediately looked for the bathroom. I finally found it down a path about 50 yards from the cabin. Yes, there was a flushable toilet as well as a shower. George describes the humor of seeing me coming up the path in the dark wearing a flowing white peignoir. *Is it any wonder that I had shingles*? I was still a virgin and very ill-prepared to be a wife. In my generation, we jumped into marriage before jumping into bed—I realize this is no longer felt necessary. We fumbled through the first night; my lips hurt from the fever blister and my painful shingles were all down my spine…but somehow I knew George would make everything between us eventually work out well.

The first morning as Mrs. George Oberle, I had to face the "modern kitchen" in our tiny cabin. George's mother had packed staples to use in meal preparation, and we had picked up a few groceries en route. George must have assumed that I could cook—did he get a surprise! Breakfast was fairly simple to prepare. My main challenge was trying to make toast in the oven as there was no toaster. I finally succeeded after burning and discarding almost a loaf of bread. (This may have been the first, but not the last of my "trial-and-error" cooking during our marriage.) George spent most of the week lounging in a hammock under the trees while I attempted cooking in that not-so-modern kitchen. *Indiana Beach left a lot to be desired and so did our honeymoon!* We spent a night with George's parents on our way back to Richmond. Adding to what would become very fond and humorous memories, so that George's parents would not hear the bed squeak, we made love on the floor.

In returning to our first home late at night, we found a full-sized refrigerator that George had ordered from Sears almost covering the 4x4 stoop at our front door. Before we could get into our unit, it was necessary to uncrate and move the refrigerator to the kitchen. Vet Village had been built to accommodate the veterans and their families following World War II. The units contained two bedrooms, a living room and kitchen. The rooms were very small and heated by a potbellied stove in the living room; this I had experienced in my childhood. I would have likely been uncomfortable in luxury living.

This was the time of the Korean War and George joined an army reserve group while in college. This required regular meetings and reserve camp once a year. This meant that George would not go into service unless the entire reserve group was called for active duty. As soon as we returned from our honeymoon, George left for Reserve Camp and I returned to work at the hospital. It had been necessary for me to obtain a driver's license in order to drive to work while George was away. Being an inexperienced driver, I soon had my first fender bender. George loved that yellow car, but thankfully was very understanding.

When George returned from Camp, I knew that he would be bringing a friend for dinner. Planning for an easy dinner, I splurged on steaks. (This is another favorite story of George's.) After the steaks had been in the broiler drawer for about a half-hour and they were not yet warm, I called George in for advice. I can still hear him laugh as he said, "You have to put the broiler pan in the oven." I was so humiliated to realize that I had been trying to cook the steaks on a broiler pan in the storage drawer. How could anyone be so dumb? So much for my first attempt to entertain! *Little Emily, my life's puzzle pieces were coming to me so rapidly, I felt overwhelmed; can this get any worse? Did I make the right decision? Can I ever be the kind of wife George expects and deserves?*

Chapter 5

Early Years of Marriage

Our early years of marriage were full of love, pregnancies and births struggling and achieving, work and play, and the accompanying joys and sorrows.

— Eleanor Roosevelt

I identify with these words included in *The Autobiography of Eleanor Roosevelt.*

I came of age in the early 1950s, so naturally I expected to be a perfect wife and exemplary mother. Every high school girl was required to take Home Economics where we learned not only domestic skills like basic cooking and sewing, but also were instructed as to our role in our (assumed) future marriage. We were told that wives should prepare themselves to feel and look refreshed when their husband arrives home from work—this may require a short rest, and tidying up one's home and appearance, it was explained. "Then, make him comfortable, and listen to him, and never complain." I swallowed this message hook, line and sinker.

In the mid-1950s we experienced the birth of rock 'n roll with hits like "Rock Around the Clock" by Bill Haley and the Comets dominating the airways. Country music and film songs were also popular. Love songs recorded by vocal groups climbed the music charts with hits like "Earth Angel", "In the Still of the Night", and "The Great Pretenders" by the Platters.

Though at the time we thought many of the antics were outrageous, the pop culture was mild in comparison to decades to follow—cramming the telephone booths, panty raids (college boys confiscating the co-ed's lingerie, and displaying it on lampposts etc.) for a "kick." Also, this was the fun-fashion decade of poodle skirts, bobby socks and saddle shoes, and rolled-up jeans.

Against the standards of the 50s, I was failing miserably as a wife. Fortunately, George wasn't complaining—to me. Determined to improve in all aspects of my marriage, I bought *The Joy of Sex*, the *Better Homes and Gardens Cook Book,* and Amy Vanderbilt's book on etiquette—in that order. Not having role models, I turned to books. Books were, and have always continued to be, my teacher, companion, and friend.

Sooner than we planned, I added *Understanding Your Pregnancy* to my library. George laughed as he often told the story that our first child was conceived with his army pack on his back when he returned from Army reserve camp. (That was the era of diaphragm use for contraception, and it was effective *when used!*)

A new boy's dormitory, Barrett Hall, was being completed; this was to be our new home. It included an efficiency apartment for the head resident. After learning that we would soon be a family of three, a wall was knocked out to give us extra space. This was indeed upscale from Vet Village, but with much less privacy. Typically, students maintained diverse schedules and we could be disturbed around the clock to take care of an array of needs.

Our lives were filled with college life. Besides attending sports functions, George sponsored most social activities on campus and I joined him chaperoning. In addition, I was working, studying for my RN State Board exam, and dealing with severe nausea which lasted for nine months instead of the usual three-month period.

George was accustomed to his home always being open to family and friends. In our little apartment, we maintained the same policy. Mostly our guests were alum friends returning to campus, my sisters, or George's family. I was stunned when he invited his family for our first Thanksgiving dinner. I remember saying, "Can't you get it through your head, George, that your wife can't cook?!" He thought that women inherently knew how to cook, iron shirts, clean house and all the wifely things. My Home Economics training was basic enough I could boil an egg, but…Thanksgiving dinner? Most of all I wanted his love and approval, so, I sought out the help of a well-loved House Mother, Ma Baker. She instructed me in baking the turkey and preparing all the trimmings that go with a traditional Thanksgiving feast. All this I did on a two-burner stove and an apartment-sized oven. Since most of the 160 resident boys went home for the holiday, we served dinner in the dorm lobby as there wasn't space in our small apartment. George's wonderful family was very complimentary. Though I felt there were many things that were far from perfect, I gave myself an "A" for effort.

I graduated from Reid Memorial School of Nursing in December, 1954. I was the first in the Whittymore family to even attend college. It was necessary to order my graduation uniform in a larger size than I normally wore because at graduation I would be nearly five months pregnant. I chose to work in the pediatric department following graduation, thinking the children would be less likely to notice my anatomical changes. In March 1955, I took a leave of absence from nursing in an attempt to catch up on all that was taking place in my fast-paced life. *Little Emily, it felt like an avalanche of new pieces in my life puzzle – they continued relentlessly.* This was the first time I had been unemployed since I was 13 years old, and of course, before that I was a nearly full-time farm-worker.

I rejoiced in the beauty of the spring. Outdoors, it seemed that everything was coming to life with the spring rains and warmer weather. Even though I was still feeling inadequate as a wife, I felt so blessed to be entrusted with a child. Just as the buds were popping out on the trees and the flowering bushes were starting to bloom, I was expecting to soon bring forth a new life. *How awesome.*

With George coaching baseball, I was able to ride the team bus to his out-of-town games. George justified this saying, "By taking Marie, I can have my son with me." He had concluded that we would have a son. Of course, this was only a guess because a test to determine the sex of a child was not available. Yet, I too felt strongly that I was carrying a boy. *It was an uplifting spring.*

Three weeks prior to delivery, I sat for two days taking my RN State Boards. It was an uncomfortable time. I had gained 40 pounds though Dr. Meredith would have preferred that I didn't gain over 20 pounds. Our baby was quite active, and I couldn't find a comfortable position in which to sit. George and my classmates accused me of having an unfair advantage on true/false questions. They teased that I was receiving signals—one kick for "true" and two kicks for "false."

With State Boards behind me, I enjoyed preparing for our baby and attending the college activities. I remember chaperoning a dance with George and really enjoying dancing the Jitterbug. I must have been a wobbly site. Ma Baker suggested we slow down until she could get a basket for the baby. *These were special memories.* I felt awkward and a bit self-conscious about being pregnant and being so huge. But George proudly said, "I think you look more beautiful now than at any other time." *He made me feel so loved, and, he was so easy to love.*

George was indeed a partner in all our preparations. He and a college friend, Jim Sedgwick, purchased my maternity clothes; I was too self-conscious. Also, he accompanied me for regular checkups. We had enormous confidence in Dr. Meredith. I knew him from the hospital, attended school with his children, and he had given me my pre-marital exam and fit me with a diaphragm. (He probably wondered why I hadn't used it.)

In my last month of pregnancy, I was having a checkup every two weeks. Dr. Meredith questioned whether I would be able to have a normal delivery or require a cesarean section because of my narrow pelvic measurements. I really hoped that I could have a natural delivery. Most of the other faculty wives encouraged me in this direction. Many of them followed the teachings of a well-known obstetrician from England, Grantly Dick-Read, *Childbirth Without Fear* (1942), advocating natural child birth. I had practiced his exercises and studied his methods. My last checkup was two weeks prior to my delivery date. That doctor's visit is so vivid in my memory, almost as if it was yesterday instead of over fifty years ago.

George was excited and a bit anxious in preparation for his first chance at a conference baseball championship scheduled for Saturday, May 19, 1955. This doctor's appointment was the Friday afternoon prior to the team's final practice. Dr. Meredith determined that our baby would need to be delivered by cesarean section and asked, "When do you want to have your baby? I can do the surgery this afternoon." Wow! Even though it was very unusual back then, Dr. Meredith had given George permission to be with me during delivery, but now, for a cesarean, he would not be permitted in surgery. I'm sure George was thinking of that important last baseball practice he had planned to hold that afternoon, but he was always one to have his priorities straight: George notified the baseball team to practice without him and he was in the waiting room when our perfect, precious son was born that afternoon of May 18, 1955. He said, "It all happened so quickly, I didn't get to finish my magazine article."

It was such a blessed miracle…seeing our baby for the first time was a profound moment. I couldn't believe this perfect, adorable child came from my body. I didn't want to take my eyes off him; his little round face with dimples, and his change of expressions (probably gas pains). *Little Emily, it was such a humbling, extraordinary experience!* (I wondered what giving birth had been like for my mother.) Becoming a mother was like nothing else I had experienced—I felt joyful, elated, empowered, and totally inadequate. It was like being a mother expanded the parameters of what love looks like…and part of my heart opened up that I didn't know existed. This kind of love was entirely different than I had for George, my mother, or my sisters. George was really "puffed up" and proud.

And now "for the rest of the story"—not only was George blessed with a son, his baseball team won the first-ever conference championship in baseball at Earlham!

In naming our son, we were torn between continuing the George H. tradition (my husband being George H. the 4th) or breaking it. I wanted our son to be named after his father, but did not want him to be called George Junior. Our solution was to name our dear son, George Douglas Oberle, to be called Doug.

Cesarean sections (as well as any major surgeries) were treated so differently in 1955 than they are today. I was in the hospital 10 days. It was not recommended that I breast-feed because of the medications I was being given. Today, I would have returned home the second or third day. Instead of being encouraged to use my abdominal muscles to strengthen my core, I wore an abdominal binder and was advised to wear a good supportive girdle for six weeks— I know this sounds weird compared to the standard practices today.

As thrilled as I was with our precious son, I was overwhelmed by the speed at which my life was changing. There wasn't time to adjust to one major event (new pieces of my life puzzle) before it was necessary to face another. *Like you, Little Emily, I longed for a mother to talk to.*

This was a period in my life that my identity was defined by others—George, his family, our baby, our friends, the other faculty wives, the community, and tradition. What little connection I had managed to build with my true self disappeared in a puff of baby powder. I was only conscious of my many roles and what I imagined were the expected requirements of each. I became a "fake." The route I chose was "fake it until you make it." I manufactured an identity separate from my true self. I worked at making myself "normal" as defined by the era, at least on the outside. By doing this, I hoped to gain everyone's approval. I couldn't even share this with George early in our marriage because I wasn't that secure in our relationship. He sensed my inexplicable depression and expressed his desire to help. I truly didn't know what would help. (Today this would likely be called "postpartum depression" and there are resources and medications to help.)

I was immensely concerned that I would be considered less of a woman in this pioneering, Quaker environment at Earlham. Those courageous women had natural childbirth and breast-fed their babies. Not only was I failing as a wife, I was falling short in the area of motherhood. All I could do was fake it and try to fix it. It occurred to me that I was fortunate there was an alternative to natural childbirth. In the pioneer days, Doug and I would both have died.

What I did not have to fake was the deep love and strong emotions I had for George and our son. We were the first of our college friends to be parents, and I was the first of the Whittymore sisters. My sisters were in other cities dealing with their changing lives. They were both in relationships and I hoped the young men appreciated them. *I missed them for emotional and physical help.* I only had George to help me adjust to parenting…and of course, books. George took parenting in stride and it appeared to come natural to him. It probably helped that he had a brother born when he was a sophomore in college. His confidence, as usual, was comforting. He had a demanding schedule at the college but was available to help with the late evening feedings, so at least I was able to retire early.

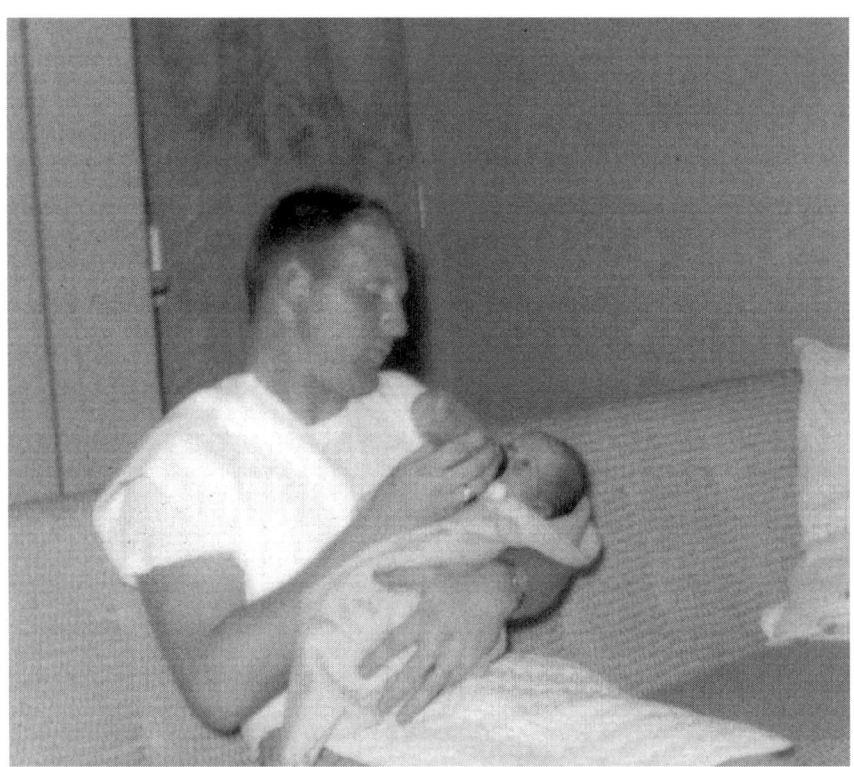

George–Doug's midnight feeding (1955)

Being trained as a nurse was a great help in caring for Doug except I was too conscious of the need for a sterile environment. For example, I ironed diapers (before the era of disposables). We didn't have a clothes dryer so I hung laundry in the dormitory basement to dry. I decided the hot iron would sterilize the diapers. In the summer, when classes were not in session, I hung diapers to dry on the dormitory porch. Occasionally, the President's office would notify me when visitors were expected on campus in time to remove the diapers. Can you imagine how much time I must have spent every single day washing diapers, hanging them up to dry, taking them down, ironing, and folding them? I guess I did that one thing enough to feel competent about something.

As I look back, I wonder what Doug would have said about his first few months of life? He probably would have preferred being back in the womb as he was not a contented infant. Believing Doug to be a colicky baby, we rocked him and walked with him against our shoulders in an attempt to comfort him. Even his experienced Grandmother Oberle couldn't make him happy.

George was in graduate school at Butler University, about 75 miles away in Indianapolis that summer. We stayed with his parents during the weekdays and back to our apartment in Richmond on weekends. It was a traumatic summer for everyone, especially Doug. During his three-month checkup, I updated the doctor on his symptoms. "Every mother tells me their baby has the belly ache," he said. "But this baby really has one." The lab reported an extremely high white blood cell count, which is a sign of infection. Little Doug couldn't tell us where he hurt, but he was constantly agitated and crying. Emergency exploratory surgery was done immediately to diagnose the problem. *Doug's appendix was near rupturing*. Wow! We had been doing the wrong thing to try to comfort him over our shoulder. Poor baby!

It was worth all the hard work in nurses training to be permitted to be with our baby in surgery. My, how tiny Doug looked on that huge operating table. I didn't want to let go of him; I wanted him to see and sense my love and feel safe. He wasn't crying because he was sedated; I wondered what he was going through. When the anesthetist put the mask over his nose and mouth, I could hardly see any of his face… I felt disconnected from him and anxious. My heart was racing and my whole body was on full-alert. I thought of George and what he was likely going through… and I prayed. All went well…the relief was immense. We even chuckled that our three-month old baby was being rolled out of the operating room just as an 80-year-old man with appendicitis was being rolled in as next for surgery. Doug's life and ours became considerably easier. Thank *you Lord!*

I gradually became more relaxed in parenting. Rhoda and I still laugh about her first experience changing Doug's diaper. It so happened that her purse was open on the bed where he was being changed. He had perfect aim right into her purse. Helen lived a greater distance away than Rhoda, but was a doting aunt.

I didn't return to nursing, but had a full life being the best wife and mother I could be—yes, relying on books. I purchased a number of books by Dr. Benjamin Spock, America's most famous pediatrician at the time.

I begin to wonder if it was fair to my dad not to let him know about his grandson. The happiness I felt now and the element of time had helped to erase some of my childhood pain. Also, I felt it was important that George meet my father. My dad had been out of my life for so long and I had been trying hard to repress those memories—it didn't even occur to me to have George meet Dad before we were married. I had shared my past with George but thought it best to leave most of my past safely buried. My feelings changed when Doug was born. Also, I was feeling more secure in my relationship with George and I felt confident that him meeting my father and his family wouldn't have a negative effect on our relationship. I saw the joy that George's parents expressed at being grandparents… I guess having a child made me more compassionate toward my father. *Little Emily, I'm in awe how the two—husband and child—gave me such a reservoir and extraordinary feeling of strength.* I finally felt I belonged somewhere (for the first time) and embraced the opportunity to give them the love and security I never had, but had so yearned for. With my life puzzle just a little less incomplete, I felt a yearning to include the past, at least a little.

Arrangements were made and both Helen and Rhoda accompanied us to Southern Indiana for the visit. Polly and Dad now had three sons, Dillard Junior, William and Levi, in addition to Polly's daughter, Ruby, and son, Harold. At first, the conversation was awkward. I felt great tension in my body, and sensed the same with Dad and others in this split family. Our conversation related to the present (small talk), even though my mind was filled with the past. *There were so many questions* I wanted answered, but I didn't know how to ask them.

Finally, Dad, still with that sad look on his face, said, "I have something for you, Doug, if it's okay?"

Still uncertain of how to act, I answered something like, "That's thoughtful of you…. Doug likes surprises." One of my half-brothers brought out a brown paper bag and handed it to Dad and he motioned for Doug. I took Doug's hand and we walked over to dad. Doug's eyes lit up as he looked into the bag and saw a little toy gun and holster. Appropriately, Doug was wearing cowboy boots.

"We better see if it fits," Dad said. Doug was saying, "Bang- bang!" at Dad as he was fitting the holster around his little waist. George said, "Would you like to give your grandpa a hug and thank him?" It warmed my heart to see my son hugging my father—the father that I don't recall ever giving me a hug or showing me any signs of affection. As Doug hugged his grandpa, there seemed to be less tension in the room. George had a way of joking and making everyone feel comfortable. I could tell that Dad liked him; what was not to like.

When we were getting ready to leave, Dad offered George a sport coat—probably the only one he had. Over and over, I've tried to understand the family dynamics of that day. It was good to see our half-brothers Dillard, Bill, and Levi, and we were pleased that life, in general, seemed a little easier for them now than it had been earlier in their lives. George reminded me that his dad was not one to give out hugs, but he still knew his dad loved him. We sisters were glad that we had taken the first step. I do feel there were a few signs of redemption in Dad's actions, but didn't get a sense that there was a place for us in his life. *I was okay with that, little Emily; we Whittymore sisters were all making a new life.*

(L-R) Helen Whittymore, Marie Oberle, Dad (Dillard) Whittymore,
Rhoda Piepenbrok, Doug Oberle (1956)

Still, I regret not asking the questions that I would like answers to. Maybe time had not insulated me enough to be comfortable with the answers to the following: *Dad, were you disappointed that you had three girls instead of three boys? Did you ever love us? Why were we punished so often and so severely? Have you had any happiness in your life? As you look back at your life (your circumstances were so harsh!), if you had the opportunity, how would you change it? How would you like my family to be in your life?*

We were so wrapped up in the lives of our family, that we hardly had time to consider what was happening in the rest of the world. Here are some of the current events of this era:

1955

Disneyland opens in California.

President Dwight Eisenhower sends first US advisors to S. Vietnam.

1956

Elvis Presley gyrates on Ed Sullivan's Show.

Grace Kelly marries Prince Rainier of Monaco.

"In God We Trust" authorized by Congress and President as US national motto.

1957

Dr. Seuss published *The Cat in the Hat,* soon a favorite of mine and the children.

European economic community established.

Soviet satellite "Sputnik" launches Space Age.

1958

Hula-hoop becomes popular; Lego toy blocks introduced.

NASA founded.

Peace symbol created.

1959

Castro becomes dictator of Cuba.

The Sound of Music opens on Broadway.

When the students returned for the 1955 fall semester, they waited in line to babysit. Lucky for us, ours was the only television in the dormitory. I think the second-hand TV was the first piece of furniture George purchased for our apartment in Vet Village. It was necessary because the World Series was shortly after our wedding, and baseball was always his favorite sport.

I soon learned that spring is the time for various professional conferences, offering opportunities for networking and professional improvement. Families of coaches can anticipate a move if their husbands (in my case) are looking "to climb up the professional ladder." George had "the right stuff" and with his charm and ambition was recruited to a position which was equivalent to a significant job promotion. We moved to Indianapolis, where George had accepted a position at North Central high school, a brand-new school, as Chairman of the Health and Physical Education Department, Summer Recreation Director, Head Baseball Coach, and Assistant Football coach.

We moved into a house belonging to Mom Oberle's adoptive parents, the Crutchfields. Her adoptive mother was deceased and her adoptive father was in a nursing home.

This was an especially happy time for us. George was near his family and had many school friends in the area. We were also closer to my sisters—Rhoda lived in Indianapolis, and Helen was in Columbus, Indiana. George and his friend and colleague, Dean Evans, took turns driving the 45 minutes to work so that Dean's wife, Vera, and I had access to a car. The Evans also had a young son and there were several other young teachers on the North Central faculty with small children. I felt that I had more in common with these faculty wives than the Earlham wives. We became active in the nearby Baptist Church and enjoyed the couple's class.

For the first time, we were near family that were available to babysit with Doug to give George and me an outing. Rhoda and Walt even offered the use of a wooded cabin in the area. It was a perfect place to become reacquainted with uninterrupted intimacy.

I had an unexpected experience in the fall of 1956 during a trip we enjoyed to Detroit to meet some of George's relatives. One young couple had a new baby girl…I left there with such a strong desire to have a little girl as soon as possible. My need was so compelling! I shared this with George. It didn't take much persuading. I prayed that my immediate pregnancy would result in the birth of the baby girl I so wanted. We were having our family earlier in our marriage than we had planned, but it was turning out perfectly. As I reflect, this was God's plan for us; our children would be about two years apart.

Helen Whittymore

We didn't feel it necessary to change obstetricians. We were only two hours from Dr. Meredith and this delivery would also be by cesarean section. In spite of nausea throughout the pregnancy, it was an enjoyable growing time for me—in more ways than one. I delighted in every developmental change I observed in Doug and spent quality time with him, knowing he would have less of my time when we had our second child.

We attended George's sporting events and treasured time spent with our families. His family had embraced my sisters and me with love and acceptance. Beautiful Rhoda was living in Indianapolis and planning a March 23, 1957, wedding. Tenacious Helen had graduated from Indiana University and was employed in the personnel department at Cummings Engine Company in Columbus, Indiana. She was planning a June 22, 1957, wedding with a very enterprising young man, Al Friel, also employed at Cummings. Helen, at 27, was a little older than the typical bride of that time. I was in awe of Helen's accomplishments though she always put her younger sisters first. It wasn't until Rhoda and I had an opportunity to seek a career that she had finally focused on herself. With little outside help, and plenty of hard work, she successfully completed college. (I went to school on a scholarship but Helen worked her way through Indiana University.)

As young girls we had decided that I would one day be Helen's maid of honor. Well, even though I was seven months pregnant, I was proud to stand with my beloved older sister as her matron of honor. She had Jacqueline Kennedy's kind of classic beauty; I told myself no one would be looking at me in my plus-size dress anyway. Helen and Al planned to remain in Columbus, Indiana, and continue working at Cummins Manufacturing Company. Helen was working in human relations and Al in the manufacturing department.

On George's side of the family, his sister, Jackie, and brother-in-law, Chester (Chet) Dorrell, had a son, Stan, who was a year older than Doug, and a son, Don, born April 7, 1956, on my birthday. They were such a close happy family. Jackie had married her high school sweetheart following his discharge from the service. Chet had a position at the Eli Lily drug company for his entire working life. Jackie was in high school when her baby brother, David, was born and took over much of his care. She delighted in her own babies.

There was only one major threat to my pregnancy. Our house was old and only had three overhead cabinets in the small kitchen. There was just enough room for Doug's highchair and a chair for me to sit in as I fed him. One of these feedings was abruptly interrupted when the largest of the filled cabinets fell on my head. I was knocked to the floor and covered with flour and sugar. I just remember Doug crying when "down went cabinets, mother and all." Fortunately, Jerry (George's younger brother) was in the guest room. He was ill and recuperating at our house so that I could give him the injections he needed. He ran to us, moved Doug's highchair away from the debris and said, "My God, Marie, what happened? Your hair is all gray!" He gently helped me up and saw that the flour and sugar canisters had opened and poured all over me. What a sight I must've been. Doug was my first concern—he was okay as soon as we dusted off the contents of the cabinets and he could see it was me. No permanent damage to my pregnancy. Thank you God!

George was enjoying his many responsibilities at North Central and growing professionally. He was completing his master's degree the summer of 1957, when I was to deliver our second child. We scheduled our delivery date for July 11. Later we found that George's finals were scheduled for July 10, the day I was to be checked into the hospital. So, I traveled the 75 miles to Richmond by bus. (Again, I had gained 40 pounds and felt like an elephant.) As he helped me board the bus, George announced to the driver, "My wife is going to Richmond to have a baby." This really made the driver nervous. He placed me in the seat just behind him. George didn't bother to tell the driver that I would have a cesarean section and was not likely to go into labor in route.

"Are you sure you're all right, lady?" the bus driver asked. "I have two kids...with the second, I barely got my wife to the hospital in time. If you feel anything, you let me know immediately." He was likely thinking, "What idiot would send his wife on a bus to have a baby?" I eased his nervousness by clarifying my situation. The whole experience became humorous. Our dear friend, Ann Kendall, met my bus and checked me into the hospital. Her husband, Rick, also spent time with me— enough to confuse the staff when George entered the scene. Who was the father here?

YES, God blessed us with a beautiful, precious, healthy baby GIRL. How awesome! I felt so blessed, overwhelmed, and inadequate for the responsibility God had given me. She had all of her fingers and toes. Her head was perfectly shaped, as was her sweet face and body. Her wide alert eyes made me melt. I can still feel her softness in my arms. I didn't want to put her down; when I did, I continued to play with her soft little hands and feet. Unlike Doug, she could be cuddled without feeling any pain. We named her Teresa Marie, after her mother and grandmother. Very soon, she became "Terri."

Proud parents with Teresa Marie (1957)

Grandpa Oberle was offering a $100 war bond to the family that gave him his first granddaughter. We were on top of the world with joy and thankfulness. We had our perfect little family now that we had the girl we so wanted. Since we felt so blessed to have our daughter, we recommended to Grandpa Oberle that he just give each of the four grandchildren a $25 bond. Terri, as we call her, didn't agree with this decision when she was old enough to understand the value of money. She is still trying to collect from the three grandsons—with interest. (As she's a CPA, I'm betting on her.)

Little Emily, I had an enormous passion for parenting. I so wanted to give my children the love, security, and educational advantages you never had. George, too, was enamored by our good fortune and the joys of parenting. I can only hope my parents had even a little bit of the pleasure in being parents that we had.

I cherish a poem George wrote late one night when the children and I were sleeping:

> God is great and God is good,
> and now I lay me down to sleep.
> These are the prayers that we teach
> these precious children, now in sleep.
> As I lie here with you at my side,
> I thank God for the love that fills me with pride.
> As you sleep with mind at rest,
> the newness of our love fills my breast.
> For the love we share knows no end,
> and keeps me strong as problems descend.
> I love you Marie with a heart so full,
> that God only knows the heart that's so joyful.
> The children we share and love so strong
> are gifts of God, and to us belong.
> May we as guides, and I as a dad,
> lead them in a way that thou would be had.
> And to Doug and Terri, I do vow,
> to provide the best that I know how.
> There will be times, I'm sure,
> you will want, and ask to procure.
> These things if you should find yourself without,
> I hope that there is one thing you will never doubt:
> I love you both with a heart that is true,
> And hope some day you may love, as your mother and I do.

We had two fun years in Indianapolis enjoying our families and making new friends. Mom and Dad Oberle made holidays really special. This was all new to me. I participated and reveled in planning and implementing holiday activities. What the Oberle family perhaps took for granted and carried out as traditions, I saw as awesome—so much love, so much food, so much teasing and laughing. I became a part of it all. My bliss was only interrupted when I thought of my mother. Why did she have to die at this joyful season? I felt incredibly sad to think that she never experienced anything like this…especially the love. As I saw the joy our babies were for Mom and Dad Oberle, I had to force back the tears. Thinking that my mother, by taking that fatal step when she was only 33 years old, was now missing what she must not have even imagined…she would never see, or hold, or kiss her grandchildren. *Little Emily, like you, I wondered, "Can she see us from heaven?"*

Even today, Christmas is my worst time of great sadness and depression. I remember, with pain, that dark Christmas that Mother committed suicide. I still want to ask her, "Why? Why did you do it… my beautiful loving mother?"

Despite my sadness, I counted my blessings. I remember her late nights of sewing to provide us with Christmas surprises. Little did she realize she took away the only thing we really wanted. The Oberles knew of my past and attempted to help compensate. No one said anything when I would tearfully leave the room. Only Helen and Rhoda could understand the depth of my sadness. I also thought of them, and said a prayer. The saddest of my Christmas experiences was seeing on television or hearing about little children in need who would not have a Christmas. Yet, I made every effort to cover up my sadness and be as upbeat as possible for the family.

Thankfully, after winter, we are always blessed with spring. Two special blessings began with the springtime birth of our godchild, Carla Jo Piepenbrok, April 7, 1958. This was nine months after our Terri was born. Yes, and on my birthday. Rhoda and I have been so very close throughout our lives; it is special to have our girls so near the same age. I felt honored with both a nephew and niece born on my birthday. The second blessing was the birth of Jackie's and Chester's third child, born April 13 and named Debra Dorrell. Terri now had two girl cousins within a year of her age. Mom and Dad Oberle were thrilled to now have five grandchildren—one arriving each year for five years. They were unbelievably loving and caring grandparents with plenty of love to go around. I wonder if they ever knew how much that meant to me, since I wasn't providing any grandparents from my side of the family. So, as my extended family grew, more of my life's puzzle pieces appeared, full of love and acceptance.

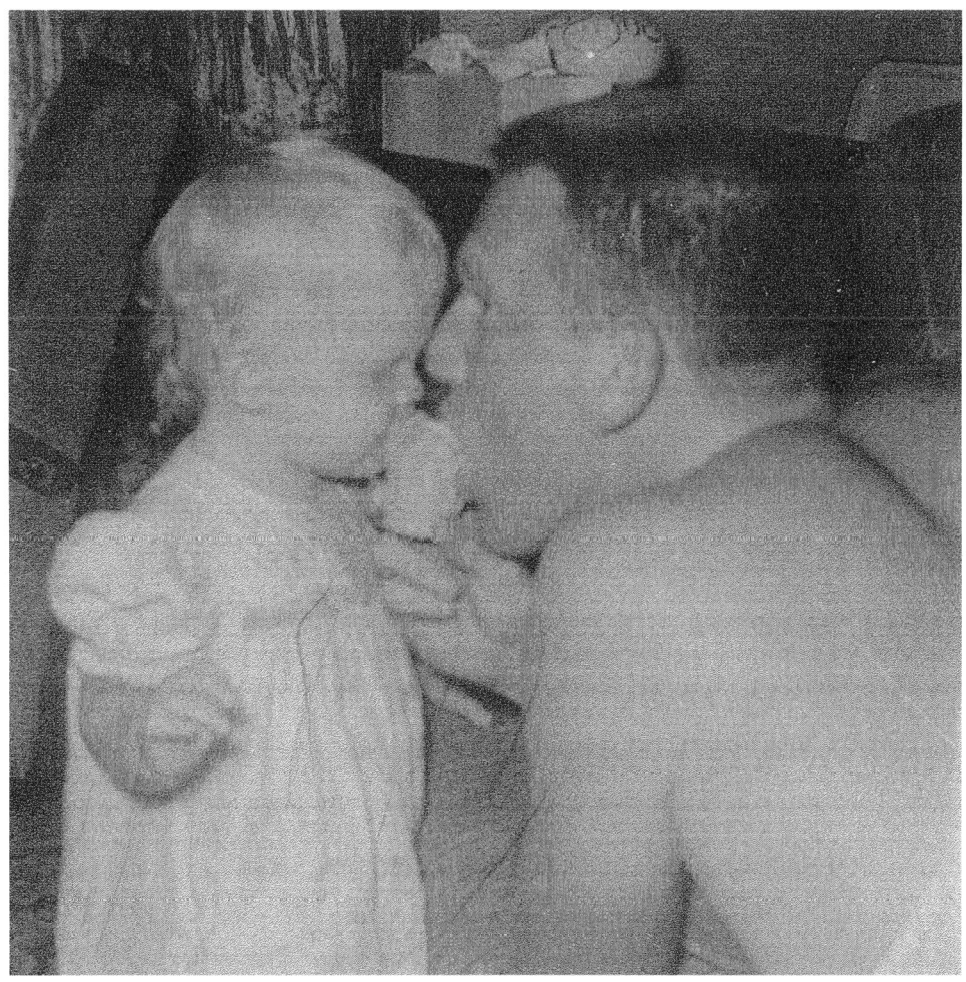

The sweetest picture! (1958)

Terri celebrates her 1st birthday with big brother (1958)

Chapter 6

Open to Opportunities

It is not the strongest of the species that survive, nor the most intelligent that survives. It is the one that is most adaptable to change.

— Charles Darwin

Characteristically, in the spring of 1958, George again looked for professional opportunities to further his career. He did not see his future as only in high school coaching. Jumping at the opportunity to return to his alma mater, he accepted a position comprised of roles as Athletic Director, Assistant Professor of Health, Physical Education, and Recreation, Head Football Coach, and Head Baseball Coach. George still held an enormous fondness and respect for Earlham, but I teased him that he was not able to "break the apron strings." This seemed to me to be too much responsibility for one position—yes, but great experience.

We moved for the fourth time in four years of marriage to an older, large two-story house in Richmond, Indiana, just across the street from the Earlham campus. The uniqueness, but undesirable aspect, of this move was that a farmer friend loaned us his farm truck for the move. Certainly, this was an economic savings, but the truck leaked and the manure was not cleaned out of the truck prior to packing in our furniture. I wasn't a happy camper.

Returning to Earlham was a bit uncomfortable for me because of unpleasant memories of how inadequate I had felt when I wasn't able to have natural childbirth. Even though I tried so hard to accept the fact that I could never compete with the Earlham faculty women when it came to being the "pioneering wife and mother," I continued to feel inferior. My courage wasn't yet strong enough to pat myself on the back and remind myself how far I had come since I left the farm. *Little Emily, this is the part of you I so desperately wanted to be free of…your identity as a feed-sack-dressed child, feeling afraid and unworthy of love.*

I was, however, a little more secure as George's wife and Doug's and Terri's mother. Our world focused on campus life, rather than the community. Since we would be participating in numerous events on campus, we had two college girls living with us. They were an absolute delight and afforded us live-in babysitters. We didn't even attend my home church, but attended services on campus. Even though it was a Quaker college, the services were adapted to diverse religious preferences. The services consisted of 15 minutes of silence, 15 minutes from an invited speaker, and 15 minutes of music. I remember it well—I treasured this quiet time—the only time during the week for me to reconnect with God, and feel that comfort and reassurance only He can give. Our babies were at home with our college girls. (A traditional Quaker meeting is silent with an occasional person feeling compelled to break the silence with an inspirational message.) I was inspired by the intellect of those who shared their thoughts. I wondered how they had become so accomplished, so full of wisdom.

I knew it was up to me to grow by improving myself intellectually and socially. The environment offered opportunities for me to learn and gain more self-confidence. We couldn't afford tuition for me to take classes for credit. (Today they have free tuition for faculty dependents.) Always the eager learner, I took advantage of enrichment opportunities. For example, every week I enjoyed the educational and religious leaders who were guests on campus for the required convocations. Also, there were many opportunities to join a small-group study on significant issues. Topics focused on the theology, efforts for peace (Quakers were conscientious objectors and this was the era of the Korean War), and a wide variety of intellectual pursuits.

Earlham had a reputation for liberal thinking even though it was located in a small, conservative town. Since a good percentage of the student body was from other countries, civil rights issues were less of a challenge than on more conservative campuses. In the 1950s when George and I were students, a national headline event occurred when "a Caucasian girl married a Negro." This highly unusual interracial marriage was widely discussed and used as a case study for Life Magazine.

In the "Tumultuous Sixties", clashes were the shocking norm. The decade that began with the election of the young, exuberant, John Kennedy became a roller coaster ride of highs and lows. Before it was over, assassinations would claim the lives of Martin Luther King Jr. as well as president Kennedy's brother, Robert. The following are highlights of the early 1960s:

1960

President Eisenhower signed the Civil Rights Act into law.

Alfred Hitchcock's film, *Psycho,* released.

First televised presidential debate (John F. Kennedy and Richard Nixon).

First patent given for a laser.

French tested first A-Bomb in the Sahara desert.

Birth control pill approved by the FDA.

The Flintstones aired on television.

1961

John F. Kennedy became the 35th US president.

Pres. Kennedy advised all "prudent families" to have a bomb shelter.

Berlin Wall construction began, cutting off W. Berlin from E. Berlin and E. Germany.

President Kennedy announced to Congress his goal to put a man on the moon before the end of the decade.

DNA genetic code was broken.

Peace Corps founded.

Vietnam War officially began; 400 US troops arrived in Saigon.

The US started underground nuclear testing.

In addition to improving intellectually, I wanted to better fit in socially. I thought it was time to do some entertaining…I so wanted George to be proud of me. One dinner was especially memorable—I had put a great deal of thought and effort into the details—only to have a faculty wife comment, "This is like a Thanksgiving dinner." I took this to mean the menu was too elaborate and not what was the norm for a dinner party. In retrospect, she could have meant this remark as a compliment and I took it the wrong way. My self-confidence was so fragile.

I was forced to learn to cook in quantity and I rarely knew how many people to expect for dinner. It routinely was the six of us. However, George would often detain some of his ballplayers after practice and then the Earlham cafeteria would be closed. Of course he invited them to join us. It was surprising how far I could stretch a chicken! The money budgeted for food was harder to stretch. I had the feeling George was still expecting me to be as competent as his mother at cooking. From my perspective, this never happened.

Parenting continued to be a pleasure. Doug was in daycare on campus three mornings a week. This gave me precious individual time with sweet, fun-loving Terri. One day each week, as was required of parents, I assisted at the daycare center. This was great as it gave me a perfect opportunity to observe Doug with other children. There was an extremely unstructured, permissive atmosphere at this daycare. For the most part, the children were exposed to a large variety of toys and activities and could choose their play interest. I've yet to understand why Doug spent most of the semester digging a hole in the playground. He enjoyed the shovel so much that we bought him one.

I sensed my own personal growth and I began to view education as empowerment. Throughout my life, I've been intrigued by the trends in both teaching and parenting. I took to heart the widespread theory that the *first* five years of life affects who you will become more than that same amount of time in any other period of your life. *Little Emily, I wonder what this means in relation to your future?*

Our live-in college girls continued to be a blessing. Both Doug and Terri delighted in the attention given to them by the girls. Terri was a joy as she learned to walk and explore. The children and I attended most of the home games George coached. The college girls usually grabbed Terri and she was totally entertained. Next to the shovel, Doug was obsessed with any kind of ball. It was easy to take him to ball games as he could always have a ball to play with. Fortunately, Doug had a friend next door, Jack Meek, two years older, who was also interested in sports. Jack's parents, Don and Jenny Meek, became great friends. Don was the basketball coach at Earlham. Looking back, our close community of like-minded friends with young families, college-girl babysitters, and a culture of learning, made this stage of our life seem truly idyllic.

I smile as I remember the spring of 1960. While a student at Earlham, I didn't have the time to enjoy the diverse activities on campus. Now, I did. A highlight that spring was the reenactment of the Old English May Day with a May Queen and the May Pole Dance. Doug, aged 5, was invited to be an attendant in the Queen's Court. Terri, aged 3, was a charmer in her frilly blue and white dress, a gift from her Aunt Helen.

Sometimes, while reflecting on the wonders of parenting, my mind would go to Little Emily and wish for more insight into her life when she was the age of my children. *Help me, Little Emily.* Looking back, I wonder how, and how much my past affected my parenting. Even though I felt the need to make Doug's and Terri's childhood a happy, free, creative experience, was I overprotective or overattentive because I never wanted them to feel unloved, lonely or abandoned?

Developmental psychologists say that when a child and mother are separated physically during the child's developmental stages, the undue stress on the child makes them vulnerable to psychological problems later in life. The experts say the earlier the separation anxiety occurs, the more vulnerable the child will be. The earlier the wound, the more the puzzle pieces which complete one's whole life picture become irretrievable, damaged, or lost. *Little Emily, you had way too many puzzle pieces missing, but you survived!*

It is comforting to know that we do not stop growing, nor do we necessarily stick with who we are at a young age. I have found that opportunities for growth and healing appear in all seasons of life. As we pass through each stage of development, we encounter opportunities to evolve new strengths, heal old wounds, enhance our creativity and spirituality, and remake ourselves into the best we can be. *This is our life goal, Little Emily.*

My introspection about parenting and childhood development sometimes made me think of my sisters. They too certainly had childhood wounds and, like me, Rhoda was a mother. I believe she too was feeling her life enriched by this stirring experience and God's gift.

Al and Helen had moved to Marietta, Georgia, where Al had started his own Cummins Engine Distributorship. He and Helen were "jet-setters" traveling far and wide for business. That was an era when wives were expected to accompany their husbands whenever they hosted clients. Helen's life was now very different from her sisters. She had now switched her career from industry to education. They built a beautiful contemporary home on a huge, hilly, wooded lot. Helen was so much like Mother in that if she did not know how to do something, she learned. At this juncture, Helen took a course in horticulture and did a magnificent job in the landscaping of their home.

Through Doug and Terri, I was living vicariously the childhood that I never had. I was able to reeducate myself to the wonder of everything I focused on. I found such joy in reading to them and even delighted in playing simple board games together. We enjoyed exploring for unusual rocks, bugs, leaves and flowers as I did my best to impart an appreciation of nature. I remember George's Aunt Naomi playing jacks on the sidewalk with the children as I made fresh peach ice cream on the front porch. We took joy in so many simple pleasures. I appreciated George's preference for me to be a full-time wife and mother. Certainly, we could have used the money, but I would have missed so much of the children's developmental changes, not to mention my delight in finally having "fun" and "childhood" exist together. *Little Emily, can you let in some of this joy? Can you ever forgive the cruel world that robbed you of so much?*

It was necessary to be creative in acquiring money to buy gifts for George. We were on a strict budget. I figured out that if I was very resourceful, I could slip some money out of the food budget without detection. We used quantities of milk and one way I saved was by mixing whole milk and powdered milk. Neither George nor our college girls seem to notice. (I later confessed.) By doing similar cost-cutting tricks, I was able to stash away enough money to purchase a projector for George's movie camera as a surprise for Christmas. I thought my secret was safe for the children to know—I didn't think they could even say "projector." Well, Doug surprised me by pointing to one on the TV screen while George was watching television, saying, "That is Daddy's." So much for surprises…ah, life was joyous.

Dr. Spock remained my preferred expert resource on child-raising. In addition to specializing in pediatrics, he did further research into understanding children and their parent's psychological needs. The more common advice in most parenting books recommended a strict, structured regime in baby and child care such as: "Picking up infants when they cry will spoil them." Spock countered that: "Cuddling babies and bestowing affection on children will make them happier and more secure." He also stated: "Parents are the true experts on their own children." I still didn't have an abundance of self-confidence in parenting; however, I was more comfortable with Dr. Spock's approach than cold authoritarianism. Above all, I wanted more than anything for our children to feel secure and loved. History reflects extensive criticism of Dr. Spock's permissive approach to child discipline, cautioning that it would lead to more teenage delinquency. Fortunately, this did not prove to be the case in our family.

In studying psychology, I learned about Pavlov's conditional stimulus-response theory, and about an extensive study being done on rats. A rat's behavior going through a maze could be controlled by either negative or positive reinforcement. The assumption was that similar external influences work for humans. In reflecting, I did partially buy into the concept. I disciplined the children periodically for bad behavior, but focused more on reinforcing positive behavior. For example, I was careful not to take an object from the children unless I replaced it with a favorite toy.

Not surprisingly, in the late spring of 1960, George was ready for a professional change and elected to try Public School Administration. His new position would be City Supervisor of Health, Physical Education, and City Director of Athletics. Again, instead of spring housecleaning, we moved—this time to Marion, Indiana, into a small rental house which I had not seen prior to walking in as the new resident. This was the easiest move of my lifetime. Moving expenses were included in George's contract, and we didn't have a lot of possessions to move. I actually took the children on an outing and when we returned, everything was packed. As I unpacked our belongings, I laughed. Even small rocks around the house plants had been carefully wrapped by "the professionals" before packing.

George's job responsibilities were entirely different than he'd had in any of his previous positions. Both his days and evenings were filled with work. Our children adapted easily with Doug entering kindergarten and also making friends with a neighbor boy who gave him the thrilling new experience of riding a go-cart in the field behind our house. Terri and I explored our new town, and I participated in my first Welcome Club. This was an excellent way to get acquainted in our new community. I learned where to shop, which doctors to use, options for churches, and a little about the different neighborhoods. In a new community, we typically visited several churches and then attended where we felt most comfortable and saw there were opportunities for the children. In Marion, we joined the Methodist Church.

We soon agreed that home ownership would be a sound investment. We bought an acre of land in an upscale community called "Rolling Hills." The lot was so rolling that we chose a four-level house design to accommodate the slant of the lot. Even then, we had to add fill-dirt in order to walk out from the lowest level. The rear of the house had huge windows to enjoy the view and rear living. To reduce the ultimate cost of construction, George was optimistic enough to believe that if we had the shell of a house built, he could do the finishing work. He worked on the house late evenings, often following sporting events, and after church on Sundays. To eliminate the expense that we were paying in rent, we moved into the basement of the house under construction while we did the finishing work. I cooked on a two-burner hot plate and in a deep fat fryer. As I look back, I'm aghast at the amount of fried food I fed my family.

That fall of 1961, Doug entered first grade and rode the bus to school. Terri participated in afternoon preschool, but we had to furnish transportation. With only one car, this took some organizing. Added to the transporting challenge, I returned to nursing. I worked the night shift from 11 PM to 7 AM. George would leave the children asleep while he drove me to Marion General Hospital by 11 PM, and picked me up again at 7 AM… an arrangement far from ideal. Even though we instructed the children on how to contact the wonderful Lorts family across the street if they needed anything, Terri told us later that at times she would hear her dad leave and was scared and cried. Periodically she would run out to try and catch him. This made me feel terribly guilty!

George and I both worked harder physically that year than any other year in our marriage. Obviously, there wasn't much time to sleep. He continued to spend any free time he had working on our home. He had helped his dad a little when their family home was being constructed, but had never laid hardwood floors and trimmed out windows. I was so amazed and pleased at his construction skills. I helped by sanding, painting, and even tiled the basement. I purchased an array of leftover tiles cheaply and configured them into an interesting floor design.

I recall meeting our next-door neighbors while we were working on our roof. "George, what kind of impression do you think we are making on our neighbors?" I asked. George, in his ever-confident and joking tone, said, "Don't be surprised if they ask us to do a project for them."

They thought well enough of us to invite us to their country club for dinner. This was the first time I had ever been inside a country club. My life that had previously been so narrow and restrictive was now filled with many "firsts." *Little Emily, I couldn't keep up with all the new puzzle piece pieces in my life!* I felt somewhat out of place, but I faked the role that I thought appropriate—I was working my way up to an Academy Award nomination, I'm sure.

Thanksgiving break, as usual, was spent with the Oberles, and with Rhoda and her family in Indianapolis area. In addition to little Carla, Rhoda and Walt now had a darling son, Chris. Walt was in the construction business (both residential and commercial) and therefore was able to design and build their large, beautiful and functional family home. Walt's mother had an apartment adjoining their home, and Rhoda did a superb job of caring for their young children and an ailing mother-in-law. Her responsibilities were staggering. I wish I had lived close by to have been of help, other than moral support.

Mom Oberle always prepared the family's favorite foods for the Thanksgiving feast. George always said, "I hope she will have her oyster dressing, and of course our favorite pies." From our perspective, there was never a better pie-maker than Mom Oberle. But, Thanksgiving, 1961, Doug had the chickenpox and we needed to just stay home. The silver lining was that instead of the traditional experience with the Oberle family, we made our own memories. The children and I made Thanksgiving decorations. I prepared a chicken in the deep fat fryer—not too healthy, but the least of our worries. We had our own little feast and a full afternoon of fun family games.

The lasting friendships we made in each community we lived enriched our lives. In Marian, it was the Lorts family. Ann and Russell were older than us, but the youngest of their four children, Russie, was between the ages of Doug and Terri. Russie was a playmate, however, the older children were also fond of Doug and Terri. Ann Lorts, a beautiful vibrant Italian lady, and I would get together frequently as Russell was with the Secret Service and traveled extensively. I particularly remember helping with her garage sale and sipping espresso coffee in her dainty China demitasse cups.

We also imported some dear friends. George was instrumental in Dean Evans, his colleague at North Central high school, moving to Marian as Assistant Superintendent of Schools. By this time, he and Vera had three boys. These are friends we kept up with for many decades.

Christmas of 1961 was filled with family visits and children's laughter. Another tradition was to go to Indianapolis on Christmas Eve. We visited Rhoda and family during the day and enjoyed the Oberle Christmas in the evening. I can still taste the German chocolate cake Rhoda made for us to take home. (I think I ate most of it.) I was especially touched with her efforts; she and Walt now had three precious children, Carla, Chris and Paul. She was an accomplished wife and mother.

Yes, we were still living in the basement, but it was "home," and we drove back to Marian late on Christmas Eve so that we would not miss Santa's visit. I noticed that, probably because of experiencing the joy and wonder of Christmas through our children, I no longer felt overwhelmed with sadness during the holidays. The pain was still there, but new, happy memories were weakening its hold on me.

(L-R) Maria, Marie and Ann (1994)

In the spring of 1962, we moved out of the basement but continued the finishing work on the house. My hard work and lack of sleep was catching up with me. I was losing weight (5'5"tall & 103 lbs), had a high fever, and ached all over. I was diagnosed with rheumatic fever and put to bed. Of course, that meant George's responsibilities doubled. We rarely lived where we could depend on family to help in such emergencies. That isn't all bad—we learned to adapt and get through life's frequent challenges with God's help and each other. Such was the case here. Fortunately, I recuperated without any residual symptoms.

Again, George did his professional networking while attending the 1962 Spring Conferences. He became excited about the opportunity to return to teaching and coaching at the collegiate level. I wasn't very happy to abandon the house we had worked on so diligently. We worked even harder to complete the house in order to put it on the market. Dad Oberle, Dean Evans, and others helped with the landscaping, and it was listed for sale. George accepted a position at Indiana State University (ISU), in Terre Haute, Indiana, as Assistant Football Coach, Assistant Baseball Coach, and Assistant Professor. *I thought, my gosh, now after the house— our first home—is completed, we don't even get to live in it. It's like leaving part of ourselves!*

Chapter 7
Putting Down Roots

I am convinced that life is 10% what happens to me and 90% how I react to it. And so it is with you...we are in charge of our attitude...

— Charles Swindoll

As you can imagine, my attitude wasn't the best when we went house-hunting in Terre Haute. We had literally put our love, sweat and blood into our first home … only to leave it as soon it was completed. It didn't help my mood that Mother's Day weekend when there was a rare snow storm in May. It was cold, cloudy and depressing. The search to find a place we could afford (we had put all our money into the Marian house) was discouraging. I was so depressed that George bought us some Ripple wine—a very cheap brand. As I soaked in the tub after a long day with nothing to show for it, I sipped, sipped, sipped until I drank a whole bottle! I seldom had alcohol and when I did it would never be more than one glass of wine or a cocktail. The next day of house-hunting was made worse because of my major hangover—I paid my dues!

We settled on a small duplex, owned and occupied by the friendly Llewellyn family, Bill and Joanne, and their sons, Bill and Brad. The apartment had two bedrooms upstairs. George and I shared the smaller one with just enough room for a queen-sized bed and an end table. Doug and Terri shared the larger room. Our new neighborhood, Edgewood Grove, was well-established and filled with young families. My attitude was improving.

A number of the families have remained lifelong friends: the Llewellyn's, Harley and Grace Gaston with their three boys and one girl; Chuck and Nancy Bradford with two boys and one girl; and Dr. Shelley and Kit Mabry with three girls. Terri attended kindergarten, and Doug was in second grade at Meadows school across the street from our subdivision. Lisa, the oldest Mabry girl, was an excellent organizer of games and children's activities. It was an extremely friendly and social neighborhood, and our neighbors were an interesting cross-section of society. The men were diverse in their occupations, but their conversations were generally about sports. The women were well-educated, unique in their talents, and entrenched in the roles of wives and mothers. The community was accepting of others very different from themselves, yet we shared many values and interests so that fun times and new friendships were part of daily life.

This was the early 1960s when lives were being affected by increased activism and rapid changes in our society. It was reported as the era that changed the country without an analysis to explain the mass nature of the phenomenon. The United Nations resolved that it would be the "decade of development" and President Kennedy launched this notion in his inaugural address; he signaled a new sense of purpose in international affairs. This brought an awareness of other cultures and a questioning of the rigidness in the U.S.

History tells us that "The Sixties" (as they were known in both academic and popular culture) was a time of revolution in social norms about clothing, music, drugs, sexuality, parenting, formalities, and schooling. The decade was also labeled as the "Swinging Sixties" because of the fall or relaxation of social taboos, especially relating to racism and sexism that occurred at this time. It was even stated that the '60s became defined by the radical and subversive events and trends of the period. We wondered how the atmosphere would be on this campus; our impressions made us think Indiana State would be a conservative University. The Midwest, ever since I can recall, has that designation when compared to northeastern schools or those in California. My assumption that we would be impacted in a relatively mild way proved to be the case.

Our lives were filled with a pleasant combination of both college and community activities. Sunday afternoons became family playtime using the outstanding facilities in the ISU Physical Education Department including: trampoline, basketball court, workout room, and swimming pool. We enjoyed them all. I do recall one frightening event. I can see it now…when Mom and Dad Oberle were visiting, Dad Oberle (who hadn't been in a pool for 50 years) climbed up to the high diving board and happily waved at the startled family. George yelled, "Dad, don't do that!" Too late—Dad was leaving the platform. We all gasped when we saw and heard the loud splash—as Dad landed on his back. Fortunately, he was okay, except for the big slap to his pride. (He didn't realize new diving boards were fiberglass and were very different from the wooden ones he had experienced.)

One advantage to living in a rental property is there is more free time on weekends; every spare moment is not spent on home improvement or maintenance. Our community activities were built around Meadows school, the Methodist Church, and the neighborhood. Of course, we continued to make frequent trips back to Indianapolis to see all the Oberles, and Rhoda and family. Mom and Dad Oberle made Easter really special. They had a very large yard in which to hide colored eggs, some of which were only found weeks later when Dad was mowing the lawn.

A positive addition to the Oberle family and the Easter Egg Hunt was the addition of four more grandchildren. Jerry's first marriage had not worked out, but he had two fine sons, Kevin and Tim. He found a second chance with Sharon and her two children, Lynn and Keith. They made a successful new life together.

My new friend, Nancy Bradford, and I shared a merchandise card from our nearby Great Scott Supermarket; it was stamped at each shopping trip. I was fortunate to shop for the final stamping. Surprise! We won $1000! Nancy and I split the winnings of my first and only lucky card. For us in 1962, this was a large windfall.

Mom and Dad Oberle, Terri and Doug (1962)

Nancy celebrated by giving a neighborhood party, after which she got pregnant. They had a beautiful baby girl…their fourth child. We teased that instead of calling her Sue, the name should be "Great Scott." Since this was money not already budgeted, George and I elected to apply our winnings to having our first family vacation.

And so we treated ourselves to a trip to California by train during Christmas break. For all of us, it was our first train experience. Traveling coach for three days with two active children required preparation and resourcefulness. Each day they had a gift to open such as new games and books. We spent much of the time in the observation car. It was an amazing trip visiting Knots Berry Farm, Sea World, and Disneyland. *Little Emily, I know this is almost impossible for you to believe, the magnificence of Disneyland.*

I was so filled with emotion, I couldn't keep back the tears on Christmas Eve. As I stood surrounded by twinkling lights, watching the smiles on the faces of people of all ages, listening to the laughter of our children (ages five and seven), and counting my blessings, I found myself thinking of my mother. *Little Emily, how you still wish with all your heart that your last Christmas with her would be a fond memory, one to dwell on with nostalgia…not the most awful day of your life.*

I was just a little younger than my mother had been when she ended her life; I was 30, she had been 33. I silently thanked her again for her love and for opening up my doors of opportunity. I felt so grateful for the life I was living, especially with our California Christmas (right out of a movie scene) feeling almost too good to believe. This vacation experience was more spectacular than I ever dreamed.

Thanks to the hospitality of the generous Lorts family (neighbors we knew from Marian), we had lodging. Otherwise, we couldn't have afforded the trip. Their son Johnny and his friends camped out at the Rose Bowl Parade site to reserve places for us to watch the parade. What an extraordinary experience being so close to the fragrant, colorful flowers designed so creatively. Such a site heightened all my senses unlike watching the Parade on television. After the parade, Johnny transported us one-by-one on his motorcycle to the site of the Rose Bowl game, skillfully maneuvering through the mass of cars. Of course, Coach George was in his element and we were all caught up in his excitement to be at the Rose Bowl.

Too soon we had to head back to Indiana, and the return train trip seemed much longer and was far less joyful. Unfortunately, Terri became very ill with strep throat and a doctor had to be contacted to come on board the train in Kansas City to treat her.

To my delight, in the spring of 1963 George was *not* searching for a new job. Instead, we sold our home in Marian while continuing to enjoy our full life in Terre Haute. George and the children gave me my first bicycle for Mother's Day. I was thrilled and was the envy of the neighborhood children. They thought it rather strange that a 31-year-old mother received such a gift. While I was learning to ride it, I couldn't blame them for laughing at my many falls.

We contracted to have a home built in a new community, Lincolnshire. This proved to be a very desirable neighborhood with young families, a park behind our house, and a community pool. Being frugal, as usual, we did our own painting and decorating. We moved into our new home in the fall of 1963—our eighth move in nine years of marriage. Some neighbors and lifetime friendships developed during this time including Bob and Dottie Henline and sons Jeff and Brad; Matt and Jackie Okeefe and children Renée and Doug; Dr. Don and Marlow Owens and children Eric and Cindy; Dr. Herb and Norma Ross and their children Randy, Rhonda and Julie.

Where were you on November 22, 1963? It was a Friday—I was doing my weekly shopping at the Great Scott supermarket when the overhead background music was interrupted; over the intercom came the announcement that President Kennedy had been shot. I was too shocked to move; finally with a great sense of urgency, I rushed home. Like many families, we spent the weekend clustered around our small console television, black-and-white of course. It was a sad time.

We watched with a combination of pride and horror—pride in the outpouring of support for this nation and for the young family. It was such a tragedy, and a horror that our idyllic life could be interrupted so abruptly by such a heinous act. Looking back at that weekend, one news release called it, "…an end to the innocence of youth, much as Pearl Harbor must have been for a previous generation. Still, it was a time when the nation was one, a pause between the divisiveness of the civil rights movement and the looming disaster that became the Vietnam War. For a time, there were no Republicans or Democrats, just Americans."

The Oberle family felt a shell of protection as we dwelled in our little Lincolnshire community. We had lived there for eight delightful years—Doug was there from third through tenth grades, and Terri from the first grade through the eighth. Doug enjoyed swimming, Boy Scouts, Little League baseball (George coached), archery and tennis. He didn't particularly take to his choice of musical instruments, the violin. However, he won't forget the violin because he broke a tooth, in unusual circumstances, the night of his violin concert.

Another accident also led to problems for Doug in his extracurricular pursuits. This time, a case could be made that it was my fault. I got on Doug's black list since I was driving when we had a severe car accident while returning from a Spring Break trip to Clearwater, Florida. (Actually, that we all survived was a miracle!) Our station wagon was overstuffed with our luggage as well as too-many-to-count toys and entertaining distractions we had allowed the children to bring for the long car ride. Since this was on our way home, we also had souvenirs and even bushels of citrus fruit strapped to the top of the car to bring back and share with friends.

I was the relief driver while George got a few winks of sleep when I realized a tire had gone flat. I started to slowly apply the brakes and pull off the road onto the adjacent gravel. George woke up and shouted, "BRAKES!" I slammed on the brakes. The brakes had recently been tightened before the trip and the abrupt lurch was more than I (or the laws of physics) could control. The luggage all shifted in the top-heavy station wagon as it careened off the road, flipped and rolled over twice. The back doors flew open and the children were thrown out onto the ground. George didn't have a seatbelt on and ended up in the backseat. My door was torn off and I was unconscious, hanging by my seatbelt. The oranges and grapefruits were spread all over the highway as well as all the children's favorite toys.

Miraculously, help appeared instantly. A physician who was in traffic was immediately on the spot providing first aid. This was in Valdosta, Georgia, on the Saturday before Easter. We were all admitted to the local hospital. George and Terri (aged seven) had only minor injuries but Doug (aged nine) suffered a fractured clavicle. I had a cervical fracture, and abrasion and bruising around the waist; the seatbelt saved my life. The guys were in one room and Terri and I in another.

The story of our ordeal spread quickly throughout the community and on Easter Sunday, the mayor's wife brought the children colored Easter eggs. The town sheriff and his family took Terri on an outing that afternoon, and my wonderful sister Helen and brother-in-law Al drove down from Marietta, Georgia, to assist us. Ours was such a human relations story, it made national news. We counted our blessings and flew back home (minus the citrus fruit and most of the children's entertainment items) to receive warm welcomes from our concerned and caring neighbors in Lincolnshire.

Of course, Doug could not try out for Little League baseball that spring. The good news was he was still selected for a team because the coaches remembered his strong skills from the previous year. To say he was a natural athlete would be an understatement. He even won the seventh-grade table tennis tournament with his left arm in a sling. (He must've taken after his mother.)

Doug and his friend Randy Ross acquired excellent tennis instruction from the Indiana State University tennis coach, Duane Klueh. In fact, in their first tennis tournament in Evansville, Indiana, they came in second in the 12-years-and-younger group. Doug continued to develop and use his tennis and baseball skills through high school and college.

There was a comforting feeling of safety for the children in Lincolnshire. We knew and trusted all our neighbors. The pool was a gathering place for mothers and children during the summer. Since there wasn't a lifeguard, a responsible adult was required to accompany the children. The children always had plenty of friends to play with and the mothers socialized to their hearts' content...this is where I learned to play bridge. Family pool parties were often part of our weekend. We also enjoyed entertaining in our home; I was becoming more comfortable in that role.

I remember hosting a Gourmet Dinner Club dinner that got a bit out of hand and became legendary, as dinner parties go. George had been in Boston for a professional meeting, and planned to arrive home with lobsters in time for our Saturday evening party. His plane was delayed so we started the party without him. The hors d'oeuvres were quickly consumed as well as a half a case of wine. Our women guests decided to go with me to meet his plane—not a good idea. Poor, tired, stressed-out, lobster-laden George was greeted by a giddy group of gals with a little too much "party" in them for him to enjoy given his current state. We drove home and were greeted by the remaining guests who had continued with the wine in our absence.

Finally, we served our lobster feast. For dessert we served strawberries soaked in champagne—also, not a good idea. By now, the highly inebriated guests were actually making a game of flipping the strawberries on the ceiling and chugging the champagne. They were a rowdy group. George and I were too sober to see that it was funny—and it certainly wasn't funny when one of the guys pulled my wig off. (I had been too busy to style my hair so I put on the wig I often wore after swimming.) I tried to get them to have coffee and cake before driving home (that didn't go over) but somehow they all got home safely.

The next morning, I found my wig in the clothes dryer, a woman's shoe in the cake pan, and someone's tie on the street near our mailbox. What a disaster! Calls of apology soon started coming ...some even offered to help repaint the ceiling. With our open floor plan, this meant painting all of the ceilings except in the bedrooms.

Marie, as "Twiggy"　　　　　　　　　　George, as "Dr. Feel-Good"

A few days later, a package of "Official S.O.S. Apology Forms" arrived with bylaws and instructions. It was a masterpiece, masterminded by Dr. Shelley Mabry, the quietest and brightest of the group. We were each to fill out the apology forms before attending our next Gourmet Dinner. This clever but sincere gesture did lighten the episode and we all found Shelley's composite of forms humorous. The guests unanimously voted it as the best party they had ever attended and continued to talk about it for years. It's a story that George and I always laughed when telling, and I'm laughing now. Other parties were quite fun as well, especially the costume parties which were frequent in this lively crowd.

I admit I did not miss my former night-shift nursing job one bit and treasured the quality time I got to spend with Terri and Doug. Since I grew up in a family of all girls, getting used to having a son took some time. (In fact, I am still trying to understand the other sex.) I laughingly told George he had to stay with me, no matter what, until Doug was raised. I felt I would not have too much difficulty raising a girl, but a boy—not sure. Doug and Terri both shared George's interest in sports. I was so pleased that Terri's friends were both boys and girls, even for sleepovers. I recall Jeff Henline, a neighbor, being careful to return home early in the morning before his older brother was up to tease him.

Terri was such a beautiful, inquisitive and delightful child who had a special zest for life. She was a good organizer of activities at the pool, in the park behind our house, and throughout the neighborhood. She often reminisces about her fun times living in Terre Haute, and especially the pool opportunities. College communities offer a variety of summer enrichment classes for children. Terri studied conversational French at St. Mary's of the Woods College, also in Terre Haute. I recall one of her books in French called *The Oberle Family*. This surprised me because George's family is German. I later learned that the area they were from was at one time controlled by the French.

George and Doug officiating their first college game together (1978)

I enjoyed being Terri's Girl Scout leader. This was all new to me, so we learned together. She also took tennis from Coach Klueh, but it wasn't her cup of tea. Gymnastics appeared to be a natural for Terri until she had a fast growing spurt and became less flexible, but her gymnastics skills served her well when she turned to cheerleading in the seventh and eighth grades at Glenn Junior High School.

In addition to enjoying the many activities of our children, George and I focused on including quality time for ourselves. I often reminded him that he still came first in my life. Although this attitude may not be so popular in today's era, I can attest it makes for a strong and quality marriage, and this proved to be such a Blessing for the many, many years George and I had together after our children were grown and attending to their own families and lives. When the children were younger, attending conferences with George was one way we were sure to get in some quality time together (more time in bed), and it helped me to be a part of his world.

We both continued to look for new opportunities. George further expanded his interest in officiating college basketball. The Dean of his department had been a Big 10 Football official. George not only aspired to be a Big 10 Basketball official, he achieved this. Of the many valuable things I learned from George, one certainly was that there is no goal which cannot be reached with enough intention and determination. Over and over, he set his sights on something, went for it, and achieved it. It must be noted that remarkably, through all his career ambitions, he never lost sight of his priority of loving his family.

George made the career decision to stay at the college level and enrolled in the Doctorial Program at Indiana University in Bloomington, Indiana, approximately 60 miles from Terre Haute. Gradually, he moved out of coaching into the role of Assistant Dean with expanded administrative responsibilities.

Ours was the generation when wives were expected to be totally supportive and involved in the husband's career. It didn't occur to me to attempt to change George's decisions in any of our moves. However, I never wanted to return to see our Marion home. I think I resented that we put so much of ourselves into it, only to leave it for someone else. Few wives had their own careers. I became involved in the University Wives Club, and like many of the club members, took enrichment courses on campus while the children were in school. I particularly enjoyed literature and sociology. Our second year at ISU, I was elected President of University Wives, the youngest president ever. I obviously fit in better with this faculty than at Earlham.

My selection was significant because ISU was in a major expansion period and a large number of young faculty were being hired. I was challenged to transform the University Wives Club from a "monthly tea" event to one with a wide variety of interests directed toward helping new faculty wives adjust to their new community. A few women faculty members were also a part of this club. This responsibility was extremely time-consuming, especially because of the care I took to include the faculty wives with long seniority into the decision-making regarding the changes. I learned that group process can be effective but requires great patience and time. We ended up keeping their monthly teas, but added many additional social activities. I was able to introduce many interest groups such as bridge, a book club, gourmet dining, and others that I had enjoyed in the Marion Newcomers Club.

Working with these bright, talented women was empowering, and I gained confidence in my negotiating and organizational skills. However, I've never enjoyed or been at ease presiding in front of a group—but this didn't stop me from pushing myself into leadership responsibilities. Even participating in Toastmasters Club helped very little. Probably my years of "acting" helped me more than anything to speak confidently even when I was very nervous.

Our neighbor, Marlow Owens, was a master at knitting. She taught me enough knitting to introduce this skill to Terri's Girl Scout troop. She also chaired an interest group on knitting and helped me knit a coat. The coat wasn't very professional-looking…into the donation bag it went. I hope at least it helped someone keep warm.

I especially remember how much I admired Charlotte Smock, wife of the Dean of Education, for her quiet strength and encouraging manner. She was responsible for my being asked to co-chair plans for National Heart Month. We organized various fundraising activities for the city of Terre Haute. This included a dance, walks, bridge tournaments, door-to-door soliciting, etc. It was a successful month of fundraising and I felt that I had done a good job.

Even today, I remain grateful to Charlotte for recommending me for P.E.O. (Philanthropic Educational Organization) membership. I had not heard of this sisterhood whose mission is to celebrate, educate, and motivate women across North America and around the world. It was because of my respect for this remarkable lady that I accepted the invitation. My new sisters helped fill the void of not having my birthright sisters near. I am honored to still be associated with these amazing caring P.E.O. sisters; since it is an international organization, I maintained my membership in every place I have lived.

At ISU, my volunteer work more than filled any spare time that I had. I felt rewarded by the confidence-building and leadership skills I was acquiring. However, I began to consider what I might want to do as a career. Our entire family appeared to be in a good place in their lives—I could hardly believe we had lived in our little home and community for five years— and we actually put down some strong roots. *Little Emily, here I was finally able to put many of my life puzzle pieces in place. It's a good feeling.*

I always assumed I would have a career as our children and home needed me less, and now felt ready to have some goals and make some plans. George was continuing to grow intellectually and I never wanted him to feel he was "outgrowing me." Also, I had taken so many enrichment courses that the professors recommended I put a degree plan together. ISU didn't provide the opportunity for me to complete my BS in nursing. This wasn't all bad because I had serious doubts about returning to nursing. I internalized and took on others' pain to the extent that I "passed out"—fainted. This is not a good trait to be able to be an effective caregiver. A satisfactory alternative was health education. This appealed to me because I prefer helping people stay well rather than treating them when they are ill.

In 1967, Dr. Walter Ney, my advisor, assisted in developing my plan of study. At the same time, George's brother, David (20 years younger), enrolled at ISU. We were enrolled in the same class, but he didn't like the professor's reputation and since his friends had advised him to avoid this class he transferred out. (Could the real reason have been that he didn't want any reports going back to his big brother?)

Though I was pursuing my career interest, I continued to plan my life around George and our children. I would study in the evening, after Doug and Terri went to bed. George's evenings were usually filled with ISU sports events, his basketball officiating, or IU classes. The times he could be with the family were *quality times*. Even though child rearing and discipline were left almost totally to me, George was in accord with my style and gave his full support. We continued to award good behavior and sound decision-making. When our children were unsure whether to do or not do something, I encouraged them to think of the consequences of the act and ask themselves if the pleasure outweighed the possible consequences.

Vacations were marvelous family times. To provide our children experience camping, we visited the Smoky Mountains. Our night of camping consisted of exploring the area, light cooking over the campfire, and preparing the tent. Terri and I elected to sleep in sleeping bags in the back of the station wagon. During the night, we had company…a big black bear was rattling the trash cans. George and Doug quickly found cover in the station wagon with us!

A major highlight of this family vacation was taking a side trip to visit the Friels in Marietta, Georgia. Helen and Al now had two adorable sons, Alan born February 1, 1966, and Kebin, born February 1, 1968. This was a major change in their jet-setting life, but one they were obviously ready for. They had so much to offer in love and material comforts for their young family. Al was successful in his business and Helen was now a Dean in the local high school. Helen having her first child at age 34 was unusual in that era, but certainly not today; now women tend to focus on their careers before starting their family. Helen was an independent thinker and didn't feel the need to fit into anyone else's mold. I regret that I lived too far away to properly spoil my nephews.

Our first vacation with another family was to West Palm Beach, Florida. We had experienced the west coast of Florida and wanted to check out the east coast. This was with the congenial Ross family; Herb and Norma, and their children, near the ages of ours, Randy and Rhonda. On this trip, we learned that marketing can be deceiving, especially noted by Dr. Ross who was a professor of marketing at ISU. Our accommodations were less than desirable. In fact, the swimming pool has been drained for repairs. After two days of driving, we were not happy campers. Fortunately, the proprietors made us reservations at the Colonnades Resort in the area, and we all adjusted. The children shared similar interests, as well as the adults.

George and I were blessed to have their friendship throughout our life and enjoyed additional vacations together. Now I am going to share a little story, and I'm wondering if our children are learning about this adult exploit of their parents for the first time. The adults were up for a new adventure, maybe even something *extra* adventurous, being in a city where we were not known. Norma and I had not ever been to an adult dinner club; I don't remember whether this was the first for George and Herb. The one we decided to explore turned out to not be an upscale establishment. The "girlie" performance was going on during dinner… it spoiled my dinner. The strippers were not physically attractive with their loose skin and saggy boobs. When one of the entertainer's bras landed on George's head… we asked for and paid our check. The husbands refused to leave a tip. We walked out, followed by the enormous bouncer who said, "You didn't leave a tip." Observing the size of the guy delivering the reminder, George and Herb didn't hesitate to pay up. We were all shocked and silent as we hurriedly drove away. I guess we were all expecting something at least a little glamorous or exotic, but we all agreed it was nothing of the kind.

Sometimes we vacationed at home. We delighted in our home being a hangout for the neighborhood children. Of course, the older they got, the larger their toys, and the more space they required. The garage was okay for a ping-pong table and place for their music, but they needed inside space during cold weather. We envisioned a room large enough for a fireplace, soda bar, space for a pool table, and for lounging. George used the skills he had acquired finishing our Marion home, and with the help of Doug the project became a reality. The 30' x 30' bonus room was a perfect activities center for family and friends.

Helen, Kebin, Al and Alan Freil (1969)

Little Emily, the 60s were tumultuous for many, but for me this time was the most secure and idyllic life I had ever known. We were fortunate to live in an environment that reinforced family values, the value of education, and respect for all human beings. George and I felt blessed that we could raise our children in such a loving, accepting atmosphere. It was painful making the move to Terre Haute, but the decision turned out positive for all the family. Thank you, Lord. Yet, we sensed change in the wind.

Commentator Christopher Booker described this era as "…a Classical Jungian Nightmare Cycle, unable to contain the demands for greater individual freedom, broke free of the previous age through extreme deprivation from the norm." Several nations such as the US, France, Germany, and Great Britain turned to the left in the early and mid-1960s. There was a push for social reform by groups like the Student Nonviolent Coordinating Committee (SNCC) and the Southern Christian Leadership Conference (SCLC).

The following are highlights of major happenings of the times:

1962

The Beatles' first record, *My Bonnie,* released.

Dr. Who, the first James Bond film, premiered.

The term "Personal Computer" first mentioned by the media.

Diet Rite, the first sugar-free soda introduced.

Cuban missile crisis:13-day confrontation between US and Soviet Union over Soviet ballistic missiles deployed in Cuba; Cold War nearly escalated into nuclear war.

1963

Martin Luther King's "I Have a Dream" speech at Wash. DC Civil Rights March.

President Kennedy assassinated in Dallas, Texas.

Women's and environmental movements gained attention and popularity.

Two-thirds of the world automobiles made in US.

1965

Medicare bill passed to provide health insurance for Americans 65 and older.

190,000 troops in Vietnam.

1966

Daylight saving time came into being.

1967

Anti-Vietnam war protest–400,000 march from Central Park to the UN to hear speeches by Martin Luther King, Stokely Carmichael, and Dr. Benjamin Spock.

Dr. Christian Barnard performs the first heart transplant.

Amid a flourishing drug culture, LSD declared illegal by US government.

1968

Martin Luther King, Jr. was shot and killed in Memphis, Tennessee.

Richard Nixon was elected US President.

Robert Kennedy assassinated in California.

Woodstock Festival drew 500,000 people for three days of live music and peace.

1969

Neil Armstrong walked on the moon, a success for NASA's Apollo 11 mission.

Wal-Mart Incorporated as Wal-Mart Stores Inc.

1972

Equal Rights Amendment passed (prohibited sex discrimination).

Gloria Steinem launched feminist magazine, *Ms.*

I was particularly affected by the Women's Movement. The roles of women being limited to wives and mothers began to be questioned in a big way by Betty Freidan in her book, *The Feminine Mystique,* and young feminists who were not part of the older, pre-war, women's groups. These equal rights pioneers encouraged the questioning of many aspects of society with the idea that society itself, not just the legal system, was unfair to women. Equal opportunity resonated with me—not so much as a matter of ideology but as simple fairness. The ideas were fueled by the increasing activism in the 1960s, which led to the development of the Women's Movement of the 1970s. Significant in changing women's lives was the Federal Government approval in 1961 of the birth control pill; my, how women's lives changed.

My life changed almost overnight. I was likely more aware of the increased activism because I was on campus much of the time. Assuredly, ISU and other mid-west campuses were less extreme in their activism than states on the East and West Coasts. Being interested in psychology and sociology, I was drawn to a course called "Group Process." It encompassed a wide gamut of human rights issues, and demonstrated how positive results could be achieved in groups of diverse individuals with "open minds." Our differences were addressed as we discussed our personal needs, individual rights, and the rights of others. REAL listening and interaction was demonstrated and practiced. I participated in my first ever retreat with my class.

In my 16 years of marriage, this was the first time I had spent three days away from my family. I wasn't comfortable in the group. I wasn't one to open my heart to just anyone. It was more like I was in the water, but not getting wet; I remained an observer. Still, there was value to me. In the open, caring environment, I was asked and encouraged to be honest about who I was *other* than a dutiful wife and mother. In my generation, being a wife and mother was supposed to be enough. *Was it enough for me?* Most of all, I wanted love and acceptance. This I believed I had—*My family was my passion! I* began to open up to other concepts such as:

What are my rights as a person?

It's okay for me to have needs that can't be fulfilled by my family alone.

It's unfair to my family to make them feel they are responsible for my happiness.

Wouldn't I be a more interesting person if I expanded my interests and knowledge?

George is getting his Doctorate. Will he "outgrow" me?

Honestly, this was the first time I had considered myself as a unique person apart from being a wife and mother. This concept was revolutionary. *It was okay for me to have needs.*

By sharing some thoughts regarding the retreat, my family acknowledged that I was a little different in my ideas, but they were so busy with their own lives that we were soon pretty much back to status quo. Occasionally there would be a comment such as, "You must have learned that at the retreat." We would all laugh.

I shared my retreat experience with Rhoda; she was always a good listener. However, my lifestyle was changing in a way that wasn't feasible for her with her four children and an ailing mother-in-law to care for. We continued to be close, and talked on the phone often. Helen was now into parenting and I was thinking of a career. We were all discovering that our personalities are formed by both the people in our lives and the events that dominate it. As children, we shared the same environment; as adults, our environments were very diverse.

My love for them continues as strong as ever. I've treasured the following quote for over 30 years, by "author unknown."

Psalm for Sisters

I lift up my eyes and smile as I give thanks for my sisters. My radiant, complicated sisters, who are more than sisters—they are friends. (Blessed is the woman who has someone like her, thrice blessed if she has more than one.)

I thank the good Lord that we were children together, sharing the same room, and for years—the same bed.

Thank you for these women who shared my parents, my past, my blood; who see my whole—the beginning, long ago, and the person I am now. My sisters, whose faults are so clear to me—and dear to me, just as my faults are to them. Yet, for all our differences, and the miles that lie between us, we will still battle the world for each other.

Dear God, please take good care of them, these sisters I love so much.

Our nine years in Terre Haute were almost perfect. Doug and Terri had the freedom to explore and develop their individual interests and talents. We were pleased they were both good students and interested in sports. Doug was more interested in competitive sports than Terri. In gymnastics, Terri had progressed to the competitive level when she became more interested in cheerleading and other activities. She, like her mother, was a good spectator for both her school and the University sports. Doug played a year of football in junior high school, but the season conflicted with tennis. Also, he was becoming interested in basketball. Neither Doug nor Terri appeared to be interested in music, but they tried several instruments.

The children and I were extremely proud of George, as was all the Oberle family, for completing his P.E.D. from Indiana University in 1969. He was the first in either of our families to achieve this level of education. Indiana University has a beautiful campus surrounded by the colorful Brown County area noted for its spectacular fall foliage and unique little shops. I had always wanted to live on the IU campus.

Since George fulfilled his residency requirements in one summer and fall semester, we elected not to have the children change schools for this short period of time. He rented a little basement apartment and the children and I remained in Terre Haute. Instead of George renting his cap and gown for graduation, the children and I purchased one as his graduation present. As it turned out, the remainder of his career was at the university level; this gift served him well. ISU recognized George's professional growth and gave him more administrative and leadership responsibilities. He was promoted to Assistant Dean and Coordinator of Graduate Studies in the School for Health, Physical Education, and Recreation.

While keeping the home fires burning, I completed my BS degree in Health Education. (Yes, this was in George's Department at ISU, but he was never my professor.)

In the spring of 1971, we were rocked out of our complacency. George accepted a position as Professor and Chair of the Department of Health, Physical Education, Recreation and Athletics at Chicago State University, Chicago, Illinois. He and I were extremely concerned about asking Doug and Terri to give up their friends, schools, and the only home they had cared about.

With a great deal of guilt on the part of us parents, we made the move to Munster, Indiana, just south of Chicago. George and I were not very popular with our children. Doug was completing his sophomore year and looked forward to playing varsity sports during his junior and senior years. His recourse was, "What about my friends? And being a new kid, I won't be able to play sports!" Terri, with a long face, chimed in, "What about my cheerleading… and I will not know anyone there except my brother!" Since I considered myself a "camp follower" I was happy for George's professional growth and achievements but hurt for the children. Yes, I would miss my dear friends. Most importantly, our family would still be together, and in my "Pollyanna" way I believed the move would turn out for the best… I prayed.

Star Athletes Doug and Terri (1969)

As I write this, I suspect young women of today might consider this Neanderthal thinking: "How could you be so submissive?" Or, "You had a *life* yanked out by the roots!" But this was the era in which I lived. I had been programmed this way since childhood and so was George. His role was being the "breadwinner" and mine was to be a "stay-at-home mom" and to be there for my husband. For us it seemed to work…though I didn't realize there were other options. Most of my women friends lived the same way. In looking back, there seemed to be less stress on marriages. I don't recall any divorces among our friends. The husband's masculinity was never threatened and he knew the home fires were tended to, allowing him to give his full attention to his career. The times were changing rapidly, and so did our family. *Little Emily, are you keeping up? Can you see how I felt that as long as I went along with George, I would have the feeling of security you never had?*

Chapter 8

Family in Transition

Twenty years from now you will be more disappointed by the things you didn't do than the ones you did. So throw off the bowlines. Sail from the safe harbor. Catch the trade winds in your sails. Explore. Dream. Discover.

—Mark Twain

The 1970s forced us to rethink human rights issues in all areas of society, including family, community and careers. The country was in transition, as was our family. Our country, after years of discussion and debate, finally passed the Equal Rights amendment (1972), which prohibited sex discrimination, calling for equal treatment of women and men under the law, and Title IX, which was intended to end gender discrimination in high school and college athletics. Everyone in our family experienced the impact of these changes, as I will relay here. National and significant events included:

1970

World Trade Center in NY completed.

The Beatles foursome broke up.

Computer floppy disc introduced.

Kent State University shootings (unarmed students killed by National Guard, who were there to control massive protests over Vietnam War developments).

First Earth Day.

1971

VCRs introduced.

Richard Nixon became the first American president to visit China.

Busing of students ordered to promote racial desegregation.

Mark Spitz won seven Olympic gold medals in swimming for USA.

Palestinian extremist group invaded Olympic Games in Munich.

MASH TV show premiered.

Watergate scandal resulted from break-in of Democratic National Headquarters and the Nixon administration's cover up of its involvement.

1973

Roe v. Wade Supreme Court Case legalizes abortion in the US.

Sears Tower built in Chicago, then the tallest building in the world.

US pulled out of Vietnam.

US VP Spiro T. Agnew resigned in the midst of criminal investigations of bribery.

1974

US President Nixon resigns rather than face impeachment following Watergate.

Patty Hearst, newspaper heiress, kidnapped by Symbionese Liberation Army.

In writing this book, I've been more aware of how our family's lifestyle and events throughout history parallel world changes. Just as we prayed that our family would evolve in positive ways from its experiences, we wished the same for our country. As I've shared, moving was routine in our early married life. This time, change was more difficult, even traumatic, for most of our family after having enjoyed nine years in Terre Haute. It was especially hard for Doug and Terri.

Though we needed to be within commuting distance for George's new job in South Chicago, we did have some area choices to make, and we put the children's interests as the primary consideration in this decision. Thus, we chose to stay in Indiana instead of moving to Illinois. Doug could continue playing tennis in the fall and baseball in the spring, which was not possible in Illinois where both were spring sports. Two communities with excellent school systems, both within commuting distance for George, were seriously considered. Glen Ellyn was the more upscale community. Doug voted against this choice, saying, "I won't have the money to date *those* high school girls." (He eventually married a Glen Ellyn girl he met at college). We purchased a large two-story home with a basement near the high school in Munster, Indiana. It turned out to be a wise choice and a functional family home.

As was true for all our moves, this one had its uniqueness. The events still vivid in my mind include:

George attending his national professional meeting in Reno, Nevada, during the packing stage of our move, and returning the day the furniture was to be delivered in Munster.

The children and I sleeping on the floor of one of the upstairs bedrooms in our new home the night before the furniture arrived.

Terri's love at first sight—a Saint Bernard puppy running out from a friend's garage. This friend (George's former student) raised registered Saint Bernards, and she generously offered Terri a purebred puppy. We couldn't say no to this love affair. Our hope was that the new companion would help Terri adjust to the move.

George immediately embraced his new challenges at Chicago State University. He was charged with facilitating a move and transition to a new campus as well as enhancing their programs in the Department of Health, Physical Education, Recreation and Athletics. I focused on exploring opportunities for Doug and Terri and organizing our home. Doug enrolled as a junior, and Terri as a freshman, in Munster High School.

In spite of Doug getting involved with his varsity sports, he appeared withdrawn and unhappy. He had a really close friend back in Terre Haute, in whom he confided by letter. I'm not proud to admit that in the interest of better understanding Doug, I opened, read and resealed one of her letters, hoping he wouldn't notice. He noticed. Holding the letter, he said angrily, "Mother, I can't believe you opened this." To this day, that is one of the two major regrets I have in child-rearing. The letter didn't provide much insight to Doug's unhappiness.

He later confessed that he was okay with the move, but enjoyed the sympathy and extra attention we guilt-ridden parents were showing out of concern.

In a very short while, our congenial, fearless, popular Terri was elected freshman president. Again, she tried gymnastics, but swimming, especially synchronized swimming, was much more to her liking. Her face would light up when she spoke of the Girls Timing Organization (GTO). This involved her in most of the varsity athletic events. Synchronized swimming was new to me, and I watched Terri perform in admiration. I could barely tread water.

After any major change (like a move), one would naturally feel stressed, but once again, I *acted* like I was calming the chaos with ease and grace. I felt it was my responsibility to help the children adjust and be happy with their new school, activities, and friends, while also cheering on George and making our new house a home. Sometimes, that burden was just too much.

Terri with Kashia (Munster, IN, 1972)

One afternoon, I picked Terri and a girlfriend up from school. We stopped at a lumber company to find shelving for a bookcase. I ended up becoming extremely frustrated trying to find boards that I thought would be suitable. A salesman approached and asked if he could help. Inappropriately, I said, "I don't like your lumber," with tears rolling down my cheeks. This very kind salesman said, "Let me help you." I was terribly embarrassed by my behavior, especially in front of the girls. Being tired and stressed was not a legitimate excuse. With the steady help of the salesman, I collected myself and made a purchase, feeling relieved later when George came home and was pleased with my choice of lumber.

The next morning, I was the only person home when the doorbell rang. It was the lumber salesman, holding an enormous armload of colorful cut flowers. "Your Monday was such a bad day," he said. "I hope these flowers will help you have a good Tuesday. I wouldn't want my wife to have your bad experience." Mortified, I thanked him, and he went on his way. Of course, George had questions when he returned that evening and found flowers all over the house. I've never forgotten this act of kindness and my embarrassment. It was such a life lesson about how neglecting one's self-care can drain one's ability to deal with normal daily challenges, and how acting non-stressed is actually counterproductive.

I guess Doug got tired of his act as well, since he no longer seemed miserable with his new life. He was so active in sports and other school activities; he was on-the-go all the time. Doug participated in varsity sports each season: fall tennis, winter basketball, spring baseball and tennis tournaments during the summer. We enjoyed attending Doug and Terri's school events and were extremely proud parents. When Doug, or any of the team, missed a shot, the crowd booed—that really bothered me. I didn't like it when the crowd booed officiating calls made by George, but to have our son booed was worse. I especially enjoyed Doug's tennis matches, and was inspired to take tennis lessons our first summer in Munster at age 40. This was one of the best things that I had done for myself in a very long time.

Interrupting my Munster routine was a surprise phone call from Terre Haute friends, asking us to join them in the purchase of a condominium on Siesta Key in Florida. This became our favorite beach (and was later voted the number one beach in the US in 2010). I was the only one in the family available to make the trip to Florida to investigate this opportunity, but we all embraced the idea. We purchased the condominium and spent that Christmas, and many other Christmas vacations, on that beautiful, white, sandy beach.

Since we traveled by car from Indiana to Florida, we were able to visit Helen and her little family in their unique home snuggled in an acre of trees and flowers in Marietta, Georgia. Helen's skillful landscaping made it a showplace. Their lives were focused on their young sons, Alan and Kevin. Al was a Boy Scout leader and involved his sons early on.

Our new home soon became a busy hub for teenagers. We equipped our basement with ping-pong, a pool table, and other teen games. It seemed easier to keep our own children safe if the crowd was in our home, where we knew they were supervised. We were no longer in our protected environment in Lincolnshire. It wasn't unusual for alcohol and marijuana to be sneaked into some of the teen parties. George, working in Chicago, was more aware of the temptations that young people faced in the 70s. Doug and Terri were encouraged to leave other places and bring their friends to our house if parents were not in attendance or anything was going on that they thought questionable. This happened quite regularly.

Since my home situation had never permitted me to be a "typical teenager," I felt especially insecure as a parent of teenagers. As is typical, the opinions of their peers were often more important to them than those of their parents. In child rearing, we had been relaxed in our rules and believed in reinforcing positive choices and playing down poor choices. It's a given that one's friends can influence the direction of one's life, and we tried to reinforce this with our teenagers. During their period of growing into independence, we often missed their good choices, but heard more about bad choices. I relied a lot on prayer and humor. "The good news is how much modern life is inspired by the wisdom of the ages. The bad news is the ages are between 12 and 21," was one quote I could relate to.

It seemed a long time since we had experienced the happiness and joy of a family wedding. In 1972, George's baby brother, David, married his petite, brunette, attractive, cheerleader and high school sweetheart, Chris. David had taken a coaching position in a high school near his West Newton, Indiana, family home. This was a blessing for mom and dad Oberle. In retirement years, they were able to follow David's team and delight in having this young family nearby. In contrast to our many moves throughout our married life, Dave and Chris lived their entire lives near both their parents and high school friends.

By the end of our first year in Munster, we were all finding advantages to the move. George's salary increase from $18,000 to $30,000 (approximately equivalent to $167,000 in 2013) gave us more freedom in our budget. We were able to buy a piano and provide piano lessons for both Doug and Terri. Unfortunately, it was not their cup of tea. In retrospect, it would have made more sense to rent a piano.

Most of the Oberles were making the best of our move to Munster. The children's lives were filled with fun and challenges. Meanwhile, I was having trouble adjusting. I missed so very much about our life in Terre Haute…our roots were deep… I had an identity there. In my Pollyanna way, I told myself to be patient, and I would find my place. I did find opportunities in our church, found a P.E.O. group to join, and was enjoying learning to play tennis. However, I missed being a part of George's world and doing activities as a family. Even though we attended the events where our children were participants, it was different. I treasured my experience accompanying Terri to obedience school for her St. Bernard, Kausia. I was needed to drive while Terri managed Kausia, a huge energetic dog. I wanted our playful family Sunday afternoons at ISU back.

I missed enjoying the stimulation of university life, but the long commute into the South Chicago campus made this impractical. For the same reason, we rarely had George's colleagues as guests in our home. Instead, George renewed old friendships in the Munster area, i.e., teachers and coaches he had met professionally. We socialized more with them rather than working to make new friends in the community.

I missed my private nurturing times with George and made a special effort to create those opportunities. I took advantage of evenings which were unscheduled for intimate dinners for the two of us in our home. (Yes, I finally had learned to cook and enjoyed it.) One such evening surely didn't go as planned, but later afforded us many laughs—even though it wasn't funny at the time. It started with a romantic dinner by candlelight, after which we ended up in our bedroom. Our well-choreographed evening ended too soon—we smelled smoke! George ran downstairs to investigate. He yelled, "Our house is on fire!" *Little Emily, my mind, after all those years, went to three little girls huddled in a corner while their house was all ablaze.*

He called the fire department. Trying to figure out what had started this awful fire, we discovered that the match I had used to light the candles at dinner was not completely out when I tossed it into the waste basket. This was an embarrassing and expensive lesson to learn. When the children returned that evening, we were wrapped in blankets in front of the fireplace looking a little sheepish, trying to stay warm since we had the entire house open to get rid of the smoky odor. This wasn't easy to explain to our children and the neighbors. As I've learned throughout my life, best intentions don't always turn out as planned.

As a family, we enjoyed hosting George's staff for an annual Christmas party. It was a lively, fun time with a great a deal of dancing initiated by an amazing dance instructor with pink hair. Yes, Peggy Dunlap not only had bright pink hair, but almost everything she owned was pink. We all grew to love her. I don't think Doug has ever had a better dance partner. George's large staff at CSU included more nationalities than at the previous universities. Our family was enriched through learning about their cultures, but was not able to share enough time and experiences with them to become close friends.

Also, as I stated earlier, George knew a number of coaches in the area, and we were able to become better acquainted with their families. The wife of one was in charge of school nurses in Hammond, Indiana, a city adjoining Munster. She offered me a position as a school nurse covering two elementary schools in Hammond. Even though I had not worked full-time since Doug was born, this opportunity appealed to me; I did have time on my hands, as I was feeling less needed at home. I was especially pleased because the school setting meant I would have the summer off to be with our children. I accepted the position.

My assignments were inner city schools with primarily black children. The principals, both highly committed black men in their late 30s, had concerns that I would have difficulty relating to their students and parents since I lived in Munster, which had few poor or minority residents. Their doubts were short-lived, as they quickly saw how much I cared for their children. My focus on health education was sorely needed. The parents welcomed the study groups I formed. I was the only medical person that many of the parents had access to, and in fact, they would often bring other ill siblings for me to see and evaluate. *Little Emily, my childhood experiences helped me to relate to these needy families.*

It broke my heart to learn of the home situations that many of the children had to endure. For example, I heard on the news about a local bar shooting—to my surprise, the children of the men involved were in school the following day. I didn't feel adequately trained, but was filling the roles of a nurse, psychologist, health educator, friend and social worker. There were not enough hours in the day to accomplish all that needed to be done. It was a real learning experience and fulfilling; I felt that I was making a difference in the lives of many of the families.

Doug and Terri were looking forward to their second year in Munster High School. Doug had been elected captain of the basketball team for his senior year. A new basketball coach was hired over the summer—in fact, it was a young coach George had recommended. Unfortunately for Doug and other seasoned players, the new coach saw more benefit in giving the younger players experience playing while the seniors sat on the bench. It was very anticlimactic for the senior players to have the coach more interested in looking ahead to the next year. Being a close family, we all felt Doug's disappointment.

He began to increase conditioning for baseball season, only to have a friend accidentally fall onto his right wrist. This resulted in a serious injury for Doug. We all thought, "More bad luck—no baseball." Fortunately, the wrist was not broken, just badly sprained. The wrist took a long time to heal, but Doug did have a successful baseball season leading to college scholarship offers. He was *that* good.

Even though Terri was two years younger than Doug, their social maturity was nearly at the same level. Her peers became increasingly important, and the more friends she had around, the happier she was. She was at ease with Doug's friends as well as her own classmates. She was an excellent student, embraced life, and was open to new experiences.

Not too long ago, Terri was sharing some school experiences with her 13-year-old daughter, Nicole, in my presence. "I was surprised that my parents allowed me to leave the house at 4 AM to T.P. the homes of popular athletes prior to a major event," she said. (This was, and, I believe, still remains a popular practice in some high schools.) "I don't think I would allow you to be out at that time without me."

As I reflect, George and I felt that we lived in a safe enough neighborhood, and as long as she was in a group, we trusted Terri. Our philosophy was that we fully trusted our children, and would until they gave us reason to question that trust. Admittedly, the time came that, right or wrong, George and I found reasons to question that trust. For example, George found a vodka bottle under the seat of Doug's car. Doug said that it did not belong to him, but would not "rat" on a friend. In later years, his friend Roger reminisced that it was his liquor bottle that got Doug into trouble. Doug laughed then, but at the time it wasn't funny.

Also, we found out from various sources that Terri would go against our wishes to keep up with her friends. For example, she was sometimes not actually where she had told us she was going. As is typical at that age, pleasing her parents was less important than pleasing her peers. Even today, I'm still surprised at events shared in Doug and Terri's reminiscing about high school days. I thought, as parents, we may have been better off not knowing.

Gail Sheehe's book, *Passages*, and other such books helped me better understand teenagers as well as conscientious, struggling parents. In one of our mother-daughter disagreements, I overreacted, lost my cool, and slapped Terri in the face. Even today, I am ashamed and continue to live with this regret. This was the second of my unforgivable mistakes in parenting. (The first I shared earlier, relating to opening a letter Doug received.) Terri and I talked about this event after she became an adult. She said, "When I got mad at you, I remember thinking that I wouldn't care if you were run over by a car." This hurt went deep. Nowhere have I read that parenting is easy. I remember thinking that there would be payback time if and when Doug and Terri had children of their own. And, they would also learn that the rewards outweigh the challenges. As parents, I know we make mistakes. I also believe that as long as children know they are loved, they will be okay.

Even with Doug's disappointments, I think he would call his senior year successful. Munster High had a reputation for strong college preparation. He made wonderful friendships, some of which he continues to maintain. He chose to attend Eastern Illinois University with the help of a baseball scholarship. The summer after Doug's graduation was both happy and sad. We were proud and happy in sharing Doug's excitement and preparation for college, but sad to have "our little boy" leaving home.

That summer, Terri's 16th birthday party was the talk of the town. Our beautiful, popular "social butterfly" was extremely inclusive with her guest list. It was an informal cookout where the numbers kept growing. This required a quick mid-party trip to the grocery store. Since it was in July, the Cross Country Team was already practicing. They ran through our backyard and helped themselves to the hot dogs George was grilling. Adding to Terri's joy was her new driver's license. She was pleased to be able to drive our two-week-old Mustang. Unfortunately, she totaled it. She said, "I turned at an intersection because a truck driver motioned me to do so. I learned that it's my responsibility to make sure the coast is clear." *Thank God she was not seriously injured!*

George was the only family member not content with life. Into his third year at CSU, he was becoming impatient and discouraged with all the obstacles to change, and questioned whether he could ever accomplish what he believed his department needed in order to attract and maintain quality students. The civil rights issues were huge at this campus. He began exploring other universities for career opportunities in his field as well as entrepreneurial offerings from his coaching friends.

Whether it was George's dream to "get rich quick" or his desire to help friends, he invested in Shoe-Inns, Inc. in Gary, Indiana with a coach friend. This enterprise would focus on top of the line, athletic shoes. Another investment George became excited about was with a coaching friend from Maryville, Indiana; Play-Co, Inc. designed and manufactured play rugs. I was getting a little concerned because of the money needed to assure our children a college education.

Doug, HS Graduation (1972)

In the spring of 1974, George attended his national conference in Las Vegas. There, he was recruited to be Chairman of the Department of Health, Physical Education and Recreation at Oklahoma State University (OSU) in Stillwater, Oklahoma. He had his initial interview in a non-traditional setting—the lobby of one of the casinos. His interest was piqued as it would be another big step up his career ladder. Negotiations were continued following his return home and he scheduled a visit to OSU for late May. Terri and I accompanied him.

The night before flying to Oklahoma, George and I chaperoned Terri's junior prom. We helped check the students as they arrived to make sure they didn't sneak in alcohol. Later, we discovered that some clever students were successful getting past our inspection. They hid alcohol in the guys' top hats and under the girls' dresses, held in place with a garter. I found a very drunk girl vomiting in the bathroom. She begged us not to take her home. Instead, we took her to our house (not very wise), gave her coffee, and walked her around until she was sober enough for her date to take her home. Terri had a wonderful time with her steady guy, Skip. We left for Oklahoma, exhausted.

My first thoughts of Oklahoma were from the stories I had read concerning the huge dust storms often causing dust pneumonia, and about herds of Buffalo roaming over the countryside. This was so completely wrong. According to Oklahoman propaganda, there are more waterways in Oklahoma than in Minnesota. Of course, in Oklahoma they are man-made, and the water is not clear, but red from the clay in the soil. We were warmly welcomed by OSU representatives, and it was soon obvious that George was their first choice for the position, with the major responsibility of implementing Title IX.

Our primary concern was moving Terri for her senior year. This seemed so unfair, since we moved her as a freshman. Also, she was experiencing her first love…the situation had the makings for her to most likely feel like she hated her parents. Since Doug was in college, it wasn't likely to affect him much. As a family, we made the decision for George to accept the position in Oklahoma, but Terri and I would remain in Munster until she graduated from high school. This was quite a sacrifice, and expense, to accommodate her, but one that George and I felt was appropriate under the circumstances.

Though we had previously told her she could make her own decision about college (she was considering majoring in accounting), our compromise was for her to start college work at OSU. George would be missing so much of her senior year; he wanted the opportunity to share her early college experiences. We agreed that if she wasn't getting what she expected at OSU, she could transfer.

The wheels started moving for George to make the transition from Indiana to Oklahoma. He decided to rent an apartment in Stillwater, and Terri and I would stay in our Munster home, but put it on the market. However, the first person I told that we were selling our home offered us a price we felt was fair and, just like that, our Munster home was sold. In retrospect, we could have probably done better working through a realtor. Terri and I found a small furnished apartment, and we shopped for a house in Stillwater. This was accomplished in a weekend. George helped us downsize our furniture prior to the move. The most painful downsizing was finding a home for Kausia. We had all learned to love her, but knew that the warm weather in Oklahoma and our non-traditional lifestyle would not be fair to her. Finally, after a great deal of work, headaches and tears, we were all in position for the 1974 school year: George in his new job at OSU, Doug in his sophomore year at Eastern Illinois University, Terri in her senior year in Munster High School, and I continued as an inner city school nurse in Hammond.

Unlike any of our previous moves, this totally rocked my world. This splitting up was a heartbreaking, painful decision for me, even though I considered it wise and practical. I wondered if divorce could have been any more painful. I seemed to be the only one taking it that hard. George was totally absorbed in this new challenge, and Doug was heavily involved in college life. Terri was experiencing her first love, and leading the life she should as an intelligent, popular senior. Fortunately, I had my work. This was rewarding, but I wanted more. By not being a couple, I felt totally neglected by my friends. *My loneliness reached such depths!*

My life had been my family, and now they didn't seem to need me. *How I ached.* After a few months, Terri acknowledged my despair and offered to move to Oklahoma. This was a wake-up call for me. I so wanted her senior year to be the best ever, and did not want her concerned about me. I needed to learn that I could survive on my own.

Who am I without my family? I had to find out. Again, I turned to books. I found Joan Erikson's books helpful. She theorized that women are partly controlled by the changing powers of their body. "Women experience phases that come every seven years and change us emotionally, spiritually and physically," Erikson wrote. "The first seven are filled with wonder. From seven to fourteen, we are hormonal; from fourteen to twenty-one we are sexual; from twenty-one to twenty-eight, we experience the desire to procreate, after which our time is consumed with mothering and putting others first; at thirty-five, however, we began to wake up and look beyond such a limited existence; between forty-nine to fifty-six, we desire to live without rules, and go away until finally we have the chance to find our individual reason for being. It is after that when we truly become who we are."

There was comfort in thinking that, if Joan Erikson's theory was correct, I wasn't the only woman at my age struggling with identity and purpose. I made a vow to myself that I would never again become so dependent on other people. It isn't fair to them, or to me. Yes, people would continue to be important in my life, but *not my total life*. I kept reminding myself with positive affirmations such as, "Unlike sponges, we are in charge of what we soak up. We can saturate ourselves with 'poor little me' or we can overflow with gratitude and appreciation."

Little Emily, do see how life can change at unexpected times, and add additional pieces to life's puzzle? Each puzzle piece is a new challenge and a lesson to learn.

I had been on my own and independent prior to meeting my "knight." But once I had someone who loved me and wanted to take care of me, I had easily moved into dependency. Many historians refer to the 1970s as "the worst decade of the post- war era." For me, other women, and minorities, a number of positive events, especially the passing of the equal rights amendment, were moving us toward greater opportunities.

The activism of the 60s continued into the 70s, particularly for women and other minorities. As the war in Vietnam came to an end, new social causes came to the forefront, especially environmentalism. Economic equality of the sexes still proved an elusive goal. Even as women moved into nontraditional jobs and big companies opened day care centers for working mothers, disparities in pay for men and women doing the same job remained significant.

Doug, Terri, Marie and George, at Theta Pond, OSU (1973)

In retrospect, our nontraditional lifestyle was a blessing in disguise. I found encouragement in Romans 5:3-4: "Rejoice in our sufferings, because we know that suffering produces perseverance; perseverance, character; and character, hope." I began dreaming about and looking forward to life in Oklahoma. Our trips to visit George were filled with joy, hope, and planning. Terri enjoyed spending time in the dormitories making new friends and getting acquainted with the campus. I realized that George was also missing his family. We were all with him at Spring Break and learned that he had arranged for a family portrait near Theta Pond on the OSU campus. He said, "I was afraid this might be the last time we would all be together." *This broke my heart.*

I encouraged him to tell us about his new life. He shared with us some of his challenges in implementing Title IX. "Change doesn't come easy in education, when things have been done a certain way for so many years," he said. "It's really hard to change a mindset." He was laying his groundwork by getting to know his staff. He had entertained them in our home. (As I looked at broken dishes, likely from the move, stacked on the tea cart, I smiled to myself, thinking, "…men don't seem to notice things like this.") I was confident that in his persistent, yet gentle, manner, he would win them over. He also shared his experience with lesbians on his staff. He had likely worked with them previously; but they had not "come out of the closet." Now he had a colleague whose significant other had been previously married and had two children. This family, knowing that George missed his family, often visited and brought him dinner. I remember him saying, "This is an experience I didn't expect in conservative Oklahoma." I began to understand his loneliness for his family, amid his new challenges. There was so very much in my life for which to be thankful. "Pity party" time was over.

This was about the time we learned that courageous Helen, who had been plagued with back problems and generalized nerve-related discomforts for several years, had been diagnosed with multiple sclerosis. What heartbreaking news! She didn't deserve this additional health challenge. I thought it would have been easier for me to manage this disability with our children being "out of the nest."

During one visit to Oklahoma, new acquaintances, Jack and Marguerite Shelton, invited me and George to the Stillwater Country Club for dinner. In learning more about the Sheltons, we discovered that Marguerite was on the board for the Indian Meridian Vocational Technical School (IMVTS). This school would serve the Stillwater and surrounding-area high school students, and was scheduled to open in the fall of 1975. Marguerite said, "Marie, I know you are an RN and have a BS degree in health education. Would you have interest in a teaching position?"

I couldn't believe I was hearing this—an opportunity to teach. I responded, "I would like to know a little more about the position."

She described the program: "The purpose of the program is to introduce interested high school students to health related careers. Also, the students could leave the program with a Nurse Assistant certificate. You would be required to develop this program." The opportunity excited me. I already knew there were not any openings in the area for high school health teachers as they had coaches teach these classes. An instructor was already being considered for the IMVTS position, but she didn't have a teaching degree. Vocational teachers were permitted to teach without a teaching degree as long as they were taking classes in pursuit of a degree. Marguerite arranged a meeting for me with Dr. Thomas Reed, the IMVTS superintendent, and I was offered the position before Terri and I returned to Indiana.

We were immensely proud of Terri for all the honors she achieved in Munster High School. Her graduation was such a gratifying time for us. We felt guilty about asking Terri to start her college experience at OSU; now, we told her that she had college choices. To our delight, Terri chose OSU, saying, "I want to attend a large university because they are likely to have a stronger Accounting Department, but I want the feeling of a small friendly campus. OSU has both." George had been farsighted in helping Terri feel comfortable at OSU prior to our move.

While the George Oberle family was focusing on our transition from Indiana to Oklahoma, Dave and Chris Oberle were transitioning into parenthood. Their first child, Derrik, was welcomed into the world in June of 1975. All the family was thrilled to have a new baby in our fold—it had been awhile.

Tying up loose ends in Munster was easy. Of course, Terri would miss her friends, especially her boyfriend, Skip. However, most of her friends would also be leaving for college in the fall. I felt I had made a positive difference in the lives of many of the students and their parents in the schools where I worked. Saying goodbye was difficult; I felt that I had been given a gift to work with those families. Also, I had made good progress toward my goal for greater independence. My self-confidence had increased, and I had more insight into myself as a person. I was becoming more competent in putting my thoughts into actions. I believe Terri was open to new experiences in Oklahoma, and I knew that I was.

Chapter 9

Turning Points

Events in our lives happen in a sequence in time, but in their significance to ourselves they find their own order… the continuous thread of revelation.

—Eudora Welty

I think of a turning point as a time of significant change or transformation. I can't speak for my family, but I have had many such powerful events. Each member of my family is represented in these events. My major turning points include going to live with my mother, Mother's suicide, meeting George, parenting, my seemingly sudden empty nest, and walking through the door of opportunity to earn my advanced degree. At the time, I may not have thought of the events as turning points; now I realize that I could never go back to who I was before that particular experience.

In reviewing my busy life, I wonder, *was my need to be busy—committing to too many people in too short a time, exhausting myself and those around me, trying to make it all happen—a struggle to accept myself?*

I had done this—goal-setting and achieving had become a way of life. Feeling unworthy and insecure, I may have created the goals in hopes that achieving them would make me feel good about myself. Yet, I can't believe this was all bad, as I grew in confidence each time I achieved a goal.

I am wondering now whether I have to feel finished in order to feel whole. Only God is perfect, I remind myself. I'm feeling more whole and I like myself—and I'm a little nicer to myself.

I am speaking for our entire family in saying that our turning points have included challenges, uncertainty, excitement, and even regrets. I felt satisfied that in spite of my parenting insecurities, George and I had raised (with the main ingredient being love) well-adjusted, happy, young people who were excited about their futures. We acknowledged we made mistakes. The statement, "There is no recipe for parenting" comes to mind. I remember saying to George that from that time on, Doug and Terri will be needing us less in their lives. Doug was completing his second year of college, and Terri ready to start her college career.

Certainly, we didn't expect to be greeted by a tornado during our first week in Oklahoma—and on Friday the 13th. Our home was at a higher elevation than the OSU campus and from our backyard we could see it touch down on the campus. Terri was really terrified as she drove home during tornado winds. She later learned that she should have gotten out of the car and laid face down in a ditch. This experience we could have lived without!

A pleasant surprise was the friendliness and open trust of the Oklahoma people. Living so near Chicago, we had become more guarded and were surprised when Stillwater businesses allowed us to take items from their stores to see what matched or fit into our home without paying or even signing for them. They would say, "Take the items home and see what works and pay when you return what you don't need." Wow. In a way, it was a small thing, but it enlightened us as to the culture of our new community and we liked it very much. The only downside was that in this relaxed, laid-back environment, we had to adjust some of our expectations. For example, during typical business hours if we needed something from a local shop, we often found the store closed with a sign on their door, "Gone fishing."

Doug was completing his sophomore year at EIU. He had become less pleased with the baseball program, but happy that he could switch to varsity tennis and still receive financial assistance. We all spent a happy summer of 1975 in Oklahoma. Both Doug and Terri enjoyed lifeguarding at the OSU pool and began making friends in Stillwater. They were introduced to the local entertainment which included "Turtle Races" at the Mason Jar, a popular bar near campus. A washtub with the bottom removed was used as a holding place for the turtles. Participants in the races would put identifying marks on their turtle and deposit them in the holding tub. The tub was lifted to begin the race and a good-sized crowd cheered the turtles on. The first turtle to cross the finish line earned its owner the prize of a six-pack of beer.

George had met a group of women tennis players at the Stillwater Country Club, only a couple of blocks from our home. I was immediately invited to join the group. Nancy Gibson, Sylvia Simank, and Adwina Covington were fun tennis buddies and became lifelong friends, though I am the only one of the four still living.

Still being interested in an opportunity to "get rich quick", George invested in Pilgrims Inn which was promoted as a fresh concept in motels that was sure to win the hearts of cost-minded travelers. (What…you've never heard of "Pilgrims Inn?") He even served on the board. Fortunately, he did not ask me to sign on any of these entrepreneurial ventures. I guess I was okay with his entrepreneurial activities as long as he kept his day job.

For me, the only downside to that summer was going to bus-driving school. This was necessary because in my new job I would be transporting students to healthcare facilities for hands-on experience. The training was held in Bartlesville, Oklahoma, a very hilly community. The bus used for the training was a long, 64-passenger bus with a floor clutch. This was a totally humiliating experience. While taking the test for certification, I was trying to parallel park on a hill near a fire hydrant; I nearly hit the fire hydrant. My Instructor said, "Lady, I don't think you have the bus under control." This was an understatement, and I began to cry. My knight came to the rescue. Yes, George made arrangements for me to repeat the test in a modern bus on the OSU driving range. Happily, I passed my driving test and only had to drive an automatic, air-conditioned minibus at IMVTS.

Stillwater was a University town, with approximately 45,000 residents. OSU was the only major industry. Our Stillwater home was much smaller than the one in Munster. It was a white brick, ranch-style, three-bedroom with a Great Room, on a cul-de-sac—more appropriate for our "empty nest" lifestyle. It was only a seven-minute drive to the OSU campus and a five-minute drive to IMVTS.

In the fall of 1975, George geared up for another school year and started officiating Big Eight basketball. While in Indiana, he had officiated in a number of basketball conferences including the Big 10, and also in a few football conferences. I started my new job at IMVTS, Doug returned to EIU for his junior year, and Terri enrolled at OSU and moved in to a dormitory. To give Terri more independence, we felt she would benefit by dormitory experiences, though she was welcome to come home any time she wished. We agreed to only call her in case of emergency. George delighted in her frequent visits to his office and periodically seeing her on the campus. He soon realized that our beautiful, popular teenager, less-trustworthy daughter he left in Munster was now a much more mature, responsible young lady. He had missed seeing her maturing and positive changes during her senior year. I feel she and I survived the anguish of adolescence with mutual respect.

Vocational education was a large part of the educational system in Oklahoma. In fact, Oklahoma was exemplary in curriculum and program development. Even though I had a secondary teaching degree, I needed a degree in vocational education and learned that this was offered at Central State University in Edmond, Oklahoma. Most of the IMVTS teachers commuted the 40-50 minutes for evening or Saturday classes. Students from Stillwater and surrounding high schools were bused to IMVTS. The students were diverse in their academic abilities as well as their level of socialization. Some were 4.0 students whose goal was to gain insight and experience in health-related fields to aid them in deciding on a career choice. They could also work in an entry-level health-related job while attending college. At the other end of the spectrum, my class included students who were only looking for easy classes to fulfill high school requirements for graduation.

It was a new, beautiful well-equipped high school offering a wide variety of vocational opportunities. In addition to the Health Service Careers Curriculum, leadership skills were stressed through vocational education clubs starting at the local level and extending to national competition. My club was called the Oklahoma Health Occupations Student Organization (OHOSO). I prepared the students to compete in health-related skills as well as public speaking, debate, and conducting meetings using Robert's Rules.

This position was indeed demanding. With George totally absorbed in his career and Doug and Terri both in college, I worked long hours. My lowest evaluation mark related to my getting too involved in the personal lives of my students. My response to this accusation was that I cared so much for the total student that I didn't know how to teach and care less. In all honesty, the evaluation was correct. Just as I wasn't a very good nurse because I took on the patient's pain, I found myself identifying with the students undesirable environments. For example, one girl was living with her aunt and uncle and her uncle raped her. When she phoned, George and I took her into our home for the weekend until other arrangements could be made. To me, this wasn't so unlike my junior high school teacher, who took us three students into her home when our mother committed suicide. Fortunately, I had enough bright, eager, well-adjusted students to help balance my emotional scale.

Terri was having a positive experience at OSU. Through testing, she was able to eliminate a semester of college requirements because of her excellent academic preparation in high school. Skip visited her less frequently. She pledged the Alpha Chi Omega sorority and became very active there as well as in many other aspects of college life.

Doug, in his senior year at Eastern Illinois University, had a full plate. In addition to the typical responsibilities of the seniors, he was in love with an attractive, petite cheerleader, Kathy McVoy. They were making plans for a summer wedding in Glen Ellyn, Illinois. This was built into his considerations as he explored career opportunities, which would likely be sports related.

Fortunately for us, Doug turned down two coaching position offers to accept an opportunity to manage Racket Time in Stillwater. Having worked summers at Stillwater, he had explored career options in the area. (During the summers, both our children had lifeguarded at the OSU pool.) These were joyous times. George and I always delighted in having our home filled with our children and their friends.

We became involved in the active tennis community. Of course, Doug, having played tennis competitively in high school and college, was rarely defeated. He played doubles competition with his dad and me. When he played with me he laughingly said, "Mother you can serve and get off the court. I will cover." We proudly displayed the trophies George and I won with Doug as a partner. I did improve enough to win some women's singles.

Terri didn't share our interest in tennis. Her love was the water—lifeguarding, synchronized swimming, snorkeling, and scuba diving. Her interest in the water may have been reinforced by her attraction to an OSU competitive diver, Dan Danner.

VICTORIOUS MARIE OBERLE
....Captures Women's Singles Title
Stillwater Press featured Marie on front page of the sports section (1976)

That special summer of 1977 was topped off by the very lovely July 30 wedding of Kathy McVoy and Doug Oberle in Glen Ellyn, Illinois. Most of our relatives enjoyed it with us, and it had the wonderful atmosphere of a combined wedding and family reunion. Driving from Indianapolis was George's brother David and wife Chris with their young son, Derrik, and Mom and Dad Oberle. To complete George's side of the family were his sister, Jackie, her husband Chet and family; brother, Jerry, with wife Sharon and family. On my side of the family was my sister Rhoda and brother-in-law Walt and family. From Marietta, Georgia, was my sister Helen, her husband Al, and family. We didn't get to see our Georgia family as often as we would have liked. This is the first we had seen Helen use a cane as, unfortunately, her MS was progressing and limiting her quality of life. Kathy's family was well represented as most of them lived in Illinois.

Since Doug had used part of his vacation days to travel and be in his good friend Roger's wedding (he is the one that let Doug take the blame for vodka being in Doug's car) just prior to his, he and Kathy had a really short honeymoon before settling in Stillwater. George and I drove a U-Haul truck with their wedding gifts to Stillwater on August 1st, our 23rd wedding anniversary. George and I felt very blessed that even though our children were grown, we all lived in the same area for the time being.

By having my summers free of teaching, I was able to accompany Helen and her family for a few of Al's business conventions; these were held at lovely resorts. I was able to have fun with Alan and Kebin while helping Helen, as her MS steadily reduced her quality of life.

After two successful years teaching at IMVTS, being selected as the Outstanding OHOSO Chapter in State competition, and completing my Master's degree in Health Occupation Education at Central State University (CSU), another door of opportunity opened. Central State University offered me a faculty position. I accepted the challenge to develop a course of study to teach teacher survival skills to vocational education instructors who were experts in their career fields but lacked teaching skills. This was a positive step for me.

As I look back and review my employment experience, it's difficult to believe that the only job I had asked for was when I was 16 years old and applied for a job at Read Memorial Hospital. All other opportunities were offered to me. There is a major change in the world of work today, 2014. Even young people graduating from college are having difficulty finding employment.

My adult students were in class to learn skills that would move them ahead in their careers. They were older and more motivated than most of my secondary students. The course was offered on Saturdays in workshop style. Each student was assigned a Master teacher from their school, to be available for daily assistance and encouragement. The downside to this teaching position was the hour commute to Edmond, Oklahoma.

Al and Helen Friel, George Oberle, Kathy and Doug Oberle, Rhoda and Walt Piepenbrok, Terri Oberle, Kebin and Alan Friel

I found tremendous satisfaction in teaching adults and George and I discussed how to expand my credentials in adult learning. "Lifelong learning" was becoming a frequently used term in higher education. I began to explore options for obtaining a doctoral degree in higher education with a focus on adult and continuing education. A more natural choice would be a doctorate in the healthcare area. The downside of that avenue was I would be a student in the department that George headed. That did not appeal to me as I didn't want anything that might interfere with our personal relationship. We were both aware that the nature of our relationship was changing as I became more independent. This wasn't bad—just different. We were evolving with the times, with our family and environmental changes.

Then another door of opportunity was opened—it must have been God's plan for me. Our neighbor, Jake Davis, working in the State Vocational Education Department, told me of federal money available to women and minorities to prepare them for leadership positions. I had mixed feelings about competing for this money because George and I could afford for me to return to college now that our youngest would soon be out of college. Also, I didn't feel good about competing for federal "handouts." Mother's advice came to mind: "As long as you can work, you don't need charity…work never hurt anyone." Nevertheless, I made application for the Graduate Leadership Development Program (GLDP).

One hundred and fifty awardees would be selected from thousands of US applications. I was 46 years old at the time and felt that would be a negative, though this was likely more of my self-effacing attitude. To my surprise, the application did not ask for my age, marital status, race, or if I had children. Important was previous work and volunteer experiences.

My belief was that all my volunteer leadership experience made me a strong competitor. We were required to give our first, second and third choices of schools offering the program. Fortunately, OSU was one of the 15 universities participating and my only hope for being a part of the program was to be accepted and designated to attend OSU. Believing that if I was fortunate enough to be selected, I would most likely get my third choice, I chose the University of Hawaii first, Ohio State University second, and OSU third. *Good strategy, Marie.*

The greatest thrill of my middle years (46) was being selected as one of the one hundred and fifty applicants to participate in the GLDP at OSU. What was especially meaningful to me was that I was selected on my own merit and not because I was George's wife or Doug and Terri's mother. *What a confidence boost!* My passion in life continued to be my family, but this recognition validated me as a person. My family was proud of me, but more importantly, I couldn't help but be proud of myself. *Little Emily, you must have at least one puzzle piece in your soul which believes in the possibility of a better life, an extraordinarily rich life, against all odds.*

The new bride and groom, Kathy and Doug, were transitioning from college life to married life and their careers. Terri was a senior at OSU and in love with an OSU graduate and practicing veterinarian. She was focusing on early graduation and a January, 1979, wedding. We talked about how this was a turning point in our lives…especially mine.

George (48) was winding up his fifth year at OSU. He had successfully completed the major goals he envisioned for his department. Actually, he often stated, "My philosophy [in regard to length of time to remain in a leadership position] is…if you can't accomplish what you wanted to do in five years, you need to leave and give someone else the opportunity." Thus, he was evaluating his professional options. My opportunities at OSU may have influenced his decision to remain in Stillwater.

Oklahoma seemed so distant from our families in Indiana and Georgia. We were missing the joy of seeing all the children's rapid changes. Dave and Chris provided Derrik with a baby brother, Chad, in August of 1978. With doting grandparents on both sides of the family, aunts, uncles and cousins in the area, these children were well-loved. Only our family was on the losing side.

Fall, 1978, found five Oberles at OSU: George, a professor; me, a faculty wife and doctoral student; Terri, a second semester senior; Doug, a Masters student; and Kathy, a graduate assistant and Masters student. Terri and I were full-time students, but the others had full-time jobs. For the most part, these were happy, productive times for all the Oberles.

It had been 34 years since I had been a full-time student. Five other GLDP students were in the special OSU leadership group; three men and two women. Our backgrounds were diverse: faculty wife and mother; divorced (Mormon) mother; single Caucasian lady; American Indian husband and father; and a single Caucasian man and a family man from Micronesia. Our advisor (I will call him Dr. Williams) was Caucasian, a single father and OSU professor in agricultural economics. His challenge was immense—building camaraderie and advising each student in their options to achieve diverse educational goals and leadership experience.

I visualized many rewards in my new journey as a student. My schedule would be somewhat flexible, there wasn't added pressure on our family budget, the most important of my volunteer and social activities would continue, and I could accompany George in many of his travels. What I didn't expect was that my sincerity and motivation for the GLDP was challenged by Dr. Williams and others. I overheard Dr. Williams in conversation with colleagues discussing the GLDP awardees. "In my judgment, Mrs. Oberle will be the first to drop out," he said. "Working with her is a waste of everyone's time. This is just a new whim for her; she will soon lose interest. Why would she want to work so hard when she could have such a soft country club life?" Well! I would just have to show them that I would succeed! At this time, it wasn't clear just how this would be accomplished. George, always my number one supporter asked, "What can I do?" Certainly, I appreciated his wanting to protect me, but I knew it wasn't good for his position and my independence.

In time, with a colleague of his (Dr. Jones) on my side, we gradually convinced Dr. Williams of my sincerity. Dr. Jones understood the Oklahoma culture of that era…a woman's place is in the home. Her department head was surprised that he had hired a female… After all, her first name was Waynne. I salute Dr. Williams; as soon as he was convinced that I was serious about the program, he opened up an array of leadership opportunities for me.

Terri moved home to live in her last semester. She was doubling up on coursework to graduate in three and one-half years. This wasn't easy with two majors, accounting and technology. She had to give up tutoring and other sorority activities to study and plan her January wedding. What great fun! Terri had excellent organizational skills, knew the kind of wedding she wanted, and made most of the decisions. Dan, her fiancé, was working in a veterinarian practice in Texas. At the end of my first semester in December, I was torn between studying for exams, doing the typical family Christmas activities, or helping with wedding plans. My solution was to ask for a deadline extension for my exams. (My family always came first.) The professors granted this option. Knowing that I had a choice relieved my pressure enough that I successfully completed my exams. Terri stayed on top of her many responsibilities and graduated with flying colors. Since OSU did not have a midyear graduation ceremony, she would participate in the spring. George and I were the proudest of parents!

The winters are usually mild in Oklahoma. Not true in January 1979. The icy weather prevented many out-of-town family members and friends from attending Terri and Dan's wedding. George's parents were able to arrive from Indiana. Their luggage didn't show up in time for Dad to change for the rehearsal dinner, but his flannel shirt just added humor. Dad said, "No one will be looking at me, anyway." The groom's family and friends rented a bus, which was much safer that individual automobiles on the icy streets. What wonderful memories!

Terri did an impressive job on her wedding details. She used fall colors and silk flowers, except for her fresh flower bouquet. Even today, I get tears in my eyes as I remember my mixed feelings watching that beautiful, bright, mature bride (our baby girl) walk proudly down the aisle. On the humorous side, Doug took on making sure guests at the reception had enough champagne by walking around refilling their glasses—and stuck extra bottles under his jacket only to have one drop to the floor. The cork popped out and we had a second champagne fountain. It was a lively reception, enhanced by Terri's favorite all-girl band which was perfect for dancing. She shared with us later that she was told they were lesbian. I asked, "Would that have made a difference if you had known?" She answered, "Certainly not. I had several friends in my dorm that were lesbian. In fact, I was asked if I was lesbian a number of times, because I'm a hugger, no matter what sex." I include this to show the contrast of that era with 2014, when gay marriages are an everyday occurrence.

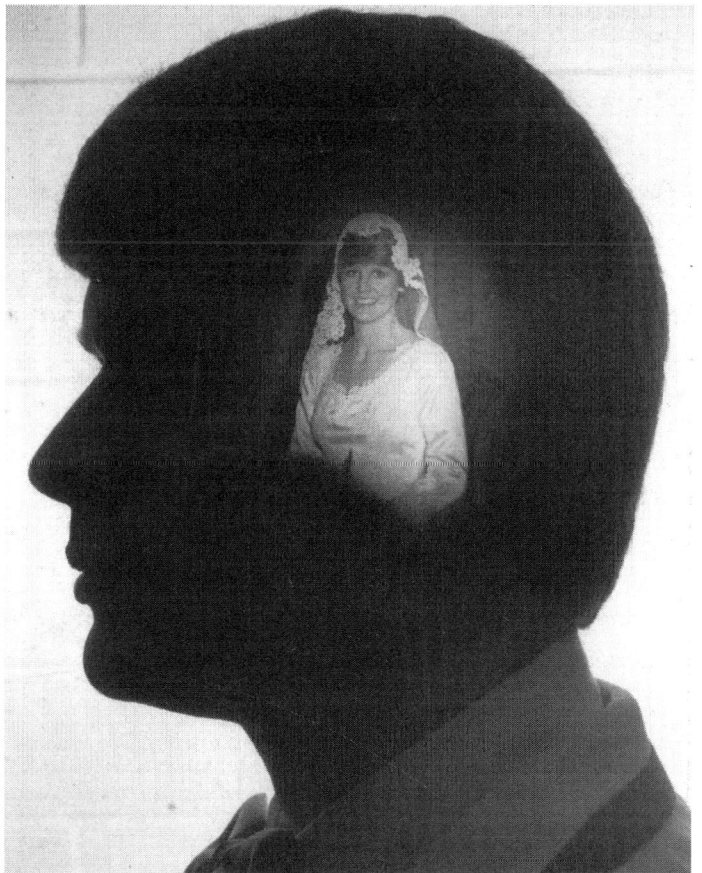

Beautiful Bride Terri with Dan Danner (1979)

The event turned out so especially nice, yet in the days following I felt pretty sad. I was left with an empty feeling, after sharing all the planning activities with Terri. Now, unlike Doug living near us after his wedding, she joined Dan in Texas. He was working with the veterinarian contracted to care for animals in a wildlife park in Arlington, Texas. She took a position with a Big Eight Accounting firm in the auditing department. She was such a people person that friends often asked, "Why did you select this career?" Her answer was usually, "It pays well and I like numbers." (She knew her parents were not getting rich in the field of education!)

My life (in 1979) continued to be enriched in a multitude of ways: we would be grandparents in June, I was more adjusted to student life, and George and I planned to go to Hawaii for our 25th wedding anniversary. WOW! Three weeks in paradise—sightseeing on all of the islands, making love any time we were in the mood, playing tennis, enjoying the beach (George bought me my first two piece bathing suit), and no responsibilities. This was a new experience... feeling carefree, cherished and risqué. Maui was our favorite island, with mountains on one side and water on the other. When we played tennis we had magical drops of water cooling our body, but the sun would dry up the moisture before it could affect the court. I had never felt so free. While embracing George, I said, "Can life get any better?" He held me tighter and said, "I'm trying to make up for giving you the worst honeymoon on record."

We returned home for another awesome experience: we were honored with our first grandchild. This brought back such tender memories of our babies. It was so touching to see the look of joy and pride on the faces of Doug and Kathy as they gazed, in wonder, at their tiny beautiful gift, Bryan Douglas Oberle. We couldn't have wished for a more perfect child. I was reminded that our cesarean section babies looked differently than those born naturally because they didn't endure the trauma of going through the narrow birth canal. Seeing Bryan, my first thought was how helpless he looked. Then, I thought his head had been a little traumatized and his eyes were a little swollen, but he had large dimples and all of his fingers and toes. This was one of the first things I checked for with all babies. (When I was pregnant I had dreams that our babies might be different.) Yes, Bryan was God's precious gift. In a week the birth trauma disappeared—his head was a perfect shape, his dimpled cheeks were rosy, and he was simply adorable. George and I felt extremely lucky to have this young family living near us. I remember saying to Kathy, "You should be glad I have school to occupy my time, because if I didn't, I'm afraid I would be an interfering mother-in-law." We had not known that being grandparents could be so very special.

Marie in Honolulu sports her first two-piece swim suit (1979)

The 1970s rolled into the 80s as we remained in Oklahoma, building more and more great memories and adapting as well as we could to changes in the country and our own world. The 1980s began with double digit unemployment and inflation. Interest rates were over 20%. Our family escaped the unemployment problem, but not the high interest rates. For example, Terri and Dan returned to Tulsa and eventually built their own veterinarian clinic. To do this, they secured a 25% interest loan.

A new concept of music recorded with video revolutionized fashion, the music industry and even how we watched television (MTV). It was the era of cassette and 8-track tapes, Michael Jackson, and heavy metal. The clothes in the 80s were described by fashion reporters as, "…clothes that depicted people who were trying to find themselves… both men and women… their creativity and individuality." The hair was big, curly, bouffant and heavily styled in contrast to the straight hair of the 70s. The television show Dynasty helped popularize the volume bouffant, gold chains and glamorous image associated with the 1980s for both men and women. Excessive amounts of mousse gave the men their desired shiny look for their hair. The band Poison popularized the mullet hair style for men, which was short on the sides and long in the back. Punk fashion began as a reaction against both the hippie movement of the 1970s and the materialistic values of the 1980s. The short, tight spandex miniskirts were popular for young women.

Clearly, I fit into the category of "trying to find myself" with my new freedom and lifestyle that the empty nest made possible. George and I were aware that our relationship was changing. I remember him saying, "You, Terri and my female staff have helped me rethink traditional life roles." We all embraced the new era in dress style, big hair for women, gold chains, lip gloss, blue eye shadow, and bushy eyebrows.

In the era of the 80s, the three premiere world leaders were Ronald Reagan, Margaret Thatcher, and Mikhail Gorbachev. President Reagan survived an assassination attempt in October, 1981. This led to an increase in his popularity and political power, resulting in the passage of his programs. Margaret Thatcher was the only female to ever hold the position and went on to become the longest serving Prime Minister in the United Kingdom. Mikhail Gorbachev changed Russia from the old Stalin dictatorship, and his policies and summit meetings with Reagan contributed to the end of the Cold War. All three leaders were influential in ending the Cold War in the West leading to the fall of the Berlin wall in 1989. Many historians label the 1980s as the era of economic development and international relations. The following are other historical events of the era:

1975

Arthur Ashe became first black tennis player to win at Wimbledon.

Microsoft founded by Bill Gates.

1976

Jimmy Carter, former Georgia peanut farmer and governor, elected US president.

1977

Miniseries "Roots" aired on television.

Elvis Presley found dead.

First *Star Wars* movie released.

1978

First "test-tube baby" was born.

WAC abolished; women integrated into regular army.

1979

Margaret Thatcher became first woman Prime Minister of Great Britain

Nuclear accident at 3-Mile Island was disastrous.

Iranian radicals stormed US embassy in Tehran, taking 90 hostages.

Sony introduced the Walkman.

Energy crisis and economic collapse set pessimistic tone in America.

Mother Teresa awarded the Nobel Peace Prize

1980

Ronald Reagan defeated incumbent Jimmy Carter in a landslide.

John Lennon assassinated.

1981

President Reagan and Pope John Paul II survived assassinations; Egyptian President Sadat did not.

Looking back, George and I were experiencing our "turning point." Our relationship was changing as family roles were less defined. I was becoming more confident and independent as I successfully carried out leadership assignments. George had been the one attending professional workshops, conferences and officiating Big 8 basketball. Now, enrichment opportunities were open to me. I think he questioned whether my sheltered life might make me too vulnerable for my new freedom.

I recall how frequently he phoned me when I was out of town. The most memorable was on returning to find beautiful roses to welcome me home. He had even called my hotel at 2 AM and I wasn't there. I wondered, "Is George remembering events and situations he has himself experienced at conventions?" I admitted that disco was new to me and I was enjoying my new experiences and attention. Yet, he could trust me to honor our marriage vows wherever I was. To me, he was the naïve one, and thought his integrity would never be questioned. For example, as a young, inexperienced teacher he had a beautiful college coed that needed to make up his class on giving mouth-to-mouth resuscitation. The only space he could find available was in the men's locker room. During the demonstration, a fellow coach walked in. This story spread throughout the campus and at alumni gatherings. George was only a few years older than his students and was a popular counselor. He must have asked himself, "Are they questioning my integrity?" when the solid door to his office was replaced with one having glass. Because of George's friendly, fun-loving nature, his convention colleagues must have felt compelled to assure me that George had fun, but never stepped out of line. There were times… I wondered.

Following one convention, as he left for work I discovered him taking women's clothes out of our hall closet. His explanation was, "Some of my female staff did not stay in the convention hotel, so they used my room to change for the evening functions." I thought, "Should I believe him?" I was a bit on edge, anyway; I had been entertaining Mom and Dad Oberle during his absence. I took special effort in scheduling outings that (I thought) Mom would enjoy. She complained that Dad didn't care for plays and concerts. It was a slap in the face when Mom said, "Marie, the only reason you keep so busy is to get back at George for being gone so much." I was hurt… and my good intentions had backfired with Mom and, even worse, I was questioning George's faithfulness—not a good time for me. With his parents there, we couldn't even have a good argument. Later, he said, "I will make sure my folks don't come to visit unless I am home." Regarding his fidelity, there were times I questioned, but in truth, if he had been unfaithful, I didn't want to know. I wanted to trust… I wanted to go through life with my soul mate.

The most challenging and rewarding activity of my graduate program was my job as program chairperson, National Leadership Development Program Seminar, in New Orleans in 1980. The seminar was for all the recipients of the GLDP nationwide. My responsibility was to seek out and secure national leaders in education to present and interact with us graduate students. The internship I selected, as part of my GLDP, was in the Department of Education in Washington, DC. While there, I had access to the desirable presenters for our seminar. This meant being separated from George for three months.

Through his contacts, I was able to rent a studio apartment on New Hampshire between the Kennedy Center and George Washington University, where I caught the Metro. It was an especially hot, but stimulating and rewarding summer. I felt privileged and special—I only had to walk across the street to enjoy The Kennedy Center's amazing concerts and theater. These were available to me at student prices. I thought, *How great to celebrate a Fourth of July in our nation's Capital!* It didn't happen. George sent me an airline ticket to come home. I thought, *Why doesn't he come to Washington?* Well… at least I experienced the magnificent cherry blossoms during another trip to Washington DC. My successful internship was over; I was happy to be returning home, having met my goals. I was excited that the presenters for the GLDP Seminar were in place—now I needed to prepare myself mentally.

Being Masters of Ceremonies at the event was truly frightening—I am not at ease speaking before audiences larger than a dozen. In a small group I can make eye contact, providing reinforcement or a need for redirection. This was an even tougher job than convincing national leaders to take time out of their demanding schedules to participate in our seminar.

In the public speaking workshop I had attended, we were given this advice as a way to be more relaxed while speaking: "You must not try to get eye contact, but look over their heads and think of something funny." I did this—I remembered having a real belly laugh when my older sister, Helen, told me of buying her ancestors… yes, buying. She and her husband Al moved to Atlanta, where she decided, "You aren't anybody if you can't brag about your ancestors. I couldn't. So I searched in flea markets until I found pictures of ancestors to match my glorifying story". The technique worked; I only had to remember Helen's story to break into a smile—this relaxed me.

During this busy time for me, George, having accomplished his major goals at OSU, turned to other challenges. He was still interested in "get rich quick" though his prior investments had not been successful, to say the least. The play rug company was destroyed by an accidental fire—without insurance; and the shoe company was not making a profit. His friends must have known he was a shoo-in when there was potential for profit. He made a major investment in a Sheraton Inn motel in Norman, Oklahoma, which required that we take a mortgage out on our debt-free home. Investing was a touchy issue between us. I encouraged him to look for safer ways to use his creativity and energy—this he did. A colleague, committed to a healthy lifestyle, got us both interested in a new concept on weight loss. This was not a large investment, and I agreed the potential reward seemed to warrant the risk. However, the daughter of the company president was in a serious auto accident and he lost interest in the business—another unsuccessful investment.

In Indiana, he had served as the president of his major professional organization and also in Oklahoma. Actually, his leadership was in demand throughout the country. In 1987 he was appointed by President Reagan, and later reappointed by President George Bush, to the National Council on Disability. He helped write and bring into law the Americans with Disability Act. A fringe benefit was being able to travel with or meet him at fun places throughout the country. We were each living enriching lives together and individually. I had mixed feelings when George said, "I am feeling less secure in our relationship as you become more independent… but you have the right to explore your own opportunities now that our children are on their own. You have been the devoted, capable loving wife and mother. I appreciate that… now it is your time". I really worked at making him feel secure while I was enjoying more freedom.

I resumed hiding love notes in his luggage when he traveled as well as other obvious places that he would find them; and I reminded him more often that he was number one in my life. Periodically, we would treat ourselves to a long weekend in our Florida condo on Siesta Key. We could instantly rekindle our chemistry in the warm sunshine, and the feeling of being caressed by nature. We found there was a constant need to nurture our relationship.

Our children were continuing to experience turning points. In 1980, Doug accepted a brokering position with his father- and brother-in-law in Denver, Colorado. It is rare that an in-law has a positive experience joining a family business; they usually remain an outsider. George and I observed Doug's reluctance to leave his position at the Raquetball Facility, but the move would mean more money and Kathy would be near her family. We would miss seeing Bryan growing up. He was such an adorable child. The proud parents had another precious son, Jason, in 1981. The same year, Doug took a related position in Houston, Texas, and Terri and Dan returned to Tulsa. Dan took a position with a veterinarian who was nearing retirement. Terri got an auditing position with a Big 8 Public Accounting firm. George and I were delighted to have them back in Oklahoma, and Doug and his family were also closer.

Best Buddies Jason and Bryan Oberle (1981)

My roller coaster life was getting more exciting by the month. In July, 1981, George was one of two American basketball officials invited to officiate University World Games in Bucharest, Romania. Even though I was in my last semester of graduate school completing my research and writing my dissertation, I was thrilled to be able to share this experience with him. I had not traveled out of the US except to Mexico. Being part of the American delegation, we felt safer than we would have traveling alone in a communist country. Without escorts, sightseeing was limited to the Olympic Village. Otherwise, we were driven in a bus with shades over the windows. Machine guns were still along the streets. This was an eerie feeling.

It was the start of Romania's austerity program to reduce the budget deficits; many people were going hungry while tons of food was being disposed of that wasn't eaten in the Olympic Village. Unfortunately, many of the young athletes preferred their native foods. Except for a few organized events for our delegation, George's time was taken up officiating in non-air-conditioned facilities. I was assigned a delightful teenage girl as interpreter; I could use her several hours a day. She said that, "A number of people from my country think you look like your president's wife [Nancy Reagan]." This was flattering. I enjoyed being a spectator at the Olympics but also took advantage of side trips including the Black Sea and Keiv. I couldn't help comparing the Black Sea with its black, rocky beach to our Siesta Key's sugary white sand; clearly different. It was too painful to walk barefooted. I resisted telling others about the number one beach in the USA.

"What was your most surprising experience while officiating, the World Games?" George's friends would ask. Without hesitancy, he responded, "While officiating my first ever women's competition—it was between Russia and Canada—one of the Russian players fell. As with men players, I helped her up and slapped her on her rear end. There was complete silence in the arena as the Russian coach stared daggers at me. I expected to be pulled out of the game… but after what seemed to be a long silence, the game resumed. To my surprise, there were not any additional repercussions regarding my stupid mistake. It may have helped that the Russians won the game. I felt forgiven when I was given a standing ovation by the audience following my last game."

A number of incidents reinforced how fortunate we are to live in the USA. I returned to our room one day to find our luggage being searched. Of course, I couldn't understand their explanation. The worst political mistake I made was giving my interpreter a dress she admired. She wore the dress to express her appreciation and was punished, I was later told. I would have liked to have given her more. It was surprising that by being part of our delegation, she was able to visit a number of local attractions for the first time. When looking for souvenirs, I was shocked at the limited options. I was told that items of any quality were exported.

On our return flight was an American couple who had been detained for three weeks because of some trumped-up charges. The American embassy was able to put them on our flight. The more stories we were told, the more eager we were to return to our great country. Knowing that there have since been tremendous positive changes in Romania, politically and economically, I wonder what it would be like to return, decades later.

George had been given a sabbatical from OSU for the 1981 Fall Semester. We planned to each do research in our area of interest throughout Western Europe. His focus would be on health, physical education, recreation, and wellness. I was interested in adult education/lifelong learning. We made our own arrangements through the European Embassies and had a contact in each country. We rented our Stillwater home to a faculty family whose new home was not completed. I would be graduating in December and my dissertation would need the final editing. Dr. Jones, chair of my dissertation committee, offered to do this. I thought, "How can I be so blessed?" In August, we were off to Europe as Drs. George and Marie Oberle. Yes… I rushed the degree a few months…the title added to my research credibility. *Little Emily, can you believe all the variety of pieces we will have for our life puzzle?*

Our well-organized trip turned out to be a nightmare! London, our first stop was just so-so. I remember saying, "George, you're no fun." His energy level was low… every step was an effort. We theorized he was just exhausted from the Romanian trip, all the preparation he did for a new OSU school year, and all the details for the sabbatical. Rest didn't seem to help. We forged on to Amsterdam by boat and train, keeping to our schedule.

At the train stop in Amsterdam, George was exchanging money while I checked out the Bed and Breakfast options. While in the phone booth, I put my carry-on bag, with all of our important items, between my legs to free my hands for the call. During those few minutes, my bag was stolen from between my legs. It was a dirty, noisy place, and the booth didn't have a door. This theft took me completely unaware. The police informed us that this was almost an hourly occurrence. Organized gangs were skillfully trained in Amsterdam to pick out inexperienced travelers to rob, even successfully cutting through purses and emptying their contents without the knowledge of the owners. We learned also that Amsterdam was the "drug center of Europe." We were devastated!

We had to regroup—no passports, credit cards, little money, and George feeling weaker by the day. The only bright side, if there was one, was that the owners of the Bed and Breakfast were from Oklahoma. Two days later my bag was found in a lake area…minus money, jewelry and everything else that could be used to acquire cash. Miraculously, they left our passports. I'm sure Amsterdam has its good points, but we experienced the bad side… parks were filled with stoned addicts using the benches to sleep, change clothes, and look for more tourists to rob.

Our next stop was Sweden. Compared to Amsterdam, was a haven of cleanliness and beauty. Regretfully, this good experience was short-lived. At breakfast, I observed George more thoroughly. His skin definitely had a yellow cast and the whites of his eyes were yellow. As a nurse I hadn't been very observant. I said, "I think you have hepatitis. We must get you to a doctor." A stop in Germany had been planned to visit with our brother-in-law's relatives. I called them and they arranged to meet us at a hospital.

The train ride from Sweden to Germany seemed like a lifetime… I was so concerned about my soul mate. I know that scary thoughts were filling his brain as well. Yes, he did have hepatitis—the most serious kind, usually contracted through dirty needles or bodily secretions. We theorized that he contracted it while in Romania, considering the incubation time. Prior to our Romanian trip, he had some oral surgery. In Romania, he didn't drink the water, but taught the cooks in the hotel to make iced tea. Boiling the water was a good idea, but he didn't think about the ice cubes being contaminated. He became so dehydrated officiating in the non-air-conditioned arenas, he drank gallons of iced tea. With his open wounds, he was a prime candidate for the hepatitis virus.

This was George's first time in the hospital. We didn't speak the language, and were terrified! My heart ached and I felt utterly helpless when he shared with me, "I don't think I will leave this hospital alive". We prayed for God to direct the doctors in the treatment and to give us comfort in our decisions. Believing this was the end, George called our children, other family members, and a few special friends. Even in his weakened condition, he was trying to take charge. The treatment was complete bed rest and proper nutrition. He lost 30 pounds in three weeks. He had a poor appetite, and also didn't like the food and was getting weaker and weaker.

I was able to stay with the wonderful Piepenbrok family in a fascinating historical home. As was tradition, the grandparents lived upstairs and the younger family downstairs. Interestingly, the family resided on one side of the house and the hogs on the other. I was surprised that there was no odor from the hogs in the residential areas. My room was converted from a part of the hay loft.

I left very early each morning by bus to be with George at the hospital. His nights were the worst. He said, "I see carts going down the hall at night with the bodies completely covered and I wonder, will I be next." Every time a doctor checked on him, he was accompanied by an entourage of students. Poor George imagined the worst possible things they were saying about his condition. It became clear to us that he would not get well in this environment. I called our doctor friend in Stillwater, Oklahoma, whom we had planned to meet in Frankfurt, Germany, for the Oktoberfest. Our dear friend said, "I'll come to see George before Edna and I go to Frankfurt." Such comforting words— we were so relieved! George even joked, saying, "He should be in the Guinness book of records for the most miles traveled to make a house call." Our friend was able to convince the German doctors that before George became weaker, we needed to get him home. He would be so much better psychologically. This was needed to begin healing. We felt that God had intervened… again.

George looked so sad and ill. "I so want to be in our home. I wish it wasn't rented." My dear sister, Rhoda, came to our rescue. In part of their large Indianapolis home was a mother-in-law suite, not occupied. I thought, "This will work…but can George make this long trip?" *Little Emily, I prayed, "God, please give us both strength to make this journey."* I was so frightened and insecure about managing George and the luggage. We had not been wise in our packing and had way too much. We had packed clothes for warm weather, cold weather, day wear, evening wear, and even our tennis rackets. Our caring hosts helped us check in at the airport hotel.

After making George comfortable, I left to check our luggage. When I returned, he looked more alive and natural. The beard he grew while in the hospital was no longer there. We both felt more optimistic. To this day, I can feel, in the pit of my stomach, the fear I felt as I moved George's wheelchair with our carry-on luggage down the steep escalators at the airport (the elevators were being repaired). Escalators were not made for wheelchairs. With the back wheels of the wheelchair on one step and me on the next one, I tilted the chair backwards with the weight of George and the luggage so we wouldn't all fall forward and tumble down the escalator. I prayed, and God helped us through.

Indianapolis was the perfect place for George to heal. We were with family, doctors we could understand, and were given a different concept in treatment. To help in gaining strength, George was encouraged to do more on his own. I bought the latest edition of the Good Housekeeping cookbook, became the family chef (Rhoda and Walt were both working), and prepared George's favorite foods. As his primary caregiver, I was the only one required to be inoculated for hepatitis. He was contagious through body fluids, so of course, we were to avoid sex or even kissing on the mouth. My cooking has never been so appreciated. As George finished one meal, he would ask, "When and what are we going to eat next?"

He quickly regained his weight and strength. Soon we were able to enjoy daily outings to visit family, friends, and places we had not seen for awhile. He was born and raised in Indianapolis. We were making the best of his rehabilitation and feeling positive about his recovery. *Thank you, God.* A colleague at OSU petitioned the University to extend George's sabbatical to a full year instead of one semester, and this was granted.

By nature, George was creative. As he felt better, we worked on the design for building a posh master bedroom suite onto our home in Stillwater. When we were able to return to Oklahoma, this became a reality; and the perfect therapy for George. The bedroom suite included a sauna, hot tub, and spacious closets. My size had varied little—I had several decades of clothes. Life was good again. We were indeed blessed! George said, "Life is a dream come true; I didn't think I would see this place again."

With my doctoral certificate in hand, I wanted to find a job. We pondered my choices while I accompanied George during his three-month consulting job in Washington, DC. In addition, he was researching a potential career opportunity for himself in the Washington area. We were able to rent the same efficiency apartment on New Hampshire that I had previously rented during my internship. I took advantage of a workshop given by a "headhunting" group. They guided me in developing multiple resumes depending on how I wanted to market myself. They helped me explore options in industry, education, and service organizations. As always, I delighted in taking advantage of the many offerings in our nation's capital. It has the feeling of a small town, but with greater opportunities for fun and enrichment. We enjoyed our first afternoon "tea dances" in a beautiful historical hotel. This was often followed by delicious dining, theater, concerts and walking excursions. It was amazing to feel this free again… and yes, sex was now permitted.

In job hunting, an advantage for me was that there were a larger percentage of professional women in Washington, DC, than any other place in our country. The high cost of living in the area was the main downside to working there. George was no longer interested in a professional move. As soon as we returned to Stillwater, I started my job search there.

First, I explored options at OSU. My resumes outlined my strengths in Human Resource Development, Management, and Teaching. After making appointments with all the OSU vice presidents, I started my interviews. They were courteous enough, but knowing them socially as George's wife was not to my advantage. Essentially, they said, "I don't have any secretarial positions open." Discouraged, I said to myself, "That's good… because I don't type."

After a long jog to relieve my stress and asking God for direction, I made an appointment with the Dean of Continuing Education. What a break. He said, "I needed you two months ago. I want to tell you my dream for a National Teleconferencing Network that is just in the budding stage. We need someone to work with the Proposal Development Committee developing the proposal and recruiting the membership. When can you start?" I listened with interest as he talked with great enthusiasm, for two hours, explaining how the idea started to grow during the February 1982 National University Continuing Education Association {NUCEA) Conference. Their premise was: academia needed to find the route to being a part of the rapid development of satellite teleconferencing. They believed, by the universities working as a consortium, this would be possible. The Dean was encouraged that 47 universities, out of the 70 invited, attended the first planning meeting. With a spirit of adventure, the group elected to move ahead to establish a viable network, despite perceived obstacles—the major being the conservative nature of academia and their resistance to change. The Dean already had a full-time job, but would find time to help. He hired me as a consultant, found me an office, and I started immediately to work with the committee developing the proposal…WOW! I was in the right place at the right time!

Chapter 10
Unexpected Career Opportunities

A pessimist sees the difficulty in every opportunity; an optimist sees the opportunity in every difficulty.

— Winston Churchill

My excitement was growing as I worked with a group of visionary continuing educators on the proposal for a national teleconferencing network. It seemed a natural evolution that educators should focus on new means of communicating that would unite academia, business and the community. The world would be "our oyster."

With my flexible work schedule, I was continuing to enjoy trips with George, both business and pleasure. In 1982, we were in the Virgin Islands when our precious, caring and totally loving Mom Oberle unexpectedly died. Thoughtlessly, we had moved from the conference location hotel to one that was only assessable by boat without notifying our family. It was difficult for the police to locate us. Yes, we learned an important lesson. We stayed in an airport hotel that night to catch the next flight to Indianapolis. I remember the hotel was so dirty we didn't want to touch anything. After spreading towels on the bedspread, we stretched out on the bed with our clothes on, held each other, cried and talked about Mom. We caught the next flight.

Little Emily, my mind went back to that dark December 25, 1947; the last time I saw my young, beautiful, lifeless mother lying on her bedroom floor. He was crying for his mother and I was crying for both our mothers.

Mom Oberle had not been well; she had heart problems and some dementia—the cause of her death was listed as congestive heart failure. She was a giant in her faith, love and compassion; her death left a terrible emptiness in the hearts of all who loved her! I was close to Mom Oberle, and felt I somewhat understood her convoluted life. She was bright, intuitive and had a talent for writing. This was recognized by a full college scholarship offer, which she did not accept. Her adoptive parents didn't want her to go to college—she was obedient.

She was given up for adoption at birth, lived in a number of foster homes before she was adopted by an older "self-centered" (her words), childless couple. Mom said, "I think they only adopted me to take care of them." *Little Emily, like me, she didn't have a childhood—just responsibilities.* When Dad Oberle came into her life, she had the opportunity to have a family and give them the loving home she had not had.

Mom used her talent in journaling; Chris, her daughter-in-law, read Mom's journals following her death. Chris said, "They were extremely insightful about her life, her family and the era in which she lived." They could have been a perfect legacy for her family. When George heard about the journals, he called his dad and asked if he could read them. "Too late—I have already burned them." That news hit George like a boulder!

Mom was persevering in locating her birth mother; she was able to locate a sister in Lawrenceburg, Indiana. She learned that her mother had died in a hospital in Cincinnati, Ohio, of tuberculosis. Her name was Hunt and she had two brothers, Dexter and Tom. Mom and Dad located them in Farmland, Indiana. They embraced her and enriched her life as she so enriched the lives of her family and friends.

I don't think she ever realized how widely encompassing her reach was. Her loving family did what had to be done, with Dad Oberle being their greatest concern now. He experienced such loneliness, continuing to live in the home that they had built, without his wife of 53 years. Fortunately, Jackie Oberle Dorrell, their only daughter, lived near Dad, and their sons, Jerry and David lived in the area. What a blessing.

After returning to Oklahoma, our minds seem to be in a quandary. Mom Oberle had been a willing substitute mother to me. She accepted me unconditionally and taught me a lot about parenting. George was so much like her in his sensitivity and soft heart—even his interest in art he attributed to her. Unlike her, he hid his feelings, but I could see his pain. "I wish I could have let go of my feelings as Jerry did," George told me. Jerry had embraced his mother's casket and literally sobbed.

We talked a lot about how to help Dad. He had been her primary caregiver for over two years. What would he do now? God always has a plan. Mom never knew that she would soon have another granddaughter, David and Chris welcomed their baby girl, Kristin, in 1983. This gave a positive boost; another grandchild for Dad to love. As I look back, neither of us had learned the importance of feeling the pain and "walking through it." In our typical way, we tried to bury it and go on with life. This was the way we knew—but not the best way. For both of us, the transition back to work was slow.

The excitement for my new job had diminished, but gradually I was reignited by the vision and enthusiasm of the continuing education directors. With a pioneering spirit, hard work and dedication, in what seemed a short time, the founding members agreed to establish an experimental network. Without requiring a permanent allegiance, membership was easier to acquire. Consortia efforts were encouraged; the network's success depended on it. The institutions were extremely diverse in their experience and telecommunications capabilities. The opportunity to grow together was a strong marketing tool, yet local autonomy was so important to institutions of higher education. They were all competing for the same students.

This was still in the decade of the "outrageous 80s." World and national events impacted us at the local level, to one degree or another. Events included:

1981

Ronald Regan succeeded Jimmy Carter to become the 40th president of the US; minutes later, Iran released 52 Americans held for 444 days, ending the Iran hostage crisis.

Prince Charles married Lady Diana in a spectacle of a wedding in the U.K.

First case of AIDS reported by CDC.

Sandra Day O'Connor became first female appointed to the Supreme Court.

1982

At the University of Utah, man received first permanent artificial heart.

Vanessa Williams became the first African-American to be crowned Miss America.

1983

First mobile phone came on the market, from Motorola.

Sony released first consumer camcorder (combining video and sound recording).

Microsoft Word first released.

Cabbage Patch Kids brand of doll first mass produced; became extremely popular.

Sally Ride became first American woman in space, on *Space Shuttle Challenger*.

President Reagan announced defense plan called *Star Wars*.

1985

First Internet domain name was registered.

Hole in the ozone layer discovered.

American singers including Michael Jackson, Cyndi Lauper and Tina Turner recorded charity single "We Are the World" to fundraise for famine in Ethiopia.

Wreck of the Titanic found.

1986

Space Shuttle "Challenger" exploded 73 seconds after launch; all seven crew members died.

Oprah Winfrey Show was launched.

Chernobyl Nuclear Power Plant accidental explosion in the Soviet Union; 800,000 people experienced radiation exposure.

1987

Aretha Franklin became first woman inducted into Rock and Roll Hall of Fame.

Stock exchanges on Wall St. and around the world suffered huge drop on "Black Monday."

1989

Berlin Wall falls.

First satellites for Global Positioning Systems placed into orbit.

US (and other nations) responded to Iraq's invasion of Kuwait, beginning The Gulf War.

1991

The Soviet Union collapsed.

1992

Riots in Los Angeles led to 53 deaths and over 2000 people injured after acquittal of police who beat Rodney King.

1993

The World Trade Center in NY bombed; six people killed and more than 1000 injured.

Our children and grandchildren can identify with the 80s music: The Rolling Stones, Michael Jackson, Lionel Richie, Stevie Wonder, Madonna, Bon Jovi, Metallica, to name a few. George and I still preferred the Big Band sound of the 40s, 50s and 60s.

I soon moved from being a consultant to being the full-time coordinator of this experimental Network. *Little Emily, nothing had really prepared me for this. I felt excitement about something so foreign to me, yet fearful, being so out of my element. I didn't know anything about telecommunications technology.* A quote from Kobe Bryant comes to mind: "Everything negative—pressure, challenge—is all an opportunity for me to rise."

OSU was contracted by the consortium to coordinate a Network which would allow member institutions to utilize audio, satellite, video and computers to reach national audiences with programs they originate. Being interested in psychology and sociology, I agreed that the concept was sound. All the institutions wanted to expand their market for the programs that they developed, but would they put the same interest into promoting other institutions' programs? The success of this consortium would depend on how willing the members were to work together for the ultimate success of all. I thought, *this is what I've been learning in my leadership training—how to facilitate group process. I don't need to know all the technical stuff.* I realized I needed to focus on how to bring together diverse colleges (two-year and four-year) with business and industry, and other public and private associations for mutual benefit. I was relieved to realize that for me, this is where preparation and opportunity had met.

Due primarily to strong member commitment and leadership, the National University Teleconferencing Network (NUTN) successfully moved through rigorous experimental and developmental stages and, after three and a half years, achieved maturity and stability. It was a rocky road; there were no simple, easy-to-learn methods for launching such a teleconferencing service to higher education. However, members believed in the concept and believed it would succeed and each member brought their unique expertise to the table. I became aware that most of my life experiences were proving useful in my new role, including nurturing, teaching, group process, and having been associated with academia all of my married life.

My office was responsible for keeping each of the member universities current about programs available for them to offer professionals in their community. Each campus coordinator had a good sense of what would be successful to their constituency. For example, Ohio State University (OSU) developed a program on "Health Cost Containment" utilizing world experts on the subject. Interested universities would create and implement their unique marketing plan and likely supplement the OSU program with their own experts on site. The most successful campuses were the ones that admitted other universities might be working on a similar project on a more advanced level. While trying to protect their turf, they were not keeping up with the times.

Changes in my home life continued to evolve as my new career required more time and travel. George was always my greatest supporter. I missed being with him in his travels, but occasionally our conferences would be in the same area—we would have amazing rendezvous! When I asked if he was okay with our present lifestyle, he responded, "You were always there for me—now, it's your turn…but change is difficult." My heart filled with love, understanding, and appreciation for his response.

Knowing that I was missing my daily workouts on my treadmill or jogging, George ordered from a television ad what was marketed as the ideal workout tool for travelers, "The Gut Buster." The commercials said, "Put it in your suitcase and workout wherever you are." It was simply a stretchable rope with handles. I was thrilled with this idea and must have overdone my workouts. When I returned home, I was plagued with pain in my right buttocks. I thought it was likely a sore muscle and treated it with ice. Evidence of this experience is still with me. This item was ultimately taken off the market.

We celebrated the birth of our third grandson, Brandon James Danner (BJ), on September 23, 1984, to Terri Oberle Danner and Dan Danner. It was a regular occurrence for Terri and Dan to join us for the Saturday OSU football games. Also, Terri was a major asset when we entertained, which was true of this particular weekend. They even joined us for Sunday brunch before returning to Tulsa. A couple of hours after they left, we received a call advising us to get to Tulsa because Terri was already in the labor room.

By the time we drove the nearly two-hour trip and arrived, Terri, Dan, Dan's parents, and precious BJ were in the room, drinking champagne (not BJ). Terri had gone into labor on the return drive to Tulsa. It had been an easy delivery. Her face looked beautiful and radiant as she looked with love at their perfect, beautiful son. George and I were both filled with love and joy at sharing this miracle. I so love babies; I was in my element when holding tiny, innocent BJ in my arms…too bad I had to share him. This was a new trend in birthing babies—a homey setting to include families. I felt this change was positive. I'm much more comfortable in this nurturing environment that I am in the business world; it was not always an easy transition—it was like being two people in one body.

NUTN had met enormous challenges and survived while many other telecommunications experiments had not succeeded. In October, 1984, it became a unit of OSU. The Network's services enhanced the already highly developed telecommunications system at OSU. The University's President said in one of his interviews, "Even an international Network is not out of our reach." He was so on-target as major developments in international relations and communications were rapidly evolving.

I was quoted at our Fourth Annual NUTN Conference, "The Sky is the Limit," hosted by OSU in 1985: "It is the Network's combined strength and capacity to keep adapting that has made the difference. This enabled us to remain viable in a changing higher education landscape with the convergence of new technological concepts." Actually, timing was the key to the success of any programming, and the timing of NUTN's development may have had more to do with it becoming a vital part of teleconferencing than anything else.

NUTN was now financially mature enough to support a full-time director. The Board started with a national search. I had access to the applicants and the resumes. In summary, all the applicants were men and, I felt, less qualified than me. George and I discussed my options. I said, "I don't want that much responsibility… it takes time away from my family". He said, "Then you'll end up with all the work but not the glory."

I agreed, but shared with him the general perception that I did not "have the balls" for the job. We asked ourselves, "What will catch the attention of the Advisory Board?" They were due on campus in a week… networking would be a must! I felt George's support as I gathered enough courage to call the business editor of the Stillwater local paper. "I'm excited about a national project I've been coordinating at OSU which distributes continuing education programs throughout the country by satellite," I said. "I think your readers would be interested, especially other women." The reporter came to my office the following day!

In the meantime, an OSU Selection Committee Member who had labeled me "the cookie baker" who couldn't possibly be capable of directing NUTN, was hosting out-of-town Committee Members. He was rapidly spreading anti-Marie propaganda. To counteract his actions, the very day the Selection Committee arrived on campus, the local newspaper carried a half-page article, with my picture, in the business section, expounding my exceptional leadership qualifications. The Stillwater NewsPress headline, October 10, 1985:

Marie Oberle Ramrods Real 'Higher' Education

By nature, continuing educators want to know as much as possible about the place they are visiting… they likely read the newspaper. God must've had a hand in the process. I was told that my nemesis made a motion that the vote for director be unanimous… all agreed. As it turned out, he was the only holdout for my selection. To adhere to his own recommendations, he had to make the vote unanimous. That must have really injured his ego… not sorry. I felt strong and empowered, even if I didn't want all the responsibility of the director role. The Stillwater NewsPress headline, October 13, 1985:

Dr. Oberle is Appointed OSU Network Director

No one was more surprised than me at the drastic turn of events when I was in my 50s. The nurse, nurturing mother and homemaker entered the cutthroat business world… despite being labeled the "The Cookie Baker" and "Pampered Princess".

"It's Time for NUTN and a Time for Marie" was the headline of a teleconferencing profile article in a national industry magazine in early 1986.

As I write this in 2014, it wouldn't be surprising—in 2013 a woman was appointed CEO of the General Motors Company in Detroit. Women have come a long way since Congress passed the Equal Rights Amendment (ERA) in 1972. (Oklahoma was one of the 15 states, mostly southern and western, that did not ratify the amendment before time ran out. Consequently, the ERA was not voluntarily enacted in Oklahoma.)

George, with the National Council on Disability (NCD), was working tirelessly toward their goal to help millions of disabled Americans to live a more productive life. This committee was holding hearings all over the country, gaining insight to their needs prior to writing the American Disability Act. On one such trip to Washington, DC, with a scheduled stop in Indianapolis to visit his father who was in the hospital for diagnostic work, George received the shocking call that his father had died. George had talked with him by phone earlier that day, sharing his plans to visit.

In his 83 years, this was his first time to be hospitalized, and if he had had his way, he would not have been there. Dad had not had a good quality of life since the love of his life died six years prior. He was ready to be with her. There were multiple reasons his family encouraged diagnostic work and so did his family doctor. The family had left the hospital and he was settling in for the night when I had phoned him from Oklahoma. His anxiety was understandable; it made me want to be there holding his hand. We talked about George coming to be him the following day, and how much his family loved him. That night, he had a massive heart attack. While a shock to his family, I thought God has his own plans for each of his children. Perhaps He saved Dad from—who knows what—future surgeries and endless treatments. Family and friends celebrated Dad's full life, saying; "Dad is where he prayed to be…with Mom."

His beloved children, George, Jackie, Jerry and David, followed through with Dad's plans for his memorial service. I felt joy in the wonderful family stories they shared. A major legacy that Dad Oberle left his children was his sense of fairness and treating them equal. This was reflected in his will; everything was divided equally; even the tools had designated names on each. His goal was for harmony in his family.

He was born in Indianapolis of German parents in 1905, and had worked hard all his life. His father died when he was in the sixth grade. He dropped out of school to help put food on the table for himself, his mother and two sisters. Having lived through the Great Depression, Dad was thrifty and believed in paying cash for everything—cars and even his home. This loving unique man continues to be missed.

George and I were of the generation where adversity was assumed; we do what needs to be done and move on. George said, "I don't know why I have felt guilt at the loss of both of my parents…being so far away from them when they needed me. Yet, I know that I'm doing just what they wanted for me…leading a full satisfying life."

(L-R) Terri Oberle Danner, George and Marie Oberle, Kathy and Doug Oberle, Bryan Oberle, BJ Danner, Jason Oberle (Siesta Key, FL, 1987)

In due time, George and I returned to Oklahoma, but George's heart remained in Indianapolis with his grieving siblings, missing them, and realizing that he was now the patriarch of the Oberle family. We both resumed our active lives.

The major change in my responsibilities as NUTN's first executive director was more travel, representing NUTN in educational conferences as well as telecommunications functions. These events usually filled my weekends. Most of my travel was in the US and Mexico. Any college or university that could pick up satellite IV was a potential member; the membership grew to 350. In 1989, I was the only female presenter in a distance learning conference in Japan. My, what a unique experience! I was a bit uneasy traveling by myself as George was unable to join me. However, once I was met at the Narita Tokyo airport, I felt safe and more at ease; more so than when traveling in Mexico. My hosts were so very courteous, helpful and appreciative. They seem to respect that I had learned a few words of Japanese and had researched the kinds of gifts to share. (Chocolate from the USA was the most popular gift.) My first stop with my hosts was at a sushi bar—a new experience for me—I enjoyed everything I tasted.

The Conference was held in the Birtie Hotel, Cheba Perfecture, capital of Japan. Perfectures are simply "governmental bodies larger than cities, districts, towns and villages." Cheba is located in the greater Tokyo area. The Convention Center was equipped with devices to hear the speakers in your native language. Whenever I had a free minute, I was surrounded by female graduate students asking about my life in America. They too wanted a career, but their country's mindset regarding women's roles was about 20 years behind the US.

Rhoda Piepenbok with her children Paul, Carla and Tom

Marie and George, socializing before George leaves for N. Miami (1993)

They seem to receive hope knowing that I had once been a "stay-at-home mother" and pursued a career later in life. *Little Emily, I was so humbled at the opportunities opening for me. As I remember you and how far I have come…all I can say is thank you, God.*

I was scheduled to fly from Japan to California for NUTN's annual conference…California was having a major earthquake. My staff was questioning the advisability of canceling our conference. After considering all the available options, we continued with the plans. Not surprisingly, the attendance was down. Most of us experienced some trembling of the earth and had to hold onto a lamp post or anything near for balance. The uneasiness we felt was not conducive to learning and camaraderie. This earthquake was reported to be the strongest to hit the San Bernardino Bay area since the one of 1906…resulting in 60 deaths. I experienced tornadoes in Oklahoma, but this was my first earthquake. By the grace of God, my peers and I came through it okay.

Helen deserved more of God's blessings. Dear Helen's MS had so completely cut short the goals she had for herself and her family, and the kind of mother she wanted to be. She was close to completing her doctorate when she was diagnosed with MS. I didn't tell her that I succeeded—she would have been happy for me, but she would have been filled with regrets. I still wonder about God's plans for dear Helen. Rhoda, as she was needed less by her family, reinvented herself and became one of the most successful realtors on Indianapolis' Southside.

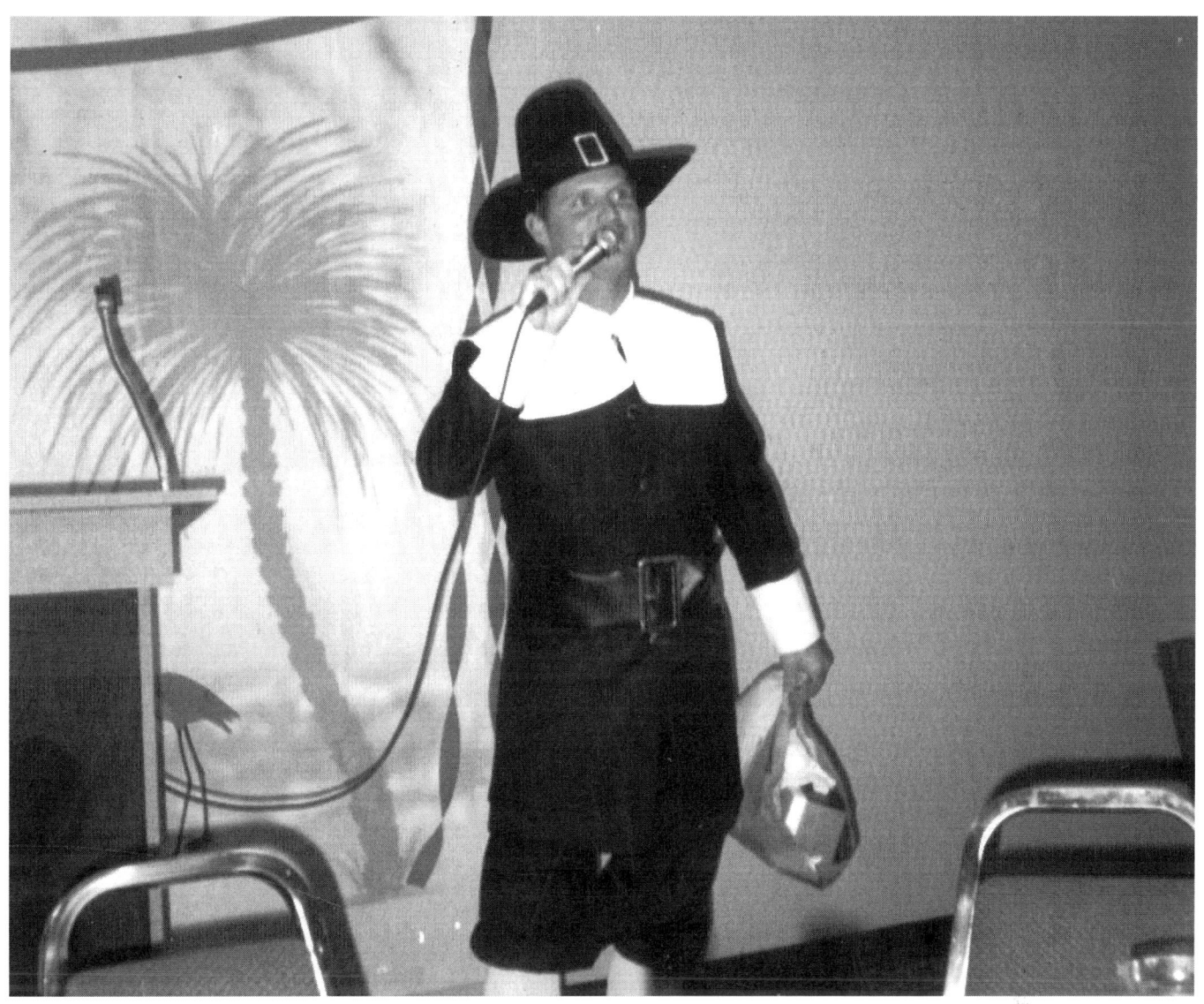

Doug Oberle roasting his dad (1993)

Yes, my career was challenging, stressful, a little bit scary and mostly rewarding, but my heart was with my family. We learned of Terri and Dan's impending divorce shortly before I left for Japan. I wanted Terri to know that I was available whenever she needed me; yet I was going out of the country. There was so much about their relationship that George and I didn't understand. Terri told us that she wouldn't have gotten married if George and I hadn't been so conservative. I remember answering her, "That's a copout." Yet, as I look at the institution of marriage and the way it is evolving decade by decade, I'm at a loss for answers. Each of us goes into marriage with different expectations. Unlike me (who wanted most of all to be loved and accepted), Terri's needs were different. She was beautiful (she was often told that she looked like Lady Diana), confident and well-educated. Why did she need a husband? She made more money than Dan, which a lot of went into his new animal clinic. She drove their pickup truck, and he drove a Corvette. Terri was responsible for maintaining the house, taking care of BJ, and maintaining the books for the clinic—in addition to her demanding corporate job. Neither George nor I were surprised at the divorce. We did encourage her to ask for child support and/or a percentage of the clinic. She said, "No, I just want out."

Energetic, adorable BJ was four years old and we loved spending time with him. George and I were proud of Terri's strength of character and her ability to provide for herself and BJ, and were glad they were able to spend many weekends with us during the transition.

Pictured here with her executive secretary, Myra Traynor, Marie was recognized at her last NUTN conference before retiring in 1994

She was Controller of the National Marketing Committee for Thrifty Rent-A-Car Systems, Inc., the highest financial position for a woman in that company. She and Dan shared custody, meaning BJ was with each parent equally. George and I wondered how this might affect BJ psychologically. Clearly, he had love and support from both sides of his family. When BJ was with his dad, his grandmother and aunt shared his care. Today, I consider him well-adjusted and happy. It seems to me that he has successfully learned to find good in everyone he meets and make wise choices for himself.

We missed living close to our older grandsons who lived in Texas, but both Doug and Kathy were good at keeping us current on their activities. Little League baseball and school basketball was big with Bryan and Jason. Doug coached their Little League baseball and was also getting increasingly involved with real estate, successfully acquiring rental properties. Kathy was teaching in elementary school. Bryan excelled in math competitions while Jason played sax in the school band and enjoyed participating in school plays. We were able, periodically, to view them in action. Our children and grandchildren were with us on alternate Thanksgivings and Christmas. These were blessed, happy times to be treasured and celebrated.

Thanksgivings were celebrated in our home with everyone's favorite foods as George's parents had done. Terri even learned to make Mom Oberle's delicious chicken dumplings. As our family grew, we had more leaves made for our dining room table; our children never liked sitting at the children's table at their grandparent's house. One special Thanksgiving, Helen and Al made it possible for their sons, Alan and Kebin, to join us; they wanted to do some hunting. Dear Helen was bedridden. This was a time of camaraderie with many activities usually related to sports, either participating or as a spectator.

Christmas holidays were celebrated in our condo on Siesta Key. George and I would arrive early to put up the Christmas tree and stock the pantry. Food wasn't a big focus—being together, the beach, pool and ocean were the drawing cards. As the ages changed, we adapted the toys and games for rainy days. Puzzles and board games were big in the evening. After a few years of getting to know the families that were regularly there at Christmas, we started a community, pitch-in Christmas dinner in the club room. Year after year, we created more wonderful family memories; these George and I compiled in our dream to retire on Siesta Key.

Transitioning from holidays with the family to the world of work was always difficult. Perhaps this had something to do with my comfort zone…they held my heart. I also had a good feeling about having an active role in communication changes during the 90s. That decade was culturally characterized by the "rise of multiculturalism and alternative media." In addition to satellite telecommunications, there was cable TV and the Internet. In 1991, NUTN received First Place for the most significant advance in distance learning, overall, by a national trade magazine. At the same time I was honored at OSU with the "Women to Watch" Award, and selected as one of the top key executives in the satellite industry.

In the meantime, George was, rightfully, taking pride in the opening of the OSU Wellness Center serving 18,000 students and 4000 faculty and staff, a unique model for other universities to emulate. For George, it was the realization of a long-standing dream and fulfillment of a personal goal, and that wasn't all: Our family celebrated with him in Richmond, Indiana, when he was inducted into the Earlham College Athletic Hall of Fame. George and I both were being recognized for life achievements.

About the same time (1992), beautiful Rhoda was shocked at Walt's fatal heart attack on the job. So goes the saying, "You never know what tomorrow will bring." I regretted being so far away from both my dear sisters. We didn't even tell Helen, whose MS was continuing to make her live a life of pain; she had more than she could handle. Rhoda's strength showed through as she adjusted to her new way of life. "I was wise when I made the decision to get into selling real estate," she said. "I've become much more confident and independent; I found something I'm good at." *Yes, little Emily, I was so very proud of her; she too—had come a long way.*

Rhoda was just getting her life back together when, one year later, her world seemed to totally stop. Her third child, 34-year-old son, Chris was accidentally shot when doing target practice with friends. This threw her into a serious emotional state. *Little Emily, I wonder if Rhoda thought about Chris being just one year older than Mother when she took her life.* To me, nothing could be worse than losing a child…not your husband, not your parents. It seemed so unfair for my little sister to go through such pain.

In 1993, George (age 63) stepped down as OSU's Director of the School of Health Physical Education Recreation and Dance (HPERD) to take a position at Barry University in Miami, Florida, as Chair of their School of HPERD. This was a three-year appointment to expand their graduate program offerings.

Of course, his OSU staff and faculty wouldn't let him depart without a memorable, loving and hilarious sendoff. They called it "The Great George Oberle Roast"… and roast they did! He had touched thousands of lives in his 19 years at OSU. Many of those individuals were on the program including our children. The program read: "Doug Oberle… Number One Son" and "Terri Oberle Danner…Number One Daughter." Doug's theme was, "Did that make you rich, Dad?" Dressed like a pilgrim (in keeping with Pilgrim Inns), he gave hilarious accounts of George's unsuccessful attempts to "get rich quick." (His venture investments had proved disastrous.) Terri presented an "Ode to Daddy-O"… so clever and funny! (See Appendix B.) Random roasting followed the official roasters. This was "payback time" for George, who enjoyed roasting and playing jokes on others. Their parting shots had us all in stitches! George left OSU with some regrets (leaving friends) but beautiful memories… even an album representative of the 19 years.

What a major change in our lives. One acquires deep roots in 19 years—we did. We embraced our change as an adventure and a step closer to living on Siesta Key, Florida, where we dreamed of retiring. The Miami area, being more multicultural than the West Coast of Florida, could be exciting. Barry University was located in North Miami. The area was not considered safe and many homes had bars on the windows for security. To us, it was a bit scary. George rented an apartment in Plantation (originally part of Fort Lauderdale), the first planned community in Florida. Unfortunately, it meant a 45- to 90-minute commute, depending on traffic. In July 1993, George moved to Florida, pulling a U-Haul truck with his library of books, clothes, and enough furniture to get by. I would be able to retire in April 1994, at 62 years of age. In the meantime, I would organize this major move, downsize, and sell the house.

During my last year with NUTN, our Annual Conference was held in Virginia Beach and hosted by Old Dominion University in Norfork, Virginia. As compliments and accolades were directed my way, I thought, "Are they talking about me?" *This was a humbling but rewarding event, little Emily.*

The most touching aspect for me was the fact there were so many the NUTN members (both men and women) who considered me a mentor. They gave me credit for their professional growth and career achievements. In their letters, I was described as "pioneering, innovative, tenacious, imaginative, resourceful, nurturing, inspirational, loyal, elegant, responsible, intelligent, charming, a giant in disguise, steady, graceful, reliable, honorable and optimistic… one of the few people who has truly made a difference… in your wildest dreams you can't know how many people you have helped professionally and personally." I did not find either "Pampered Princess" nor "Cookie Baker" in their letters. I did hear that my nemesis now called me the "Dragon Lady." I thought, *you've come a long way baby!* I also thought, *if they only knew how insecure I felt trying to fill the big shoes required in my position.* Only the Dean, who took a chance on me—a woman with a new Doctorial Certificate and little experience—and the NUTN staff knew of my personal demons. I must've played my role well … NUTN was successful! To me, developing and managing NUTN was frightening, exciting, and, at times exhilarating, but always challenging. I felt honored to have had such a challenging and amazing experience.

It was my good fortune (even though unusual) to gain approval for my request that OSU grant me permission to run the NUTN office from Florida. The remainder of the NUTN staff would remain in Stillwater. I interacted with NUTN's network of colleges and universities via the phone and email. Of course, I continued my travels.

Our family created occasions to get together. The Texas family hosted us for Thanksgiving that year prior to my moving to Florida. While there, we planned a trip to Washington, DC, as an opportunity for George and me to enjoy our grandsons and introduce them to our nation's capital. It was a destination we both found enriching, full of opportunity, and it held beautiful memories of our times.

Terri joined us on our DC trip. She had told us about a man she was totally impressed with, John Floistad, whom she had met at their Thrifty Convention in Dallas. He was working with Thrifty Car Rental in Indianapolis. They agreed to meet in Washington (his sister and family lived in Virginia) so that we could all meet John. George and I were duly impressed. It was an enjoyable family time with experiences we continue to reminisce about. I returned to Oklahoma to tie up loose ends, while George returned to Florida.

Living apart from George during this period of time was far less traumatic than when he had moved to Oklahoma while I remained in Indiana. I continued to feel incomplete when separated for long periods of time from my soul mate, but now I felt stronger and secure enough to work our plan—acknowledging that what we both had agreed to was best. Intellectually, it all made sense…but I did have occasional "pity parties." Plans fell into place and I joined George in Florida, in October of 1993.

Chapter 11

A Life to Savor

The heart of marriage is memories; and if the two of you happen to have the same ones and can savor your returns, then your marriage is a gift from the gods.

—Bill Cosby

George and I dreamed that we would retire on the West Coast of Florida, Siesta Key Beach. This move to North Miami was a step closer to our retirement dreams. The East Coast is more fast-paced and multicultural than the West Coast. We were accustomed to this pace; still, there were necessary adjustments.

The one-bedroom apartment had been perfect for George. Now, we needed a home. We elected to live in a new community in Fort Lauderdale on the edge of the Everglades, Weston. I was in awe of the beauty of our surroundings—a variety of colorful plants in bloom, graceful palm trees artfully placed, and beautifully manicured lawns. Man-made lakes were throughout the property, and we were only 30 minutes from the Atlantic Ocean.

I was able to combine business travel with a visit with Helen and her family in Marietta, Georgia. I regretted not being with her as often as I would have liked since my work became so demanding of my time. Al, her devoted, loving husband, was carrying out her wishes for her to stay in their home, although her MS was severely reducing her physical capabilities. Their sons, Alan and Kebin, were no longer living at home. She had to be fed and assisted with all her personal care. My guilt was always heavy as I visited with Helen. I wanted to blame something or someone. I remember saying, *God is so unfair. Helen had so little happiness in her life.* When her condition was finally diagnosed in 1976, she was working as a high school counselor. Helen was a true warrior, so driven to be the best in anything she tried, and she usually succeeded! Sewing was her passion, and she excelled, even adding her own labels to her masterpieces. She was probably inspired by our mother. Rhoda and I continue to wear a few of her beautifully tailored dresses.

So little is known about the cause or cure of MS. Helen seemed convinced that she was being punished for something she had done in her life and made efforts to seek forgiveness. She continued to be optimistic, fight and pray; she was open to any therapy (tested or untested) to get well. Helen had so many outstanding gifts to offer the world; how frustrating it must have been for her not to be able to use those gifts. Her vision was affected, but she could watch television even though it was blurred. One of her favorite shows to watch was "The Home Shopping Network." She had her healthcare workers order clothing items that she would be able to wear when she got well. Real optimism! Obviously, Al had to return the items, but he didn't deny Helen the pleasure of shopping. My heart warmed as I witnessed his care and thoughtfulness toward Helen. As I left her, I assured her that I would return soon, since I now lived much closer and would soon be retiring.

I returned home feeling sad and powerless. There wasn't anything I could do for her except pray and continue to love her. George was my pillar of strength. We talked at length about our blessings and ways to give back to the world that had seemed to favor us.

About three weeks after my visit with Helen, we were enjoying a visit from George's brother and sister-in-law, Dave and Chris, when we received a shocking call from Al. My beautiful sister, my dear warrior, Helen, had choked to death, June 28, 1994. My whole body seemed to go numb; I reached for a chair as George took the phone. My numbness was quickly replaced with anger as I thought of motherless Alan and Kebin and faithful, caring husband, Al. I have read that for many married couples faced with MS, the challenges are so great that the relationship cannot withstand the struggle. I can only imagine how frightening those years were for both Helen and Al, but he never failed her. What a painful way for my perservering, optimistic sister to go…she deserved so much more of "the good life." I remember saying, *Al will surely be rewarded with jewels in his crown in recognition of his loving care for Helen.*

Helen was laid to rest in the military cemetery in Andersonville, Georgia. It was comforting to hear the accolades showered on Helen; she was honored as a loving wife and mother; she had such classic beauty; she was a charming hostess, gourmet cook and on and on. I hold in my mind an indelible image of Helen as she was depicted in a large portrait hanging in their guest room (my room when I visited); so lovely…so in control. Rhoda and I owe her so much more than we could ever repay. *Little Emily, these puzzle pieces are painful to include in my life puzzle.*

After Helen's death, Al plowed much of his energy and time into scouting. He was quoted in *Scouting for Youth,* August 1999: "My sons led the way. Both of them made Eagle." Scouting took him all sorts of places, including Russia, where he took a group of local Scouts in 1994. Boy Scout Troop 1011 dedicated a Helen W. Friel Memorial Pavilion in her honor.

With a heavy heart, I fulfilled my obligation with NUTN. I remember saying to George, *God is so unfair. Why did he pick Helen out of the three sisters to challenge with MS; our children are older than Helen's. I believe that I could have more easily adjusted to a diminished quality of life.* As I did with Mother's death, I could not help but feel guilty. He held me close and said, "We will continue counting our blessings and keep Al, Alan, and Kebin in our prayers." Then, I asked myself, *who am I to question God's plan?* When I think more rationally, I believe God has a plan for each of his children. In my Pollyanna way, I told myself that at least Helen would be with our dear Mother and out of pain.

On a happier note, my sister Rhoda and our daughter Terri came to Florida to celebrate my 62nd birthday and my retirement. George treated us to the theater and exploration of Coconut Grove, a lively tourist town, near Miami. One of the most clever birthday gifts I have ever received was the 62 notes that Terri and Nicole had composed stating reasons why they thought me to be special. It became my own personal treasure hunt; I still have the ones that I was able to find in pockets, drawers, underneath furniture, in jars and so forth. I was very appreciative of such a loving and time-consuming project. For weeks afterwards, I was still discovering notes in their well-chosen hiding places.

In the pleasant Florida environment, I was grateful to be retired and be able to play (and play I did) tennis, sometimes twice a day. Also, I was active in the Newcomers Club and explored my new world. George was able to join me in fun weekends and was pleased that I was taking advantage of my new opportunities. He said, "I'm in my element when I can be creative and build new programs. Your new job is to pamper yourself." *Little Emily, I took this as an invitation to take the time necessary to figure out who I used to be, and how I got to where I was.* I had enough of a medical background to make me believe that many of my physical problems were, at least partially, a result of the guilt and pain I had unsuccessfully tried to bury deep in my memory. *Little Emily, the time had come for me to acknowledge your existence. Do you understand what is going on inside me as I open up to the truth?*

Physically, I had been plagued with chronic pain in my left hip, piriformis syndrome, for 13 years. This is a painful condition in which the piriformis muscle traps and squeezes the sciatic nerve. The nerve runs from the lower spine to the back of the lower calf. My pain is in the upper buttocks on the left side, radiating down the thigh. I explored an array of treatments including surgery. I discounted the surgery as it would be exploratory, and a positive result could not be promised. Physical therapy helped, but this, combined with my frequent headaches, limited my quality of life. I acknowledged years earlier that as hard as I tried, I could not handle my emotional problems without professional help. I thought, "How many people have the luxury to use their time in this manner?" I was blessed to have the time and the courage to embark on such a journey. Trying to deny my issues by taking on more work and constantly keeping my mind busy had not been the answer.

Through hypnosis, counseling, and instructing me to write about my past, my psychologist helped me start peeling back, a layer at a time, some of the buried pain and guilt of my childhood. The process was uncomfortable and laborious. At times I questioned whether I was making any progress. The psychologist kept reminding me, "This isn't something you tried to forget last week, last year, but over a lifetime. The process can be slow and painful, but I encourage you not to give up." George continued his loving support.

It was either God's intervention, or just being at the right place at the right time… I was offered help for my piriformis syndrome. A new neighbor who played baseball with the Florida Marlins, and a new friend in Newcomers shared their success with magnetic energy for chronic pain. Thinking as a nurse, I thought, "This sounds like a snake oil story." In nurses' training, the medical doctors had warned us to beware of such propaganda. Yet, I was becoming less skeptical of homeopathic medicine, and with my friends' sincere encouragement, I tried it. It took about three weeks of wearing magnets in my shoes and directly on the originating site of pain before I started to feel results. Soon, for the first time in 13 years, I was without pain. Hurrah! Having less stress in my life could also have helped reduce the pain. I believe the mind, body and spirit work in tandem.

An uplifting event for our family was Terri and John's beautiful happy wedding on April Fools' Day, 1995. I was surprised that my mother and father were also married on the first of April. I thought, *Is this God's plan?* I had felt such a deep loss in no longer having our courageous Helen in my life. We all experienced renewed joy being with this newly joined family. George and I felt good about this marriage—Terri was more mature and knew what she was looking for in a relationship. She had shared with us their instant attraction during the first evening they met: at a Thrifty [car rental business] Conference in Dallas, they hit it off and spent hours just talking. I was reminded of something that I had read earlier. *So, we must try as many times as necessary until our many loves become the one love, until our dreams become the one dream, until heart and path feel the same* [author unknown]. I prayed this was the case for Terri and John.

Terri and John did all the wedding planning and paid the bills. Terri said, "You paid for my first wedding and I want to do this on my own." We had to be proud of her independence. John moved to Tulsa from Indianapolis and easily found employment at International Thrifty Car Rental where Terri was employed as Controller.

The couple's sense of humor and uniqueness was apparent in the wedding planning and atmosphere. For example, Terri had her bridal bouquet designed to toss, and it would return…an April fool joke to those trying to catch it. Also, an unusual sight was John transporting Terri on his Honda Gold Wing motorcycle—flowing gown and all—from the wedding site to their reception. This was held in a lovely historical home in Tulsa, surrounded by colorful spring flowers from forsythia bushes, dogwood trees, and lilacs.

Terri and John spent their honeymoon night in a local motel and allowed a few of John's out-of-town friends to use their house. As an April fool joke, the bride and groom returned to find their kitchen cabinets completely rearranged. Terri and John, not to be outdone, reciprocated by sewing up the sleeves of their guest's jackets and other articles of clothing. Terri has a knack for finding or creating fun wherever she is.

Aunt Rhoda, Terri and her proud mother (April 1st, 1995)

Words cannot describe this beauty

Mr. and Mrs. John and Terri Floistad head from ceremony to reception

Terri Oberle Floistad dances with her dad, George Oberle, at reception

BJ was 11 years old, the age I was when Mother gave my sisters and me a new, more hopeful life. John has been an important figure in BJ's life. His interests were very different from our other two grandsons. Bryan and Jason shared Doug's interest in baseball and tennis, while BJ shared his dad's passion for soccer and was playing on the traveling team. He also became fascinated with dinosaurs and his keen mind devoured all the information he could find. At the time, I questioned the decision of the court that BJ would alternate the months staying with his father and mother. It worked. I think it was the love that was showered on him from both sides of the family.

With George still employed, our travels were mostly in the summers. Following our trip to Oklahoma for Terri's wedding, we enjoyed the Special Olympic World Games in Connecticut and both treasured the times spent with the amazing Special Olympians. Annually, we reunited with college friends for joint adventures. After each of the couples had hosted the group in their homes, we selected resort areas to vacation.

Earlham friends (L-R) Marcie Robbins, George Oberle, Martha Dickman, Marie Oberle, John Sauffer, Cliff Dickman, Lewis Robbins, Marie Moore, Peg Sauffer (2001)

After three years at Barry University in Miami, George decided to join me in my new lifestyle. He retired in June of 1996 after completing 44 years of teaching, coaching, officiating and administration. Since his favorite sport was baseball, we added a plaque to the bottom of a painting of a baseball scene containing Babe Ruth which said: "In recognition of your outstanding accomplishments in the career you loved". He had often stated, "I enjoy my job so much, it doesn't feel like work." I don't think many people can make that statement. His parents encouraged him to be a medical doctor or a dentist; but he followed his heart. For George and me, retirement meant more time with family and working on our "bucket" list.

Spending time with Rhoda was important to both of us. She had been widowed two years and was an extremely successful realtor in Indianapolis. We were so proud of what she had achieved after raising four children. Through her career, she met a handsome widower, Dick Johnson. Coincidently, Dick (Franklin College) and George (Earlham College) had gone head-to-head on the football field. They told such entertaining and exaggerated stories of their prowess and skills (and got by with it) even though we did question at times. Dick cherished Rhoda and won our hearts. They were married on Labor Day 1996.

Rhoda, Marie and Dick (1996)

As couples, we enjoyed sharing fun vacations including fall foliage tours in the Northeast, visiting the Grand Canyon out west, and traveling to Western Europe and seeing the famous Oberammergau Passion Play in Austria. This elaborate, awesome production is 6 ½ hours in length and is only held every 10 years. The first play was performed in 1634—it was a once-in-a-lifetime and unique experience.

While George and I were on holiday in Orlando, Florida, a dear friend, Anne Hall, called to encourage us to stop in Sarasota and view a property prior to returning to Fort Lauderdale. We could hardly believe this experience. This was our dream retirement home! We fell in love with the penthouse on the 10th floor overlooking the gulf, the inter-coastal waterway, and the skyline of Sarasota. Every room had a water view except the kitchen, which could be changed. Wow!

Little Emily, this was more amazing than in my dreams! I thought, *can we actually afford this?* We only needed to cross the street from our driveway to enter the driveway of the Sandpiper Beach Club, a time share facility on the number one beach in the US, where we also owned and vacationed every Christmas. It was a place filled with heartfelt memories.

As I wrote earlier, the sand is phenomenal (99.9% quartz crystals and never hot to the feet). I said, *Thank you God...can this really be? This is so perfect.* George and I had decided that we did not want to live year round right on the beach; the view of the water was breathtaking during the day but at night it was all black. By owning at the Sandpiper, we had access to their beachfront facilities—bathrooms, lounge chairs, cabanas and umbrellas, year round.

Grandsons BJ, Jason, and Bryan with fish tales

Not fully trusting our judgment in the purchase of the condo we were in love with, we consulted Rhoda because of her real estate knowledge. She agreed it would be a sound investment, even though it was more money than we had ever paid for a house. She surmised that property on Siesta Key would likely hold its value. George and I agreed. For us, this was not just a house… it would be our last earthly home, and in the location of our dreams. As always, there was much to be done before we could move. We tackled the projects with eagerness and joy. George took on the responsibility of selling our house and scheduling movers. I helped get that house ready for showing and took care of other details to accomplish our final move, one we dreamed of making, to Siesta Key, our favorite beach. I call this "another of God's plans".

Suddenly very busy, I still felt it was important for me to continue sessions with my psychologist. I was slowly making progress in freeing myself of some of the pain and guilt of my childhood. He recommended therapists in Sarasota and also suggested that I should move to our new location as "Emily," instead of "Marie." George said, "I'm not sure I can handle this. I've only known you as Marie." Even though we both thought this was drastic, I did so. The psychologist believed that since I was "Emily" during the childhood I had repressed and now wanted to reclaim and honor, it might help.

Over our lives, each of our moves had been different in the kinds of challenges it brought, as was this "final" move. To start, the movers arrived 12 hours late, short of help, and already exhausted. Doug had arrived from Texas to assist us and saved the day by helping to load the truck. They assured us that our belongings would be locked and safe during the night. Again, they were 12 hours late for the unloading and they were tired and already late for another job. Not good. Contractually, they were to put the furniture in place, assemble the beds, and plug up the appliances. We were uncertain as what to expect.

Doug positioned himself near a waterway for fear they would toss items there instead of carting them up the elevator to our condo where George and I were, directing. Doug called up to say the movers were leaving. George said, "No way! They still need to assemble the beds and move the freezer from the middle of the kitchen floor to the pantry." George asked me to call the police as he hurriedly grabbed his car keys and blocked the driveway so the movers could not exit. This was about two o'clock in the morning. We soon heard police sirens and condo residents started coming out onto their balconies questioning what was going on. The police could not do anything without a court order. Another moving disaster! Our move was the topic of conversation around the condo. (Not the best way to meet your neighbors.) Even though we were assured that our belongings would be safe in the truck, many items were missing, including a painting on loan. This was an expensive move in more ways than one—but we comforted ourselves by saying this is our *last* move.

At a time in our life when we were excited about our retirement home, our children were adjusting to major life changes. Bryan, our oldest grandchild, was graduating from Spring High School in Texas. He was honored for his successful baseball and tennis records in addition to outstanding leadership activities. Because of the school's high academic standards and scholarship assistance, he selected Trinity University in San Antonio, Texas, to pursue his interest in business and finance. Jason, two years younger, was ready for his junior year. He was interested in tennis, performance (theater) opportunities, and leadership activities. Doug was working hard in real estate, construction, and coaching his sons and other boys in baseball. Kathy was teaching and trying to keep up with all of her men. Terri, John, BJ, and their German Shepherd, Hollywood, moved into their new home on three acres in Broken Arrow, Oklahoma. It was a timely move, as they would be welcoming their baby daughter in the spring, 1998. When we received a bouquet of pink balloons, we knew we would have a granddaughter. George and I celebrated… our first granddaughter! We felt totally blessed by being given such a wonderful family.

Our creative friend and renown party giver, Anne Hall, helped with the remodeling and decorating of our condo—we told her this assured she and Tom had permanent access to the guest room. Anne commented the first time she saw the condo and stepped out onto the balcony, "I don't know where you're going to be on the Fourth of July, but I'm going to be here." Thus, we started our annual Fourth of July parties. We line chairs up, theater style, on the 74-foot lanai, giving guests a panoramic view of exploding fireworks from the beach and four other major displays throughout the city. It's a spectacular event, with just the right-sized crowd, and free!

Tom Hall was such a close friend to George, and they were so much alike, they often claimed they were "twins." They would finish each other's sentences. Tom achieved success at Indiana University in the tough game of football—yet he has a huge heart, like a gentle giant. When George died, Tom said it was like losing a part of himself.

To God, the glory… is what I think about my view. Sunsets are unbelievable in their magnificence—bursting with combinations of yellows, reds, oranges, blues and grays. The colors and designs change by the seconds… from a ball of fire to streaks and swirls and other formations. Sunsets with clouds assure more color. The formations remind me of the Rorschach test (used by psychologists) where you are asked to identify what the abstract designs reveal to you on the pages of the test. We enjoyed hours by ourselves, and with friends and family, timing the sunsets, and looking for the green streak as the sun sets into the gulf (called "the green flash") and identifying designs in the cloud formations.

Anne Hall					Tom Hall

As I write this, at my desk in late morning, the gulf water varies in color from robin's egg blue to aqua and dark blue. The boats are leaving a trail of white ripples in the otherwise still water and the para-sailers are colorful in the gray blue sky which is dotted with a few marshmallow clouds. I never take this ever-changing scene for granted. When there is a day that I miss the sunset, I regret it. I carry the memory of a panoramic sunset in my repertoire of scenes to pull from during visualization exercises in my private retreats.

We knew right away we had made the right decision to move to this haven. Life was good for George and me. We were finding joy in exploring the Sarasota area and what it has to offer. During the many years we had vacationed in Sarasota, it was for rest and relaxation and we rarely left the beach. We were now enjoying the art, music and cultural activities for which the area is renowned. I cherished my early morning walks and meditation on the beach.

It seems that we can't live long periods in a state of joy until we're hit with periods of sadness. Interrupting our delight in having a healthy, perfect, beautiful granddaughter was the illness of George's only sister, Jackie Dorrell, passed away because of a brain tumor. She was 63—one year younger than I was—and had lived a full, richly blessed life with her special guy, Chet. They had loved each other since high school. Chet retired early from the Eli Lilly Pharmaceutical Company and they were savoring the good life they had built, including three children and seven grandchildren. Her well-lived life is an amazing legacy to her family.

Little Emily, it wasn't easy living as Emily in my public life and Marie with my family. I was in a constant state of confusion, and faced with questions like, "Why does George call you Marie?" or, "Which name do you prefer?" I found myself saying, *it is a long story—I will answer to either Emily or Marie.* In time, I discovered that I actually started to feel comfortable being called Emily. *Little Emily, do you see the path ahead for us?*

Nicole Marie Floistad's christening, with George and Marie Oberle, BJ Danner, John and Terri Floistad, and Rev. Eugene and Iris Floistad

In April of 1998, George continued with our remodeling while I traveled to Oklahoma for the birth of Nicole Marie Floistad. Since my birthday is April 7th, I was hoping that she would select that day to be born—instead it was April 15th, the day that the Department of Revenue will not let us forget. Terri and John were often asked why they didn't name her "Iris" since Terri was a CPA and John's mother's name was Iris. I thanked God that there were now three generations of Whittymore women. BJ, now 13 years old, adored his little sister. Their relationship has only strengthened during the years. What a beautiful, spiritual and blessed family!

Sarasota's nickname is "paradise" and its motto is: "Where urban amenities meet small-town living." It is a city of around 53,000, on the southwest coast of Florida. As I've mentioned, it is known for its cultural and environmental amenities, beaches, resorts, and connections to the Ringling family. In 1907, the Ringling Bros. merged with the Barnum and Bailey Circus to create a virtual monopoly of traveling circuses, becoming famous as "The Greatest Show on Earth." Siesta Key, where I live, is included in the boundary of Sarasota.

Big brother BJ with Nicole (1998)

Our whole family feels at home on Siesta Key. Since 1972, we had enjoyed almost every Christmas vacation here and also other times in the year. We still own our time share condo at the Sandpiper, across the street from our present condo. In the fall, 1998, I was serving on the Sandpiper Board of Directors when we discharged the manager and needed an interim manager while we searched for a replacement. George asked, "Why don't we take a chance that Doug can get away from his responsibilities in Texas to help the Sandpiper during this period?" When this became a reality, I resigned my position on the Board to avoid nepotism. Doug's skills were indeed transferable to those required to manage the Sandpiper. I remember one of his first comments. He said, "I feel at home here, and I think it would be good to be near Dad and Mother during their retirement years."

Doug has managed the Sandpiper since 1999. At the onset, Bryan was already in college and Jason would be graduating from high school that spring and would be entering Stephen F. Austin College in Texas in the fall. We were thrilled. Doug had lived most of his adult life in Colorado and Texas—now he was just across the street. George enjoyed working on projects with Doug; observing their re-bonding was a delight for me. Early on, Doug said, "Living at home, I did things your way… now you do things my way." They made a good team.

George and I were feeling positive about our lives, those of our children and our grandchildren. Our youngest grandchild, beautiful, energetic little Nicole (two years old) was a delight to all our family. Her brother BJ was in the 10th grade and passionate about soccer. Their parents were both doing well professionally at Thrifty International. Terri was the highest-ranking financial woman in the company and the only woman to have a company car. John was exploring international markets for Thrifty. Doug was enjoying his challenges at the Sandpiper and Kathy was exploring her new environment. Jason, a college freshman, had just pledged Sigma Chi fraternity, and Bryan was a junior at Trinity University, having a positive college experience playing on the tennis team and studying business and finance.

Jason, BJ, Bryan and Nicole: The complete set of grandchildren, with custom T-shirts, Christmas at Siesta Key (1998)

Marie (Nana) with Nicole and BJ (2000)   Little Princess Nicole on her 3rd birthday

It is said that, "...your seventies is a time for reflection." This was true for George and me. I was gaining more courage in facing my past with honesty, compassion, and humility. George continued to be productive, using his creative skills in consulting assignments in-between our travels. I felt proud and honored when he asked me to introduce him at the event when he was presented Earlham Colleges Distinguished Alumni award.

Little Emily, I mustered up enough courage to attend my 50th high school reunion in Richmond, Indiana. God knows where I got the strength... This was a first… It was part of the past I had buried, and was now revisiting. I still thought of myself as one of the poor little Whittymore sisters—the girls I imagined the whole city of Richmond thought of with pity and/or disgust. I thought that everyone at the reunion would be thinking or even saying to one another, "Don't you remember when her mother committed suicide?" I reasoned, "After 50 years, there should be less stigma attached to mental and emotional conditions". It helped to have my sister, Rhoda, attend with me. As typical as it sounds, I was very self-conscious about how I would look to my former peers, and I attempted to look successful as well as give my best shot at faking my confidence. It must have worked. The reception I felt was nothing like I had feared, and I actually enjoyed reconnecting with many of these good people. I felt I had taken a major leap toward owning my past… the good, the bad and ugly.

I don't know if it is related to the "middle-child syndrome" or just the nature of my environment, but throughout my life I've been plagued with a lack of self-confidence. I'm being encouraged to look at this in a different light, and maybe acknowledge it could be the power of negative self–centeredness.

Perhaps I have been wrong in the grandiose assumption that I could have controlled the events leading to my mother's suicide. I have read that, "…in extreme moments of negative self-centeredness, we can even assume magical proportions of burden, in which we feel acutely responsible for a loved one's illness or misfortune because we weren't good enough or perfect enough." This concept is continuing to make more sense as I examine my life. After all, I was only a 13-year-old girl… how much power could I have had? Another concept I am examining goes deep. "To assume that other people's inner moods hinge on my presence is an eco-centric way to keep myself in a cycle of sacrifice and guilt." *In a way, I guess, little Emily, this could be a case of codependency. I'm thinking that to find the peace I so desire, I have a long way to go... I can do this.*

In the broader picture, the decade of the 1990s generally continued the theological and socio-economic changes; they started in the 1980s and accelerated in the 1990s. After the fall of communism in the 1990s, globalization was a strong force going into the new millennium. The US enjoyed an economic peak. The growth of the Internet was one of the prime contributors of globalization, making it possible for people to interact with other people, expressing ideas, introducing others to different cultures and backgrounds, use goods and services, sell and buy online, and research and learn from others around the world like never before.

This period also ushered in the distress of "information overload." Being bombarded with news from around the world took some getting used to. Never before had there been a 24/7 news broadcast like CNN which (though it launched in the 80s) became popular in millions of American homes. During that period our country was marked by colossal events that changed our lives. I remember as if it was yesterday: while watching the young Tiger Woods surprise the golfing world with his skills, the TV program was interrupted to announce the tragic bombing of the federal building in Oklahoma City. It was a place we knew well, and we didn't want to believe it was happening!

The following are major events that affected most families in one way or another:

1995

A federal building in Oklahoma City was bombed, killing 168 people.

Apple's Macintosh PC launched.

Soviet leader Gorbachev and US Pres. Reagan met for the first time.

1996

During Summer Olympics in Atlanta, GA, Centennial Park was bombed, killing 2 people.

President Bill Clinton (incumbent) defeated Republican challenger, Bob Dole.

1997

Scientists cloned sheep.

Microsoft helps save Apple Computer by buying $150 million shares.

1998

American embassies in Africa bombed, killing 224 people; linked to Osama bin Laden.

Titanic was the most successful movie, ever (and won a record 11 Oscars).

Google is founded in California by two Stanford University graduate students.

1999

The euro became the new European currency.

The Panama Canal was returned to Panama.

Columbine High School shooting; 15 deaths; started a chain of copycat shootings.

2000

George W. Bush (the second "Bush") elected president.

Hillary Rodham Clinton elected to the U.S. Senate, becoming the first First Lady of the US to win public office.

2001

On September 11, terrorists attacked America (deaths in NY, PA, and Washington, DC). Osama bin Laden first denied involvement, then later claimed he personally directed followers to attack. Dubbed as the "day the world changed." Nearly 3000 people died.

As terrorists seized control of four airplanes, Ben Sliney, chief of air-traffic-control operations at the FAA's command center in Herndon, Va., gave the unprecedented order to ground 4,000-plus planes across the nation and redirect any in the sky to the nearest airport. It was his first day on the job.

2003

Invasion of Iraq by US; concerted campaign to remove Saddam Hussein from power. Ultimately this war cost the lives of 4,400 American soldiers.

2004

A tsunami from the Indian Ocean following an earthquake killed 250,000.

2004

First African-American US president elected, Barack Obama, a senator from Illinois.

2005

Pope John Paul the second died.

Hurricane Katrina hits New Orleans and surrounding area; 1,835 people died.

2008

The economic crisis, the largest since the Great Depression in 1929, hit the world.

Fidel Castro, Cuban President, retired 49 years after seizing power in an armed revolution; handed over the leadership to his brother, Paul.

Obama elected for the second term as US president.

2010

President Obama signed a $940 billion federal health care plan.

This era of terrorism, upheaval, and recession greatly affected our family, yet certainly not as seriously as the Great Depression in 1929 affected families. I'm wondering how many people living today experienced both? As noted earlier, I was born in 1932, three years into the Great Depression. Then, young people, fresh out of college and eager to take on the world, experienced doors closing on their dreams and opportunities. Now, our oldest grandson, Bryan, with a degree in business and finance and additional training in financial planning, was filled with hope and expected success—only to have the World Trade Center destroyed by terrorists.

He said, "Entry-level financial planners typically begin their careers doing cold calls" and was willing to do whatever was necessary to get his career going. Even with his training and personal charisma, the economic climate of the time meant investors were leery to trust his recommendations. This negative experience was one of many that continue to plague him. Thankfully, our younger grandson's were more fortunate in their career choices.

Our daughter, Terri, Controller at Thrifty Rent-A-Car Systems, Inc., was replaced by a male counterpart when her company merged with Dollar Car Rental. She was given more marketing responsibilities. Later, she and her husband, John, lost their jobs through downsizing. It wasn't easy, but they both drew on their strong faith and believe that God had a plan for them. They tightened their bootstraps, revised and changed priorities for the betterment of their family. We couldn't be more proud! Terri said, "This can be a blessing. I now have more control over my work hours so that I can have more quality time with Nicole and for doing God's work." She continued to use her CPA skills in contractual opportunities, and John became a distributor of automotive products, covering designated areas in Oklahoma.

They felt a calling to do therapeutic foster parenting. Three young sisters (ages four, six and seven) soon became a part of the Floistad family. Nicole supported her parent's decision and was a tremendous help with the young girls. This was a major undertaking as each of the girls had different emotional issues and physical needs. This experience ended on a positive note—Terri phoned and excitingly said, "I have great news! A loving, compassionate family adopted all three girls." We all cheered the good news. *Little Emily, what a blessing that the girls were able to stay together, as with the Whittymore sisters.* It would be hard for Terri to imagine, as wise and heart-centered as she is, the impact of the lifesaving gift she and her family provided those girls.

Next, the Floistads welcomed two young boys who were older than the girls and not brothers. Unfortunately, they did not get adopted; their anger issues were taking their toll on all the family members. Finally, it was a family decision to regain serenity in their home. The boys were returned to family services…we all felt at that point that all we could do was to pray for them.

George and I were among the millions who had saved for retirement only to have much of it disappear during the deep recession. Fortunately, our financial planner, Barry Havener, rearranged our investments to minimize future losses in the market.

The terrorism of 9-11 left everyone in shock. Each of us was either directly or indirectly affected. The whole country was on alert, acknowledging that this could occur anywhere. No one was safe in their homes, at work, or traveling. Most airports were temporarily closed, and events were canceled.

George and I had a trip planned to commence the first day that the Tampa airport reopened. We expected security to be tightened, and knew to expect it to take longer to board. To compound our challenges, a hurricane hit our area the day before our departure. Can you imagine how eerie and frightening it was without electricity, elevators, or streetlights, and debris all around us? We managed to get dressed and pack by candlelight, struggled to get our luggage down 10 flights of stairs, avoided the debris on the roads, and finally reached the airport. At the airport, the lines were unbelievably long since the airport had been closed for several days. We were suspicious of everyone that looked a little different, worrying that perhaps there was a terrorist in our midst. We counted our blessings when we reached our destination safely. We both said, "We are too old for this."

In addition to adapting to the negative impact of world crises, our family faced pain and heartbreak closer to home. In 2001, our newly married nephew, Derick Oberle, the oldest of David and Chris's three children, was hit broadside by another vehicle, leaving Derick in a coma for weeks. His family, including his new bride, Kristin, never left his side. Prayers were encouraged… and a miracle did happen. That amazing young man is enjoying his beautiful family—wife, Kristin, and two daughters, Kate and Annie.

This decade of family challenges continued. Doug and Kathy ended their 25-year marriage in 2002. We saw them periodically when they lived in Colorado and Texas; they always put on a positive front for us. Bryan, their oldest, had graduated from college and Jason was going into his third year. Statistics tell us that even though couples have grown apart, they often stay together for the sake of their children. Even though we are living in a society increasingly permeated with divorce, the adjustments necessary in each broken home don't appear any easier. It's safe to say that 100% of us are impacted by divorce in some way or another. Divorce and remarriage are common fodder for television shows and movies. They make it sound so commonplace. As I said earlier, each decade offers its own set of challenges impacting us as individuals and the institution of marriage. George and I worked at not interfering in the private lives of our children. We prayed they would make sound decisions in their road to happiness, reassuring them they would always have our unconditional love. It is impossible to walk in someone else's shoes.

The following year, George started the first of five orthopedic surgeries: both knees (one redone), right hip, and left shoulder. In his characteristic joking way, he said, "Next I'm considering a brain transplant, if they can find one small enough." His years of playing sports, jogging, and officiating had taken a toll on his body. He was courageous throughout the ordeals and pleased to do his rehabilitation at home. Also, during this time he was very supportive to me as I searched for treatment of my migraines—they were very debilitating and I spent much of my time in a dark, quiet room.

In 2004, we were fortunate to be able to make the trip to Indianapolis to see George's Aunt Helen, 100 years old, just before she went to be with their heavenly father. We believe she wanted to linger long enough to say goodbye to her oldest nephew… George was holding her hand as she took her final breath. She had not been blessed with children. Nicole shared with us later that her class was asked to bring a century-old item to school; she chose to bring a photo Terri had taken of Nicole with her great, great aunt Helen. I thought that was really special.

The unexpected death of George's younger brother, Jerry, took its toll on the family. Since childhood, they had shared their interest in auto racing, having grown up living near the Indianapolis 500 race track. On July 29, 2005, Jerry died of a heart attack while driving to a race in Michigan. George said, "I have been blessed these last few years by having Jerry and Sharon winter near us in Florida." I couldn't help but think *George's mother, father and younger brother have died from heart problems… What does that mean for George?* It had been eight years since he had a stent put in. The youngest of his siblings, David, had a health scare in 2004 while vacationing at the Sandpiper; he had a stent put in and is enjoying a good quality of life. The Oberles surely have a genetic tendency toward heart problems.

As with all families, we had some really difficult times and some amazingly wonderful times. It was a life to savor. This was a time in our lives that much of our prayer time focused on happiness for our wonderful children and their children. The same year (2003) that Jason graduated from Stephen F Austin University, Texas, Nicole started kindergarten and her brother, BJ, entered Oklahoma State University. BJ continued his passion for polo. He was able to captain a team at OSU and spend the summer in England, caring for horses and playing polo. Academically, he majored in finance and minored in religion. Even though he received his MBA, he focused on another passion—youth ministry.

The Oberle brothers: Jerry, George and David

Doug Oberle, Marie Oberle, John, Terri and Nicole Floistad, and George Oberle, on Doug's boat (2004)

Following graduation, Jason worked briefly with Special Olympics in Florida as he moved into marketing sports memorabilia. Platinum Marketing was the name of his company. He moved his business to Boston, where he also became Executive Director of the Josh Beckett Foundation. (Josh was a highly successful baseball pitcher for the Boston Red Sox.)

Doug was adapting to single life. Seeing that the Sandpiper maintained its "Gold" status was almost a 24/7 job. How special it was for us to have him so close. He and his dad even shared the same physical therapist when Doug underwent a partial shoulder replacement as result of a medical condition.

George and I continued to be active, but began to spend more and more time reflecting on and appreciating the many decades of life we had enjoyed together. George and I were both overwhelmed by the love and effort Doug and Terri put forth for our 50th wedding celebration. It was a glorious occasion! The actual date of that anniversary was August 1, 2004. However, since it was our year to have the family for Christmas, we chose that time to celebrate. Doug and Terri planned and orchestrated a grand and memorable event, an occasion bringing joy for a lifetime. Most of our immediate family was in attendance.

George, Marie, Rhoda climb to ancient dwellings, Ute Tribal Reservation in Arizona- photo by Dick (2001)

It was many, many more times elaborate than our wedding. We had been told it would be on Siesta Key Beach, and the time…that was all. I remember saying to George, following my early morning walk on the beach, "I don't see any signs of preparation for our celebration." He just said, "The beach is so busy, you can't do much in advance." The weather cooperated. It was a sunny day with temperatures in the mid-70s. As advised, we dressed in formal attire. Rhoda directed us when it was time to go downstairs for transportation. I said, "We can walk across the street to the beach." Rhoda said, "Just do what you're told." I thought, "Bossy sister!"

We were assisted into a shiny black limousine and we drove south, heading away from our beach, and kept on driving. Finally, George said, "I believe he is lost… I think I know where we should be going." He was on the mark. The driver backtracked to a magnificently beautiful, white house owned by a friend of Doug's on Siesta Key Beach.

We were greeted with cheers by our great family and many close friends. (I have tears of joy, as I write this.) We descended the limo and were ushered to the rear of the house where an amazingly gorgeous scene met our astonished eyes. A beautifully decorated archway led to an elaborately decorated gazebo facing the blue, shimmering Gulf waters. The gazebo was enhanced with a bouquet of three dozen perfect white roses and a champagne fountain…leaving room for George and me and our dear friend, the Rev. Jerry Dennis, who led us in renewing our wedding vows.

George did not make a copy of his vows, but I said the following:

George, there cannot be a better place to enjoy the sunset of our lives than right here. As I walk this beach almost every morning, I thank God for all my blessings. What amazing gifts He has given me—He gave me you, our wonderful children, precious grandchildren, very special sisters, the loving a caring Oberle family and dear, dear friends. I treasure each and every one here today.

George, you came into my life when I was so very young and insecure. You were my "knight in shining armor." Even though there were times that armor became a little tarnished, and I even wished I had parents to go home to during that first year. We honored our commitment and have grown together. The rough spots and challenges have led us into mature love. I feel deep and enduring love for you, as well as great respect and commitment. Your unconditional love and support were there as I made mistakes and struggled to become the confident person I am today. Even though I have played many roles over the years, my favorite has been that of wife and mother. My family continues to be my passion.

Thank you for 50 years for being my lover, husband, friend and soul mate. Each additional day I have with you is a blessing from God. I pledge my continued love and commitment to you for as long as I live.

50th Anniversary Celebration for George and Marie

(from back L) Jason, Chad, and Derrik Oberle, BJ Danner, Doug and Bryan Oberle, Terri and John Floistad, Cliff and Linda Spears, Dick and Rhoda Johnson, Marie and George Oberle, Nicole Floistad, Jerry and Sharon Oberle, David and Chris Oberle, Chelsea Smith, Lynn Murray, Kristin Oberle, Kristin Badger, and Kate Oberle

Bill Whittymore, Rhoda Johnson, George Oberle, Dillard Jr. and Jalynn Whittymore,
Dick Johnson, Reba Whittymore, Alma Whittymore, Marie Oberle, Polly Whittymore, Ruby Lee

I felt blessed, joyous, appreciative, humbled and proud of all of our family and friends for the time, money and effort they put forth for our 50th celebration. WOW!

George and I talked endlessly about our blessings, and were eager to live our remaining years productively. As the world struggled to maintain a semblance of peace, we were able to turn our hearts to God, family, and friends for love and strength. As we grew older, each became more important to us. *Little Emily, I continue to feel a deep and nagging pain, as I remember the three lonely struggling Whittymore sisters, when all we had was each other.* Yes, God has blessed me abundantly! These are puzzle pieces that I will delight in putting in my life puzzle.

As a means to reclaim and recover my past, Rhoda and I (again) reconnected with the Whittymore family, and along with George and Dick we visited them in Scottsburg, Indiana. Two half-brothers, Dillard and Bill, were very gracious, as well as their wives. Polly at that time was very fragile. It pleased me that they had good lives. During that visit, they all helped me remember more of my past. This made Rhoda and me feel a little better that Dad had some remorse in our leaving—other than just "no one to pick the tomatoes." Dillard Jr. said, "Dad cried for three solid weeks after you girls left." Other family members came over since they knew we were going to be there and we were able to get a group photo.

In researching a number of options for us to spend more time with our Oklahoma family, we hit on one acceptable to the Floistads, and to us. Aunt Helen had generously split her inheritance with her nieces and nephews; she was childless. George said, "I think Aunt Helen would be pleased that we used her money as a means to spend more time with family." We added to Aunt Helen's gift and built a house on the Floistads three-acre property in Broken Arrow, Oklahoma. Building our retreat home in Oklahoma was a joy.

George and I were able do the fun things like selecting the design and materials. Terri and John did the tough job of monitoring the construction. In fact, the whole project was a family affair. Doug even packed up his tools and flew to Oklahoma to lay the tile and help with the wood floors. We decorated the house in a multi-cultural theme with family donations and from garage sales. It was completed in time for the Floistads to use our kitchen while their kitchen was being remodeled. Also, it was a convenient guest house for them.

Nicole, age eight, was the only grandchild still in school. We were able to enjoy more of her growing up activities, even having her and her friends in our home. She had her own bedroom decorated in purple (her choice), but she preferred sleeping in her own bed. Our ever-extending dining room table was at home there; we had moved it from Florida. Putting extensions in that table was one of the best family things we ever did. I have beautiful, happy memories of the many, many family gatherings around that long, oval, welcoming, wooden table. The first big family dinner in that house was for BJ's birthday. We were even able to observe the first time he went solo skydiving. I remember saying, "I will do that for my 80th birthday." Everyone laughed.

(from back L) Bryan Oberle, John Floistad, George, Doug, and Jason Oberle,
BJ Danner, Terri Floistad, Marie Oberle and Nicole Floistad
(2010)

Chapter 12
A Test of Faith/A Family Affair

To live, is so startling it leaves little time for anything else.

— Emily Dickinson

This is the way I felt in 2009. I put this book on hold. *No one knows what tomorrow might bring!* It seems timely, and I feel it's God's plan, that I write this unexpected chapter while I'm feeling unbearable pain and heartache. I pray it will be good therapy.

George had completed his rehab following a second surgery on his left knee. Even though I thanked God that I was able to be George's caregiver, I needed a break. George's quality of life was less than we had hoped. Nevertheless, I scheduled a short vacation in Indianapolis with my sister Rhoda, her daughter Carla, and our daughter Terri. There is only nine months difference in Terri's and Carla's ages. We are all very close and often enjoy short vacations together.

While in Indianapolis, I talked with George frequently and sensed that he was concerned about the way he was feeling. In one phone conversation I noticed he didn't sound very good and I asked him how he was feeling. "I just have a little indigestion," he said. "I have an appointment to see a gastroenterologist." Concerned, I said, "I can come home any time. Carla suggests you try eating some beets. This is one of her homeopathic treatments. Let me know what the doctor has to say." He laughed and said, "I'll try anything." The next I heard, he was admitted to the hospital and scheduled to have his gallbladder removed the following day.

I returned home in time to be with him the day of surgery. George was discharged, but still had the same discomfort. He saw another gastroenterologist, who did a scope and biopsy. The biopsy was negative. The discomfort continued. George saw a third gastroenterologist, who was supposed to use more sophisticated equipment for the scope and biopsy. Even though this biopsy was also negative, the physician suspected pancreatic cancer. He said the cancer was likely in an area that wasn't observable with a scope.

George's typical reaction to physical symptoms was to be worried and stressed by the unknown. Once he had a diagnosis, he immediately would take action. I'm reminded of a quote he often used: "The game of life is like football. You have to tackle your problems, block your fears, and score your points when you get the opportunity." He quickly made plans for us to go to the Mayo Clinic in Jacksonville, Florida.

After George had a battery of tests and extensive lab work, we returned to Sarasota. While we waited to hear the results, we continued to make plans for our cruise. On the Saturday prior to our scheduled Sunday cruise departure, George was diagnosed with pancreatic cancer—between stages three and four. The whole world suddenly turned black. We were devastated! We held each other and wept convulsively.

As soon as we regained at least some control over our raw emotions, we both started researching the Internet to become better informed on pancreatic cancer. There it was..... *Pancreatic cancer is one of the most serious and fastest spreading types of cancer.* At the stage of George's cancer, *the likelihood of living more than six months is rare.* I saw such anguish in George's face—I thought, Lord, why are you doing this to the love of my life, to my soul mate? We prayed, "What do we do Lord"? The future looked bleak! This was truly a test of our faith.

Instead of taking our cruise, life was sending us in a new direction. We prayed for increased faith and God's guidance as we made life and death decisions. (I say "we" because after living together so many years, everything about our lives was tightly linked). I believe God heard our plea.

After reading that a surgical procedure, a pancreaticduodectomy, could be an option, George quickly affirmed he would not be the "norm" of six months or less to live. He was certainly not ready to throw in the towel! Hopefully, with God's help and the skills of a good surgeon, we could continue to work on our "bucket list" and enjoy our family. We canceled our cruise and started searching to determine if he was a candidate for this complicated procedure, referred to as "Whipple surgery" after an American surgeon who refined the technique back in 1940. Even though George had made up his mind to fight for his life, I wondered if after reading some of the research, he might change his mind. It stated that "...surgery separating conjoined twins is the only surgery more complex than the Whipple." It generally isn't an option for anyone his age. (George was 79 years old.) Together, we believed that with his tremendous drive to beat the cancer and his otherwise healthy and fit body, and with God's help, he would survive the ordeal.

Doors were starting to open that were in our favor. A friend who played golf with a nationally renowned pancreatic cancer specialist appealed to the specialist to guide George in the right direction. This compassionate doctor advised George to move quickly to get an appointment with the best Whipple surgeon he could find, a surgeon who performed the procedure daily, not just occasionally. George immediately started his research. These skillful surgeons were practicing in John Hopkins Hospital in Boston, Massachusetts, Andy Anderson Hospital in Houston, Texas, Moffett Hospital in Tampa, Florida, Indiana University Medical School in Indianapolis, Indiana and the Mayo Clinic in Minnesota. The final decision was based on which hospital could see him the quickest.

Through his brother David's contacts, George was given a consultation within the week at the Indiana University Cancer Center in Indianapolis. Dr. Keith Lilimoe, head of surgery, personally called George in Florida to discuss options. George was immediately impressed with this caring physician. Dr. Lilimoe had left his position at John Hopkins Hospital five years earlier to open and be the head of surgery at the new Indiana University Cancer Center. We felt God's presence in our lives. I believe he reveals His presence, compassion, and control in every storm of life. Not only was George getting one of the best Whipple surgeons in the US, he and I both had family in the Indianapolis area. We would have the moral support we needed. I would be embraced and welcome to stay with my sister, Rhoda, and brother-in-law, Dick Johnson.

With renewed optimism, we made plans for an extended trip to Indianapolis. From our perspective, the only downside to Indianapolis was the weather in January. Fortunately Rhoda met us at the Indianapolis airport with my fur-lined trench coat that she keeps for such occasions. It was so comforting having Rhoda and Dick's love and warm hospitality. We all talked about how quickly our lives can be changed, and acknowledged that sometimes it takes a major tragedy to learn what we're made of and find out what is truly important.

David met us at the hospital for the consultation. He and George were extremely close, as I shared earlier. David had been born when George was a sophomore in college. To David, George was both a big brother and a father figure after their parents died. Of the four Oberle siblings, just George and David were left.

We were all apprehensive as we waited for Dr. Lilimoe. His appearance, demeanor and sincerity helped to put us at ease. It was soon evident that they were all sports fans. With this in common, George was clearly where he should be. *Thank you God.*

George was diagnosed as a young 79-year old and indeed, a candidate for Whipple surgery. *Hurrah*! We were all encouraged about George's future, even though Dr. Lilimoe warned us not to underestimate the seriousness of the surgery. We shared what we believed to be good news to the family. Doug had traveled from Florida and Terri from Oklahoma to join us in our journey through the unknown. A huge snowstorm greeted them.

David, with his four-wheel drive, was able to transport everyone to their destinations. Since George was required to be at the hospital by 5 AM the day of surgery, he, Terri and I registered at the hotel adjacent to the hospital. The evening before surgery was highly emotional. Following warm hugs and words of encouragement from Rhoda and Dick, David arrived to take us to the hospital. George wanted some time to spend with David. The snowstorm was so severe, we stopped at the most convenient fast food restaurant. Both David and George ate large bowls of chili and downed a milkshake. Not my choice, but I understood it was comfort food and brought back good memories. We all need these at this time of uncertainty. After tearful embraces, Dave dropped us at the hotel and went to the airport to meet Doug's plane.

Doug stayed with David and Chris, and the next morning they all arrived before George's surgery, scheduled for 7 AM. As a result of David and Chris's contacts, and the caring staff, we were made comfortable in the waiting area with food, pillows, and blankets for the long anxious wait. Following a joint prayer, we continued with our individual prayers and concerns.

I prayed for wisdom, strength and increased faith to believe in God's plan for George. Even so, I felt positive about the success of the procedure in the hands of such a skilled and caring surgeon. Unknown was the convalescence and rehabilitation necessary to give George, in his remaining years, a tolerable quality of life for us to share. I kept repeating to myself, "I can do all things through Christ who strengthens me" (Phil.4:13) …He did this. Another prayer was not to have a migraine headache. My primary triggers are stress and noise. I wore ear plugs and tried to put myself in a meditative mood…not easy.

We were all in the state of thankfulness and joy when, after what seemed to be an eternity, Dr. Lilimoe arrived with great news, "I have removed the tumor and George's margins are negative. More biopsy results will be available tomorrow. Then we will know if the cancerous cells are in the lymph nodes". I felt compelled to give Dr. Lilimoe a hug and say, "Thank you; thank you for giving us more time together". Also, Dr. Lilimoe said, "I could see from George's internal organs that he lived a healthy lifestyle… they looked surprisingly young. Heavy smokers and drinkers are more likely to have pancreatic cancer". George had never smoked and rarely had a cocktail after his bout with hepatitis C in 1989.

George's time in the hospital (over two weeks!) was a nightmare for all of us. Family was with him 24 hours of the day, mostly me. Both Doug and Terri relieved me until they had to return to their home responsibilities. Our Indianapolis family also filled in. When he was in intensive care, I only had a straight chair to use, but otherwise, I had a cot in his room. He was in and out of intensive care with atrial fibrillation and other complications. Much of this George did not later remember, but I remember vividly. It is usually against hospital protocol for visitors to sit on the patient's bed… not this time. To calm him, the nurses allowed me to lie with him in bed and cuddle him like a baby. He was frightened, shaking, disoriented, anxious, and in severe pain. Some of this was the result of adverse reactions to his medication. I don't think I would ever have the courage to go through this procedure that George had endured. I prayed that George could put his anxieties in God's hands.

Any peace we momentarily felt was totally shattered with a new pathology report of cancer in the lymph nodes. This news was overwhelming. George was going through such pain to give us a little more time together, and now that time was shrinking without mercy. We could only pray that the cancer wouldn't spread rapidly, and speculate on what part of George's body would be invaded next by this insidious disease. As I cuddled George, I said, "You are an exceptional human being!" He was too disillusioned to react. God only knows how much I loved this man! Even in his pain and discomfort, he was appreciative of everything anyone did for him.

George's progress was slow and he was easily discouraged. He seemed to take three steps forward and two steps backward. Family and friends wanted to help, but all any of us could do was pray.

Jason, our grandson, made a surprise trip from Boston in attempt to cheer him up. I felt sorry for Jason; he expected a cheerful smile and hello, however, George was too ill to respond in a positive way. Most of his internal organs had to learn to function differently. He could not even retain sips of water on his tenth day post-surgery. He had constant IVs, a stomach tube and heart monitors.

Even when George was confused, we had daily devotions and several times a day I read to him from the book of Psalms—such soothing content. Each day I wrote in my diary. When I left the room for only a few minutes, I returned to find him more anxious. Following devotions one morning, we were able to talk about feelings. He shared that much of his anxiety was a result of being in the hospital environment. His painful memories of being hospitalized in Germany wouldn't leave his mind. I assured him that together we would continue to fight this insidious cancer a day at a time.

We talked about how when life is so severely threatened, it prods us into stepping back and really appreciating the value of life and we take from it what we can. I said, "Honey, I hope you know that you are an exceptional human being." He answered, "I will continue to celebrate the three F's … faith, family and friends." Gradually, he was able to eat a little oatmeal, milk, and ice cream. Little by little, his bodily functions started to work, the tubes were removed… and we were all a little more optimistic, again.

Finally, on February 12, 2009 (15 days after surgery), Dr. Lilimoe said three beautiful words: "You are released!" Medication had not been able to lower George's blood pressure, but after hearing those words, his blood pressure returned to normal. Again, Rhoda and Dick welcomed us into their lovely home during an additional monitoring period before George was allowed to return to Florida. Here, we were both pampered. Even with all George had gone through, he didn't forget my traditional dozen of mixed roses for Valentine's day—even if he did have to have Dick responsible for making it happen. Such a dear man.

During George's last checkup in Indianapolis, Dr. Lilimoe said, "The Whipple surgery put you 80% ahead of pancreatic cancer victims without the surgery. You will need to follow up with chemotherapy, and/or radiation. I am optimistic that you and Marie will have a few more years together." It was difficult to read George's expression. He said later, "I was praying that I wouldn't require further therapy." In expressing our appreciation to Dr. Lilimoe, George offered, "If you ever get to Florida, we have a guest room." The doctor said, "As a matter of fact, I have a professional meeting in Sarasota in two weeks. Cheryl and I will give you a call."

It was during this period that I wrote the following in my diary: *I feel a miracle has taken place—God and our doctors… have given us more time together. Thank you Lord! Much good has come out of this dreadfully painful, challenging time. Our relationship has strengthened as has our faith. We will learn to 'live in the now' celebrating each day and praying that God will continue to walk with us and open our eyes to his plans for our future. It is awesome to recognize His hand in putting us in the right place at the right time so that our needs—especially George's—were met by the best doctor, and that he was in the right place for healing. How wonderfully blessed we are to have had caring family nearby who reached out in love and support in so many ways. Dave met all of our flights into Indianapolis during a snowstorm. He and Chris were constantly at the hospital as were Rhoda and Dick. Our children left their families and their work to be with us. It is so comforting to have family and friends praying for George's healing.*

Home in Florida, at last, we were grateful our lives were so full of love and welcoming. Almost immediately, we were off to see the oncologist. He recommended chemotherapy—no radiation. I expect anyone reading this has experienced friends or loved ones struggling through this process. It is like a roller coaster ride… ups and downs, highs and lows. We never knew from one day to the next what to expect. My life became very, very contracted. All I focused on was maintaining my strength, faith and optimism, for George's sake.

When George had the energy, we enjoyed short outings. It was a major joy for him when he could spend time on the beach. I started the outing by pushing him in a wheelchair from our condo across the street to the beach. He would walk down the boardwalk by holding on to the railings to Siesta Key's gorgeous, white sandy beach. We then both stretched out on lounge chairs, feeling the warm spring sun embrace our bodies (temperatures in the mid-70s to low 80s), and listened to the therapeutic, rhythmic sounds of the gentle surf. Our son, and sometimes Amy, his significant other, were there to greet George. Periodically, he was able to see friends that he knew on the beach. Even though this helped his morale, it was exhausting for him. We were able to gradually increase the length of our outings, and it wasn't long before he was strong enough to do without the wheelchair. This was a giant confidence boost.

Sure enough, Dr. Lilimoe called from the Ritz Carlton and made arrangements to visit us. George was able to walk down to the beach and we enjoyed a captivating sunset with his amazing surgeon and his charming wife. (This reminded us of our doctor friend who came from Oklahoma to Germany for a house call when George had hepatitis.)

Much of my time was spent making sure my guy had the right nutrition. The chemo was damaging his entire body, even his taste buds. He had lost a lot of weight. My heart ached with love and sympathy when I looked at this skeleton of the robust man I married. It was common for me to spend hours in meal preparation, only to have it rejected. I would prepare something else. George was always appreciative and praised me lavishly. He said, "I will try to eat anything to get well … yes, I'll even drink wheat grass juice. I want to beat this." I understood good nutrition was critical to his recovery. I was using a cookbook, *Beating Cancer With Nutrition,* recommended by the Cancer Treatment Center of America (CTCA). Everything was made from scratch using organic foods. Clearly, my efforts were a labor of love.

And God gave me the strength that I needed. Over and over, we gave thanks for the therapeutic environment we lived in—we could see the beach from every room, even while lying in bed.

Following George's prescribed chemotherapy, we flew to Oklahoma. He received treatment at the CTCA to help repair the chemo damage throughout his body. We found this facility welcoming, caring, and patient-centered. It was located only 15 minutes from our Tulsa home. Most patients stay on the property. George was happier living in our home and taking advantage of their wide range of offerings from a multitude of disciplines including nutrition, psychological counseling, acupuncture, physical fitness, spiritual counseling, recreational activities and the typical medical and surgical facilities. Families are also welcome to many of these services. It made my life easier by taking most of our meals at CTCA. Also, we had the love and support of our daughter and family, living next door. Terri would often go with us to doctor appointments. They were preparing all of us for the inevitable… only God knew when. We all delighted in seeing George's energy, sense of humor, and love for life gradually returning. We would all like to forget about the year 2009.

In August, 2010, we were back to working on our bucket list—a trip out west to include Mount Rushmore, and the Crazy Horse Memorial. Awesome! The sculptures were carved out of mostly granite and quartz. The ground sparkled with quartz crystals. From there we went on a spiritual journey through the Grand Teton National Park and Yellowstone National Parks—both spectacular. Old Faithful was erupting as we arrived at the Yellowstone Hotel. We saw animals in their natural habitat, a double rainbow reflecting on the mountains, sparkling waterfalls, and rivers to wade.

Sadly, it was necessary to shorten this trip…George's symptoms returned. I could not hold back the tears when George reached for my hand and said, "We are indeed blessed to finally share these majestic experiences." I responded with a warm embrace. This trip had been planned for an earlier time, but was postponed for one of George's orthopedic surgeries. There was a great deal of walking to get the maximum benefits from the trip.

The night we returned home, it was necessary to call 911. In the emergency room, George was losing so much blood rectally—I fainted and was placed on a gurney beside him. (I mentioned earlier that I left nursing because I take on everyone's pain to the point of passing out.) We called our son, and Doug and Amy were there in no time to take charge. We were so blessed to have him living across the street. Since I had promised George that he would spend his final minutes… take his last breath, in our home… calling 911 was a common occurrence. My training as a nurse has been beneficial but not sufficient in so many critical situations in which we recently found ourselves. There was so much I didn't understand about George's condition and what we had to expect. They told us very little about what caused George to lose so much blood. They just said, "Take life a day at a time." We tried to do this, but felt insecure in doing so.

Again, he gradually recovered his strength. A must-do for George was taking our granddaughter, Nicole, to Washington, DC, to help her enjoy and appreciate our capital. This was in June 2011. We had enjoyed a fun vacation with our three grandsons, Bryan, Jason and BJ during an earlier time, before Nicole was born. Fortunately, Terri and John accompanied Nicole. They took over when I needed to take George back to the hotel. He was remarkable. We all treasure that trip.

Our plans were to visit dear friends, Tom and Anne Hall, in Pennsylvania on our way home. Again, the trip was cut short. I called ahead and our internist made an appointment with a pulmonologist at a hospital to be examined. Again, our world was rocked—George's cancer had returned, now in his lungs. Even though we knew this would occur, we were all devastated! Yes, this was truly a family affair. The family rallied and we did what needed to be done. The Sarasota pulmonologist examined George and provided his recommendations. George elected to have a second opinion at CTCA in Tulsa.

Even during his illness, he wanted our life to be as normal and enjoyable as possible. He even insisted we continue with our traditional July 4th party while he was still in the hospital. We would leave for Tulsa following this event. Fortunately, he was released the morning of July 4. What a trooper! I don't think the 40 guests realized what a harrowing, roller coaster of a life we were leading. A few days later we left for Oklahoma. We would share our home with John's parents from Minnesota. They were there to be with John for his open heart surgery, repair of the left ventricle valve. Thankfully, John's surgery was successful! He was only 46 years old and otherwise in good health.

George was miserable! Fluid was accumulating in his lungs, causing labored breathing and coughing. A pleuroscope was performed, with the pleural area drained into a drainage tube left in place. Biopsies showed the cancer was widespread and a tumor had developed in the lower right lobe of his lungs. His quality of life was increasingly reduced. We continued to have family dinners at home and at the CTCA, attend church, and count our blessings. Elevated temperatures, arterial fibrillation ("a-fib") and difficult breathing kept George in and out of the hospital.

On August 1, our 57th wedding anniversary, George was home. Terri brought us flowers and a movie to watch. We watched the movie, snuggled in our bed. I found myself thinking about the chemistry between us—the power George continued to have over me…his touch, his smell, his walk, his laugh, his strength, and his gentleness. *What will it be like not being able to be in the arms of the man I have loved for a lifetime? Too soon, he will leave me. This will likely be our last anniversary celebration on Earth.* I wondered what George was thinking. As if reading my mind, George said, "We are lucky to be celebrating 57 beautiful years together." We held each other and wept, and finally fell asleep.

We were all pleased that Nicole had back-to-back summer camps during this traumatic family time. George didn't want Nicole (age 13) to remember him in his present condition. After all, he was her fun loving, active "Pop O."

George's team of doctors recommended more chemotherapy (Gemzar and Abroxane). Bad experience… elevated temperatures, nausea and extreme weakness. We all prayed for increased faith and peace of mind, not knowing what to expect next. We soon knew—Pericarditis (swelling and irritation of the pericardium, the thin sac–like membrane surrounding the heart). Heavy-hitting antibiotics, oxygen, and intravenous fluids (IVs) were started.

August 7, Doug and Amy arrived. All the family came to the CTCA for dinner and spent a little time with George. I rarely left his side. Even though he was very weak, they let him return home to be with family. That evening we were all in the living room trying to make things as normal as possible. There was tension, but mostly love, even some joking. We were all touched when Doug got out of his chair, walked over to Amy, got down on his knees and proposed. Doug said, "I wanted this to be a family affair." It seemed to give us all new energy as they talked of wedding plans. This was Amy's first visit to Oklahoma, but they spent more time doing chores for us than exploring the Tulsa area. Saturday, August 13, was a day to treasure. We enjoyed a champagne engagement brunch prior to Doug and Amy's return to Florida. It went without saying that this was an incredible gift to George to be part of an important and happy family event.

On Sunday we wanted to go to BJ's church. He was to report on his mission trip to Bolivia. Also, we wanted to congratulate him and Jane Aldred on their engagement. Very soon, BJ would be leaving that church in Skiatook for one in Tulsa. I admired, and still admire, BJ's strong faith. He and I often discuss this. I remember asking him, "How do you see God?"

"Like a mist of fog that engulfs us. We can't touch Him but He is there," BJ told me. This I could relate to my feelings of being surrounded with love and a feeling of peace. I have felt this in times of silence—in church, walking on the beach, or sitting in my little corner of my patio.

We did not get to church that Sunday as George was too weak, depressed, and feeling the need to return to our beautiful Florida home where he wanted to spend the rest of his life.

We needed to make this happen. George wasn't strong enough to fly commercially as there were no direct flights. Even Angel flights would have stops. The only option was to charter a private jet. Jason, our grandson living in Boston had helpful contacts. He volunteered to do research and report. Rhoda and Dick drove from Indianapolis to see George and help us prepare for our return to Florida. As we organized our leave, we were saying to each other, out of earshot of George, "How sad that this will be George's last time in this Oklahoma home where we all enjoyed great family times."

I begin to wonder if he would live long enough to make the trip back to Florida. His temperature became very high and he had to go back to the hospital for emergency care. The origin of his infection was E-coli bacteria. I was given wound care education. He had a rash all over his body, due to a reaction to the strong antibiotics. Chemotherapy was put on hold. We had a flight scheduled in two days. The day prior to our leaving Oklahoma, Rhoda and Dick, Terri and John, and the newly engaged BJ and Jane had lunch with us at CTCA.

Thankfully, Jason's arranged private jet transported George, Terri and me to Sarasota in 2 ½ hours (a commercial flight would have been 11 hours). How blessed we were to have Terri's help. She and I took turns getting George to his many doctor appointments. He was diagnosed with subcutaneous emphysema (air under his skin). As this condition increased, he looked like the lead actor in the movie, *The Nutty Professor*.

My warrior was back in the hospital again. Terri stayed with her dad while I interviewed health care agencies for a nurse to be with George from 10:30 PM to 6:30 AM. Our family would cover the remaining hours. George so disliked hospitals, and during the recession, healthcare facilities were reducing staff. I didn't want George to want for anything in my power to give him. As I said, I had promised him he would be home, at the end.

Our children were wonderfully loving and supportive as were other family members and our friends. This was such a despairing, overwhelming time for George and for people who loved him. It didn't seem fair that he was forced to endure so many traumatic obstacles in his long journey. A wonderful, caring friend, Jerry Dennis, who had performed our 50th renewing of our wedding vows, came to the hospital daily to read and pray with George. I usually left the room so George could ask questions or share any spiritual concerns with Dennis. Our church was without a full-time pastor; it was a blessing to have Dennis in our life at this unsettling time.

Doug and Amy set an earlier wedding date—Doug wanted his father and best friend to be Best Man. Terri, a CPA, reviewed our Trust, Long-Term Care insurance and other financial papers before returning to Oklahoma to catch up on responsibilities there. She planned to return for the wedding. My dear sister Rhoda came from Indianapolis to provide her capable loving assistance.

Friends were encouraging us to explore our local hospice services. Admittedly, we needed help…we were treading unfamiliar territory. It broke my heart to observe George when he heard this recommendation. With tears in his eyes, he said, "Am I there?" His belief was that patients have less than six months to live when they consider hospice services. As I held his hand, I said, "Honey, this is not true in Florida. I understand some patients have received hospice services for five years or more. Would it be okay if both of us learn more about Florida hospice? We can have a nurse from Hospice to visit with us, or Shane Dresen (a Hospice Chaplain and part-time pastor at our church). He thought about it for a minute and then said, "You may call Shane." This was a positive step.

Shane assured George he could continue with his present doctors and their treatments and also take advantage of the hospice resources. This was one of the wisest decisions George made and a blessing to me. I was provided with procedures to follow, and assured they could be contacted 24 hours a day. This was comforting to both of us. Shane interacted with George in a positive, understanding and compassionate way, and he too was available to George 24 hours a day. To my surprise, George continued chemo treatments which were just making him weak and too nauseous to eat. He still held onto hope—hope that he could defeat this cancer; George was as tough-minded as any gladiator in the ring.

George's brother, David, visited from Indianapolis… a timely visit. This gave George a boost emotionally and they discussed plans for George's memorial service in Indianapolis. This was painful for everyone. George had already started a folder of what he wanted in his "Celebration of Life." We would celebrate the positive difference George had made in the many lives he touched in his 44 years in education, as well as the enormous impact he had on family and friends. His life needed to be celebrated—big time. Even as he faced the task of planning his own memorial, it was clear this didn't mean he was giving up his fight for life. His choice was to have both a celebration in Sarasota and in Indianapolis. A headstone was already in place, near other family members, in Memorial Park… it would be shared with David and Chris. (Dave and Chris would have a traditional burial, and George and I elected to be cremated and ashes placed in an urn.)

I was so thankful for Rhoda being with us. We both loved and appreciated her. She helped me select something to wear for Doug's wedding. I showed it to George before taking it to be altered. He said, as we hugged, "I'm so afraid I won't be here for Doug's wedding". This completely broke my heart. He looked so thin and fragile, not like the jock I had married 57 years before. We cried and held each other for a long time. I finally said, "Let us pray that you will. I truly believe you will be the proudest Best Man ever". We continued to snuggle close, each having our own memories. Family and friends were helping us have as pleasant life as possible. There was joy and optimism… and there was deeply agonizing pain.

Rhoda and Amy worked with the caterers and details on the wedding. Amy had experience as a caterer and knew what she wanted. George and I went about our daily routine. I prayed that God would give George the strength he needed to participate in the wedding. I was impressed with Amy's skill in orchestrating such a beautiful, tasteful, catered wedding and reception in our condo. I was helping George dress and prepare as if he was going into the arena for competition. He was mustering up all the strength possible… he wouldn't let Doug down. He looked mischievous (I love that look), and asked, "Do I dare play a joke?" I hugged him and answered, "It wouldn't be you if you didn't."

We joined the group at 7 PM. The condo looked welcoming and beautiful. The lighting was romantic, and there was a magnificent violinist playing in the entry as guests arrived. Amy looked soft and lovely in a sleeveless, pale gray dress that had a shimmer like seashells and was enhanced with a silver metallic design around the scooped neckline. She carried a bouquet of elegant white roses. Doug and the other guys wore dark pants and light-colored sport shirts. I wore a long, two-piece, aqua blue silk dress. We all had red eyes due to this emotional event.

The ceremony was serious until George began his search for the ring. It wasn't long before Doug began to laugh. He knew his father… the tension in the room lessened. This was the most loving and emotional event I've ever attended! There were tears of joy and tears of sadness. I couldn't believe that George lasted until 10 PM. I think Doug wanted his dad to know that he would have a partner to share his grief. The guests included Terri, Bryan and Jason, Rhoda, and a few of Amy's family and friends.

Bryan, Doug, Amy, George, Marie and Jason Oberle (2011)

The immediate family stayed through Sunday and we attended church together. Doug and Terri made brunch while George and I rested. We were surprised when they announced that it was Grandparents Day. Jason and his significant other had compiled a scrapbook titled "Beautiful Life." Impressive! Jason had used my email list to request letters, notes, pictures and so forth from our friends. I'm continually amazed and touched at my thoughtful, creative, loving family.

I think what stood out most in the scrapbook was the love and respect Jason had for his grandpa. His grandpa had helped him get his first job after college with the Special Olympics. Also, George's surgeon from Indianapolis took a position at Massachusetts General Hospital in Boston and with George's recommendation, used Jason for his realtor. This had been a springboard for Jason in real estate.

Rhoda, Bryan and Jason left; Terri remained. We were concerned that Nicole needed her… not to worry, as John did amazingly well. He even shopped for a formal dress for Nicole's "photo shoot." Terri was still involved as they shared pictures via her telephone, enjoying the convenience of technology. She continued to handle all our business and insurance concerns so that I could be with George. Also, George was sharing with us what he thought should be included in his memorial services. She and Doug were sharing responsibilities—thankfully, they had taken charge. Lists were made for everyone before she returned to Oklahoma.

With all the fight George had left, he was continuing chemo. Major damage was occurring in his body. His blood sugar was high and he now required insulin. I adjusted his diet in relation to the insulin and learned to give his injections. *God, give me strength to keep up with George's needs. I'm so exhausted!* This routine, and being in and out of the hospital continued for several weeks as further complications occurred. An unbelievably caring pulmonologist made house calls. He taught me to drain George's lungs when his breathing became labored. I continued to take instructions from the dietitian and from Hospice. We celebrated George's 81st birthday. Doug brought in dinner from Bone Fish restaurant—George's favorite, shrimp fettuccine—and I made him his traditional birthday ice cream pie. For years, our family has preferred the black bottom ice cream pie instead of cake for birthdays. George chose cherry nut and chunky chocolate ice cream for his birthday pie. He ate very little, but was appreciative.

In the few weeks that remained, I rarely left George's side. When I left him, another family member was there, touching him and offering love and reassurance. We read the Bible, we prayed, and we relived the beautiful life that we had shared. We spent many evenings surrounding George in our king size bed, watching videos of happy events: His retirement roast, the last basketball game he officiated (and it was with our son), and our 50th wedding celebration.

On November 18, 2011, Doug said, "Mother, you look so tired. I will spend the night here and be responsible for Dad's medications." Rhoda was with us, as was Amy. George had made his last call to his family and others close to him. We had told him that he did not have to live in pain, that we would be okay, and would join him in eternity. I felt his struggle… not wanting to leave his family, but ready to go to his heavenly home. We can only go so far in understanding the pain and experience of another. I held George's hand and watched as he appeared to move in and out of my reality. I could tell by his eyes and the change in his touch that he was gradually moving from our bed and touch into the arms of our Heavenly Father.

I finally went to sleep with my arms around George. He was on my right side and Doug was on my left in our king size bed. I was awakened by Doug saying, "Mother, Dad has gone." Even though I thought I was prepared, I have never felt such emptiness and despair!

Doug called hospice. They pronounced George's death at 4:05 AM September 19, 2011. Rhoda took me to her bed in the guest room and tried to comfort me. Doug and Amy took charge. I cried for hours for the loss of my soul mate, my wonderful lover, my best friend, the father of Doug and Terri, the grandfather of Bryan, Jason, BJ and Nicole. I couldn't imagine life going on without him!

Chapter 13
Grief… A Necessary Process

The life ahead is uncharted and uncertain, but it is to be lived, and through it, you are to grow.

—Doug Manning, *How to Walk Through Grief and Learn to Live Again*

George's memorial services were a gift of our family's love and a celebration of the full life George lived. His wishes—to have a celebration in Sarasota and one in Indianapolis, where he grew up—were carried out. The agenda was somewhat nontraditional. Since our church, Beneva Christian, no longer had the minister we knew, George had elected not to use one. Our family would conduct the services at Beneva. However, George became so fond of Chaplain Dresen (also a part-time pastor at Beneva), he was asked, and agreed, and became a significant part of the celebration.

We developed a four-page flyer summarizing George's life, including the pictures he selected. During his career, he creatively and successfully marketed himself, so it was only natural that this be continued for his life celebration. It was printed and distributed with the celebration agenda. (See Appendix C.) Chaplain Dresen, sitting with us around our breakfast bar and discussing George's memorial, surveyed the diversity of our art collection and asked, "Do you think we could display a few pieces of George's favorite artwork in the sanctuary? Few people know his love for art." Doug made this happen.

Doug opened the service, and other family members who felt they could emotionally participate were part of the celebration. At the end of the services, Chaplain Dresen ceremonially "passed the rod" to our son, and then our grandsons. The closing song was "Tenderly" (our special song since our dating days). In a spontaneous manner, Terri said to Doug, "Why don't you dance with mother?" Doug pulled me into his arms and we started dancing. In turn, so did our grandsons. "Our song" always brings warm feelings of being in George's arms. George had not planned this part…but I know he must've been touched; he loved to dance. As guests left the church, they were given colorful balloons to be released and lifted up with prayers, thoughts, or blessings for George and others who have gone before. A celebration reception followed at another location.

It was important to me that, even though our loss was painful, we viewed George's death as a natural part of God's plan. My previous experiences with death had been so disturbing and negative—my mother's suicide, a friend's botched abortion, and so forth. In a sense, George gave me a gift in the loving and peaceful way he went to his eternal home. Despite the aching in my heart, and fear and terror of living without him, somehow, I was able to see beauty in what we had been through together. I no longer have a fear of death. This is the way, I prayed, the rest of the family felt.

Following the celebration, we returned to our condo and shared loving "Pop O" stories. George was famous for his large selection of colorful sweaters. Remembering this, Nicole asked, "Can we see Pop O's sweaters?" We each modeled one of George's sweaters for a picture. Of course, they didn't fit everyone, but if they did, they were encouraged to take them home. We all enjoyed a Chinese take-out dinner. Jason's idea to start a "Drs. George and Marie Oberle Scholarship" was implemented. With tears in my eyes, I said, "I am so proud of each one of you and I know George is as well. You have assumed so many of the responsibilities for George's celebration and your love has given me the strength to do what I needed to do. We will do it again in Indianapolis in a few days."

Doug had worked with David on the details for our celebration in Indianapolis. Not all of our immediate family was at both celebrations. Of course, both Doug and Terri were there. The service was similar to the one in Sarasota—it was a family affair, with Dave's pastor giving the closing prayer. At the Cemetery, Dick Johnson's burial team performed an impressive military salute. Part of George's ashes were placed in an urn on the headstone, which was already in place. David and Chris opened their lovely home for a large reception and Oberle reunion. I was in such a fog. I remember very little of what occurred. I did laugh when my sister reported a conversation she overheard at church the next day. The lady said, "Can you believe I attended a memorial service yesterday where they ended the service with the song 'Tenderly,' and they danced?" Also, many guests were heard to say that it was certainly a unique service. It was designed by George, and he was unique!

I don't remember much about the next few weeks. I was haunted by our life together. It spooled across my mind like thread from a sewing machine to a garment. Vivid... Heartbreaking...Passionate... Comical... Beautiful... Frustrating... I welcomed those memory-filled times. They usually came at night in that space between memory and sleep. I ached for his touch, his smell, his laugh, all of it. My grieving was all-consuming. My first thought each morning was, "When will it end?" Then, I remember Chaplain Dresen saying, "It never goes away entirely."

With the help of Doug and Amy, I got through Thanksgiving and Christmas. I was pleased to have Rhoda and Dick with me for part of the Christmas holiday. They divided their time between me and Dick's son and family who live nearby. On December 23, 2011, I had a major "eye-opener." I was invited and attended the Unique Dinner Group—all women, mostly widows. That was the first time I realized, "I am one." No longer would I be invited to couples' functions. This was a distressing thought, but too true.

Into the year, 2012, I kept myself busy. I buried my pain and prayed that God would give me the strength and clarity of mind to take care of the necessary business. Terri came to my rescue and left a list for me to follow up on. It was so painful, removing him from my life on paper. He would never be removed from my heart. I followed up with all of the Boards that George had served on and shared his files. Still, I felt driven to complete our "bucket list." Doug and Terri were understanding when I showed them our unfinished list:

Remodel the guest room and bath.

Replace the kitchen and hallway tile with cork.

Take the family on a cruise (this was planned for our 60th wedding anniversary).

We agreed that working on this list was a good plan to keep my mind occupied and help me move on. I didn't trust my judgment, but knew that Terri and Doug had my back. They wouldn't let me make a mistake.

Since Terri and John often used our guest room, her ideas were especially valuable. Even Jason showed up to help with some of the decisions, and I soon found I agreed with his decorating tastes. Doug used his remodeling experience to guide me in the right direction. He decided what he would do and contracted the remainder of the project. It was a joint decision that I go to Oklahoma during the remodeling. By early April, most of the decisions were made, and I would be in Oklahoma in time for my dear niece, Carla, and I to celebrate our joint birthdays on April 7—my 80th and her 54th.

George and I had made this trip every spring and fall since building our Oklahoma home in 2006. We typically stayed four to six weeks to enjoy our Tulsa family. It was important to us to attend as many of Nicole's school activities as possible. She was the youngest of our grandchildren, and our only granddaughter.

Terri met me at the Tulsa airport. She knew it would be difficult for me to be in our Oklahoma home without George, and it was. I declined her offer for her or Nicole spend the night with me. It seemed important for me to be alone with my bittersweet memories. That night, I dreamed of George and even felt him sitting near me on the bed. It was comforting to feel that he was still looking after me.

While taking a walk in the neighborhood, I encountered a neighbor who offered his condolences. He had been widowed 14 years. Talking with him was quite comforting. He told me he was a grief recovery volunteer. He loaned me his handbook and encouraged me to attend the group sessions—another of God's plans.

I enjoyed my 80th birthday more than I had expected. My family, under Terri's leadership, made it special. Rhoda and Dick were there from Indiana and the other family members lived in Oklahoma. I always thought it was special that I had both a niece and nephew born on my birthday. My grandson, BJ, and I made plans to fulfill my desire to go skydiving for my 80th. We each had a trainer and were on the same airplane. Terri fortified me with a Bloody Mary. Actually, she was more nervous than I was. I was not frightened, and my only concern was the jolt on landing. My trainer said, "Just put your feet on top of mine, and there will not be a jolt." This worked, and I landed on his soft body. What I didn't expect was the strong force of wind when the door was opened for my descent. It took my breath away. Aw, the view was heavenly. The experience was exhilarating!

Marie and grandson, BJ, celebrate her 80th birthday, skydiving

Marie soars over Oklahoma   A perfectly good plane to jump out of

The birthday celebration over, I settled in and began working on my goals (I don't know how to function without goals): to enjoy family whenever possible, work through the *Grief Recovery* handbook by John W. James and Russell Friedman, and focus on improving my health.

Even though the handbook on grief recommended that I work with a partner, I elected to work through the exercises on my own. The first concept did indeed hit home: "Unresolved grief is cumulative." I had lived most of my life with feelings of guilt, thinking that my sisters and I must have caused Mother to commit suicide. I know I wasn't as helpful and appreciative as I should have been. Finally, after I retired, I worked with a psychologist. I remember him saying, "The dictionary definition of guilt implies intent to harm." I said, "There is no way that I would ever want to harm my wonderful mother. I loved her with all my heart. Perhaps I didn't tell her often enough how grateful I was that she took us out of an unhappy, painful environment. Being with her was my childhood dream." My dream came true, but it lasted less than two years.

There wasn't any question that I handled my mother's death incorrectly. It wasn't until I sought help that I was able to be honest in my interactions with others inquiring about the cause of my mother's death. I had been so ashamed that I had lied and said she had a heart attack. George and I both tried to justify my cover-up and intellectualize my feelings, saying, as educated as I was, I should be able to handle my loss without telling the world. In that era, there was generally embarrassment in seeking psychological help. Now, I acknowledge how toxic cover-up can be.

George's death was entirely different. There was laughter and love mixed with the painful challenges that accompany pancreatic cancer. I felt honored, and there was a joy in being a caregiver to my "knight." He was so appreciative to be cared for in our home. The family and I did the best we knew how to give him a desirable quality of life, given the limitations of his cancer.

My next assignment in *Grief Recovery* was "discovering and completing what is unfinished for us in our relationship." At the end of George's long suffering, I felt a sense of relief that my soul mate's suffering was over. At the same time, I realize that I could no longer see or touch him. This was very painful! A goal in recovery is to claim your circumstances, instead of your circumstances claiming you. It was so important to me to be an example for my family, and to deal with loss directly. Loss is inevitable. I was learning that seeking help to recover from my grief was more about what was right with me, not what was wrong. I do not feel any stigma attached to receiving grief counseling. Yet, I found myself keeping busy, burying my pain, and seeking distractions, trying not to feel my loss. Old ways are hard to change.

Even though each of my family members had a different and unique relationship with George and would be handling their loss in ways that they felt was right for them, they were totally there for me. Most friends appeared to have more problems with knowing what to say and how to give support. This I understood. I did need help understanding my lack of energy, inability to concentrate, memory loss and listlessness. Obviously, I needed help in my grief recovery. Over and over the book reinforced that I need to be more in tune with my grief and let it happen. Should I not own my grief, it would accumulate, and the symptoms would remain.

I conscientiously worked through the exercises, often sharing them with Terri. The last exercise was writing a letter to George. I wrote the letter five months following his death. I was to make note of any unfinished emotional communication that we didn't have prior to his death and make any apologies that were lacking. The following is my letter of April 19, 2012:

My Darling,

I miss you—your touch, your smell, your laugh—just everything about you! Five months ago today, you left to be with your heavenly Father. My heart aches terribly! I'm crying as I write this. You're still my first thought in the morning and my last thought at night. I even think of you during the night and feel you sitting on our bed. I believe you and God are looking over me. Our wonderful children, other family members and friends are there for me. I'm so very blessed with all that you and I worked for and accomplished together. You left me in comfortable circumstances. Thank you, my "Hero" and love of my life. I thank God for giving us so many beautiful years together.

In this exercise, I am to make note of unfinished emotional communication that we didn't have prior to your death. As I review our life together and our many evenings of sharing during your long illness, we covered almost everything. I'm to make any apologies to you that I haven't done. We have laughed over all the mistakes we both made as inexperienced partners. Nevertheless, George, I apologize for anything I said or did that may have hurt you. There were times when I needed to "vent" and you would walk away because you couldn't handle confrontation. I'm sorry for "blowing my cool."

We often talked about my major challenges during our marriage. Some were the result of my feelings of insecurity and lack of self-confidence. Honey, I forgive you for not being more perceptive in our early married life in the four areas that troubled me:

Our failure to communicate effectively

Your "flirting—on the make" style of friendliness with women

Being left alone so many nights while you were officiating

Perception that I didn't come first in your life

We finally resolved all are areas of concern. I learned that sharing my frustrations in writing worked better than face-to-face. How grateful and blessed I feel to have had 57 years to work through perceived problems and grow into "soul mates." It is so very difficult to think of me without you. We had almost become one in the same. I still sign cards and the like "George and Marie."

I want you to know, Honey, how proud I was of you as a husband, father and human being. You accomplished an incredible amount of "good work" in the field of education. Your work and networking took you away from your family much of the time during the "breadwinning" years. You were wise to encourage me to be a "stay at home mother," and you supported me in the way that our children were raised. You were totally there for your family after retiring.

Darling, I want you to know that I was honored to be able, with the help of our family, to carry out your wishes to remain in our home until the end. It was beautiful and sad... even that last night with Doug and me sharing the bed with you. Honey, there was so much that was good in God's plan for the end of your life on this earth. It was truly a "family affair," just as God intended it to be. I believe you are helping to prepare a place for me. I am ready any time God chooses to take me. Until then, I will conscientiously make an effort to move from grieving to a more productive life. I shall continue to treasure my memories as I work at finding what God wants me to do with the rest of my life, until I join you.

Before leaving Oklahoma, I had worked through the entire handbook. Yet, I realized that I was not even near the end of my grieving. What occurred when I returned to my Sarasota condo, so filled with memories of George, was that I became totally engulfed in pain and despair. It was as if the efforts and progress I had made in my grieving process while in Oklahoma did not exist. My body hurt all over. I was in a mental fog, and could barely get out of bed. I didn't want to live. My family and I wondered, "What caused such a drastic physical change?" Looking back, it seems that upon my return home is when the absoluteness—the finality—really set in.

Fortunately, a very dear caregiver that had been such a blessing to George was able to be with me. She, as well as family and friends, drove me to doctor's appointments and therapy sessions. My wise internist didn't appear surprised. "You have totally neglected your own health," he said. "I have observed your commitment and the energy required to be the 24-hour caregiver to George. Now you need to focus on your own health. I will give you prescriptions for depression and to help you sleep. There's such a close connection between our mind and body. It's difficult to know what to treat first." I said, "I'll try anything." He continued, "First, you need to accept the messages your body is sending. Stop pushing yourself, and let people take care of you."

Doug and Amy recommended I see her chiropractor. I tried several sessions, but I couldn't tolerate being touched. Hospice Chaplain Shane Dresen, now a dear friend, helped me understand how unique grief can be depending on individual circumstances. Shane said, "The process will not be easy. But you will eventually, in your own time, walk through your grief and learn to live again. Life will never be the same, but you will find a new normal." He encouraged me to try the Hospice Grief Support Group. I did, but it didn't work for me. I left each session with a migraine headache because of my tendency to take on every person's pain. Individual counseling was more helpful. My counselor said, "You are where you need to be, at the 'scene of the crime.' Now, give into your grief." She helped me to see that being so goal-directed—focusing on completing our bucket list, and forcing myself to get on with my life—wasn't working. It didn't work following mother's death and it wasn't working for George's. I focused on a new prayer: "God, don't take my grief away...just help me walk through it."

My life turned into one of just existing with excruciating mental and physical pain. I was open to any and all suggestions for treatment. I was having physical therapy at home, moving about the condo with a walker, and seeing a pain management specialist, as well as a neurosurgery and spine specialist.

I was diagnosed with spondylolisthesis (overlapping of lumbar vertebrae) and spinal stenosis. The physicians varied in their treatment recommendations. I was told that, even with surgery, they couldn't assure me that I would be pain-free, and they said my bones were too soft to try inserting a metal rod into the spine and fusion, a procedure sometimes employed. I elected to be conservative in my treatment. I tried nontraditional "physical medicine" that used a number of machines, including one to stretch the spine. I was using a Tens Unit to control pain, and wearing a back brace and knee braces. After several weeks, my pain had even increased. An MRI showed my spine to be in worse condition than when I started the therapy. (Now, I am supposing why this facility wasn't approved by my insurance.)

Starting to go to a physical therapy office where they focused on exercises to strengthen my core muscles (to support my spine) seemed to actually help. Thankfully, I was making progress toward being stronger emotionally and physically. At this point, I experienced a dramatic breakthrough in my grieving process. I shared it with our Beneva Church family. I was in church on Sunday, November 18, 2012, one day before the first anniversary of George's death. Our new minister was inducted and a church dinner was to follow. My dish was prepared and in the car. Without warning, I started to cry and couldn't stop. Caring friends left their seats to sit and embrace me. They saw me to my car and took my dish into the kitchen. I cried all day.

That night I relived the last few days when George had been with us. It was bittersweet. I felt joy in his being at peace, and sadness in my losing my soul mate. I struggled through the next day. At sunset, Doug and I met with friends to honor George. I read the following letter, while others spoke what was in their hearts:

Honey,

It has been a year since you joined your heavenly father. I still miss you terribly, but I am determined to do something worthwhile with the rest of my life, but still hold you in my heart. I remember our beautiful life. As you likely know, I'm reading this standing on the Sandpiper landing that you and Doug built for this purpose. Doug, Joe and Barbara are with me. Terri, Rhoda and Carla and Amy have called and are holding you in their hearts. I'm visualizing you at peace with loved ones—Mom and Dad, and Jackie and Jerry Oberle. I will always love you! So long, my darling, until we meet again, to never again be separated. I know where I will end up, but I don't know the path God has planned for me.

Then I experienced a week of deep depression that I couldn't control. It was Thanksgiving week, and Doug, Amy, Bryan and Jason were very attentive and loving. Jason had to return to Boston, but Bryan accompanied me to church. It was the first Sunday of Advent. Beneva is such a friendly church; as I got out of the car holding Bryan's arm, members greeted me with warm embraces…I felt loved. The pastor's sermon was on "Hope." The change in my demeanor was dramatic! I felt hopeful for the first time since George left me. My spirits continued to improve week by week, as I experienced sermons on Love, Peace and Joy. Our family joined me for Joy, the last of the series on "God's gifts to us"—another one of God's plans.

Each of us picked up on "Joy" as our theme for our Christmas week together. It was emphasized in uniquely individual ways. For example, Bryan's beautiful Christmas greeting was on joy. There was such joy and laughter in sharing gifts. It gave me tremendous joy that Jason committed to adding $1,000 a year for five years to the Drs. George and Marie Oberle endowment at OSU. He said, "Grandpa O, this is your finder's fee for the house your doctor purchased from me." We were all joyful as we planned a July 2013 family cruise, the last item on our bucket list. The final example: Nicole left me a touching art piece with her clever drawings, saying, "JOY" and "I love you, Nana."

"I will not leave you comfortless: I will come to you." John 14: 18

Though feeling a little better, I was seeing my grief counselor periodically. She encouraged me to continue expressing my feelings to George by letter. This I did.

Another letter, following Christmas 2012:

My Darling,

I receive comfort by believing you are all-knowing about my life and that of our family. This was a Christmas I dreaded but found ways to feel you with us. As we gathered on Christmas morning, enjoying our traditional "pull- apart" cinnamon rolls and getting ready to open gifts…the kitchen door open by itself. In unison, we said, "Pop O has joined us." We wanted to believe you were with us. Another example: our bedroom fan periodically comes on without anyone touching the controls. I tell everyone, "George wants my attention." As I write this on New Year's Day, 2013, I feel you with me. My New Year's resolutions are to wake up every morning looking for joy wherever I can find it, and to start back on my book. Do they make New Year's resolutions in heaven? I know that 2013 will be a better year, emotionally and physically. Your love continues to give me strength. So long for now, my love.

A bright spot of joy in 2012, at BJ and Jane's wedding: John and Terri Floistad, BJ and Jane Danner, Marie and Doug Oberle, "Groomsperson" Nicole Floistad, Amy Oberle

I felt optimism at the start of the new year, and I had some goals to meet. Doug was making our cruise arrangements. I pulled out my book chapters and explored some options. My mind was in less of a fog, but I didn't feel mentally up to par. I expected to have the book completed by my 80th birthday, with George's support, but God had other plans. First, I needed a professional to look at what I had written and make recommendations. Chaplain Shane was also writing a book. He became one of my strongest supporters and recommended his editor. I emailed my draft of the five completed chapters to his editor, Barbara Dee, and asked for input. Her feedback was positive in nature. I would try to move forward on the book.

With the help of the family, I made another big decision: to rent our home in Oklahoma. I had not been there for a year and a half, because traveling was a physical challenge for me. I did make the trip, removing our personal items and renting our home furnished. Terri and John took over full responsibility for the management. It was another step to accepting and simplifying my new life.

Ready for the zip line in Jamaica, family cruise (2013)

Grandmother with all her grandchildren, family cruise (2013)

I'm increasingly convinced that nothing happens by luck or accident. *Little Emily, as hard as it sometimes is to understand, God has his plan for our lives.* I saw his hand at work in my life that week of our family cruise, the trip that George and I had planned for our 60th wedding celebration. I so wanted the cruise while I was mobile enough to enjoy it with our family. One never knows what another year will bring.

The following is the letter I sent to my family upon returning home:

My wonderful family,

The cruise—such a positive experience for me! When I left home, I had mixed feelings about the trip. I was looking forward to spending time with each of you. Yet, I had fear of being a "wet blanket," as I was continuing to live in the past. As I recall, this only occurred once. regarding the family picture. I was reluctant to have one taken without George. Terri, as she often does, pointed out another point of view. She said, "You are living in your memories, and we are making memories." It is so important for each of you to be honest with me. I want to know where you are in the reality of your lives.

While driving to church this morning, my mind was filled with thoughts of our family experiences. The first person I encountered at church was Chaplain Shane. He said, "How are you?" My response was, "Great! Being with my family was amazing!" He said, "I can see a difference in your face. Would you like to share with our church family?" When Chaplain Shane asked if there were celebrations, I surprised myself and shared a bit of my experiences on the cruise. I felt that God and my family were at work in my life. Through your love, encouragement, respect and energy for life, I was literally jarred out of my feeling of complacency and quiet suffering. I've been praying for direction in my life, to find out who I am without George. Being with the family has jump started my efforts. I want to thank each of you and remind you how very special you are! I pray for your happiness! Love and hugs, Grandmother O and Nana

Following our family cruise, Bryan began researching paintings by George's favorite artist, Leonardo Nierman. He surprised me with a lithograph by Nierman, titled, "The Moment of Ignition." It is powerful! On awakening, my mind went to that painting. I felt that ignition… burst of feeling… and better understood the meaning of the painting. Art, books and music are beginning to be important to me again. I am finding great pleasure in Mark Nepo's recently released book of poems, *Reduced to Joy*. Mark Nepo encourages us to "lean into life and hold nothing back." Ultimately, he encourages us to "live wholeheartedly, so we can inhabit the gifts we are born with and find the language of our own wisdom."

Beneva Christian church, my home church since moving to Florida in 1997, has been trying to find its "new normal," following situation after situation which almost led to its demise. It is far from the large, active, family-centered church it was when George and I placed our membership there. We were active in the efforts to keep God's work alive at Beneva as various factions in the church divided the unity we felt. During George's illness, the congregation voted to welcome another church to take over Beneva. The membership was so low, we didn't have the resources to keep it going. While we were spending time in Oklahoma at the CTCA, Beneva was gaining in life and energy, thanks to remarkable leadership. When I became active again, Beneva had a part-time pastor, was promoting a major giving campaign, and was looking for a full-time pastor. To make a long story short, Beneva conducted a successful campaign, hired a full-time pastor and retained the part-time pastor. The membership has increased, especially among young families, and Beneva has maintained its reputation as "the friendly church." I am finding great comfort in each and every Sunday mornings message. Attending Beneva is one of the highlights of my week along with being with Doug and Amy when they are available, attending P.E.O. "sisters" meetings, and enjoying dinners with friends.

I'm reminded of the similarity of Beneva coming to life again, just as I experienced being jolted out of my complacency, and I am looking forward (instead of living entirely in the past). Both Beneva and I are experiencing God at work. I look forward to seeing what God continues to reveal in his plans for Beneva and for me and my family. With God as my anchor, I will live a new chapter, but not in my book. I believe God will direct me in expanded ways to continue to give back.

"You are that which you are seeking." —St. Francis

Chapter 14

My Authentic Self

"I was born to be me, not a copy of you
be you parent or teacher or friend,
Be you husband or wife, I was given this life
and it's mine to create until the end.
I was born to be me. But I've learned in a lifetime
I never can make it alone.
Far too much of myself needs the giving of others,
    the parts I can't see until I'm shown."

—William Flinders

Little Emily, when I ask myself what I have learned in writing this book, I hardly know where to start…it's almost like I'm not the same person as when I began. It has turned out to be the path to a greater and deeper healing, both physical and mental, than I would have thought possible. It has been the process of taking all the separate bits and pieces of my history—my thoughts, dreams, feelings, regrets, and hope—to weave myself toward wholeness. I had become skillful at hiding my struggles, protecting myself from shame, judgment, criticism and blame by seeking safety in pretending and perfection. I am surprised by how I have changed; I have more compassion and forgiveness for myself and others, have a greater sense of freedom, and more respect for what I have accomplished in my life. The process has been painful, tedious, grueling, discouraging, encouraging, enlightening, laborious and liberating.

You have also helped me accomplish my primary goal; to reclaim my life… yes, all of it. With your help, I've been able to find my authentic self that had been harbored in the folds of my mind. I found the courage to write the truth, to take a chance. What would happen if I told my story? I have experienced layers of transformation in reconciling my childhood and building a bridge from the past to the present. It seems to me the more we have lived through, the more difficulty we have in surfacing. My self-discovery is giving me a stronger belief in myself and greater contentment.

I have missed the love and support of my soul mate. Also, I had to work around my health problems (there were days I was in too much pain to write a word), including my increasing short-term memory challenges. I'm at a place where I want to let go of the struggle process and let change continue, while being patient toward all that is unsolved in my heart; I am, still, a work in progress.

Finally I understand what my professor once told me in my Group Process Course; he helped me see that my learning style was to "study the rivers without getting wet." I could ponder the group without ever feeling it; this was unfair to the group and to myself. Now I'm willing to enter the stream and be part of the action; even if it makes me more vulnerable and open to criticism. Sigmund Freud wrote, "...out of one's vulnerability comes strength."

I was my own worst enemy, dogged by lack of confidence, guilt, shame, insecurity, and a desire for perfection in all areas of my life. Throughout this book, I've been asking myself—*why did you punish yourself for a lifetime? ...you had very little control over your childhood.* I think guilt ate into my soul far more than any of the other feelings. It was guilt that destroyed my confidence, damaged many relationships, and left me stuck in the past.

But I put on a façade of confidence. Brene Brown's book, *I Thought it was Just Me,* helped me to see that I was not alone with my issues. "We all experience shame—it is a universal emotion. Shame is a silent epidemic…it is the opposite of joy." She further identifies shame with fear, blame and disconnection. To acquire shame resistance, we need to "respond empathetically to others, and also be receivers of empathy." She states in doing this, "we expand our courage, compassion and connection…we become more authentic—natural, sincere, spontaneous, open and genuine."

I wonder if one can ever make a difference without believing in themselves. At last, I do! I can identify with Robert Frost; toward the end of his life he was asked if he had hopes for the future and he said, "Yes, and even for the past—we are all products of our past."

Little Emily, with your help I have come a long way in my grueling journey toward authenticity; more than eight decades of living—the good, the bad and ugly. I don't think I had a plan for my life; just the basics in Maslow's hierarchy of needs in which to continue building. Most of all, I wanted to be loved and feel a sense of belonging. I've lived so many roles: a farm hand as a child, a troubled adolescent, employed as a "soda jerk" before I was old enough for a Social Security card, a struggling college student, a nurse who never quite fit in, a wife in a truly loving marriage, a woman blessed twice with the beautiful gift of motherhood, and an achiever of advanced degrees. Later my roles included an unexpected career, retirement, savoring memories with my soul mate, and, finally, widowhood. Each life experience left an indelible mark on my soul as well as a layer of memory on my spirit.

Yes, little Emily, we have lived through a fantastically interesting era in all of history. I lost count of how many US presidents I've seen come and go. I have been through wars, depressions, recessions and inflation. I've experienced an era of incredible and rapid advances, from splitting logs to splitting the atom, from crystal sets to satellite television, from mustard plasters to heart transplants, and from washtubs, ice boxes, blackboards, and crude biplanes to microwave ovens, laptop computers, and space flights to the moon, Mars, and beyond.

In my early years, we were so isolated from the outside world that it was impossible to keep up or really be a part of our changing world. Winston Churchill recognized this in his book, *My Early Life.* "When I survey this world as a whole," he wrote, "I have drawn a picture of a vanished age—the character of society, the foundation of politics, the methods of war, the outlook of youth, the scale of values…have all changed."

Now, I feel that I am a part of Mr. Churchill's vanished age, as I read and listen to the news. In my search for joy and peace, I have periods during which I avoid the news—too frightening and negative: terrorist attacks, school shootings, child abuse, unemployment, high percent of homeless people, even families. Tonight, the local news reported that 44% of our families are just above poverty level; they can hardly make ends meet.

I have found throughout my life that being with young people (especially my grandchildren) and listening to their dreams is energizing. So much of that is even changing. The so-called millennials, aged 18 to 29, struggle with an unemployment rate of nearly 14% which approaches the level of that group in the Great Depression. Having been born during that time, I feel my life has come full circle in so many ways.

Parents and grandparents are at a loss in advising their frustrated, better educated, young adults. Most of the older generations would admit their job opportunities came from networking. But the greater opportunities for the millennials are in jobs unheard of in earlier generations, such as technology and space. The Great Depression damaged the self confidence of the young, and that seems to be what is happening now, according to the pollsters, sociologists and economists.

A bright, handsome young man I met at a friend's party (I will call him "Jack") shared his story as we talked of differences in generations and the issues they face. A college graduate, 24 years old, Dean's list and academic excellence award-winner, Jack was unemployed and living at home. He said, "I spend my mornings searching corporate websites for suitable job openings. When I find one, I e-mail off a resume and cover letter—four or five a week."

When I inquired how that was working, he said, "Over the past five months, only one job has materialized." Before I could ask how that was turning out, Jack added, "It only paid $40,000 a year. I didn't take the offer. It would have been a dead-end job. I'm holding out for corporate position that will draw on my college training and permit me to climb the corporate ladder."

I wasn't in a position to advise him… nor did he ask for advice. But I thought…*back in the 1930s, doctors worked as janitors*. Now, many hard-pressed millennials are falling back on their parents. In 2008, the first year of the recession, the percentage of population living in households in which at least two generations were present was 16%, according to the Pew Research Center. (The high point of 24.7% came in 1940, as the Great Depression ended, and the low point was 12%, in 1980.)

As I write this in 2014, the Bureau of Labor Statistics reports the unemployment rate nationally dropped to 5.9% in September. President Obama claims much of the credit. In spite of this, his approval rating (according to The Rasmussen Reports) shows that 21% strongly approve of President Obama's job performance, while 40% strongly disapprove. During the recent 2014 midterm election, the Republicans won enough seats to have control of the Senate. They already control the House of Representatives. Interpreters of the election felt strongly that results of the vote showed disapproval of the federal government in general, not so much approval of the Republican Party.

My book started with world events in the 1930s and will end with 2014. Note the following:

2011

US military formally ended mission in Iraq.

Terrorist bombing of Moscow airport; more than 30 died.

Osama bin Laden, leader of terrorists responsible for thousands of Americans being killed, was killed in Pakistan during an incredibly well-executed Navy Seal mission.

Earthquake scaling 8.9 caused tsunami and massive destruction in Japan.

2012

Gunmen assaults Connecticut elementary school; 27 dead.

North Korea launched a long-range rocket.

President Obama is elected to second term.

America's "Curiosity" rover landed on Mars; exploration showed evidence of a lake and stream system there billions of years earlier.

2013

Nelson Mandela died, age 95; worldwide mourning occurred for this Peace Prize winner.

Detroit filed for bankruptcy.

Huge, two-mile-wide tornado hit Oklahoma and killed over 50 people.

Scientists successfully cloned human stem cells.

Music in the 2000s was (for the most part) nondescript—no emergence of any new and unique styles. Two public opinion polls listed the 2000s as the least favored tune decade of the last 50 years. Convergence of different styles was one of the more defining features of the decade. MTV rated Usher Raymond as the most unstoppable force in popular music and Beyonce was named as the top female. Although my tastes in music were formulated long ago, I at least am familiar with, and enjoy limited selections of, styles of this new era: hip-hop, rappers, rock, pop rock, power pop, nu metal, liquid funk, UK funky, and artists like Taylor Swift, Carrie Underwood, Josh Groban, and Celine Dion. Electronic music (EDM) continues to be big; there is fusion between hip-hop and electric.

In the 1930s, I mentioned I was isolated from the outside world—no radio, phone, TV or newspapers. Today I find myself wanting to be isolated—needing to be—in search of joy and peace. I will mention some of the current concerns of the world which somehow find their way into my haven, as cocooned as I try to remain.

The threat of the Ebola virus is spreading worldwide. The containment of this deadly virus in some areas of Africa is, as of this writing, unsuccessful. This brings back the memories of the crippling polio virus in the early 1950s. On the onset there was no cure; people were fearful of touching others, being in groups, sending their children to school, or even being in the hospital. Just as the world celebrated Dr. Jonas Salk in 1953 for his discovery and development of the polio vaccine, the person(s) who discover the vaccine for Ebola will make their mark in history.

I sound optimistic about this because I have become used to the tremendous and rapid advances which are being made in the medical area. Genetic engineering is playing a huge part in reversing HIV. Research on stem cells for therapy engenders a great amount of attention. It's called regenerative medicine: Stem cells can be guided into becoming specific cells that can be used to regenerate and repair diseased or damaged tissue in people. It is being used with spinal cord injuries, Type I Diabetes, Parkinson's disease, Alzheimer's disease, heart disease, stroke, burns, cancer, and osteoarthritis. Research is wide open in this area.

The world has become so connected via the Internet and available technology that the world is our neighbor. The US has reason to be concerned, with terrorists attacking at home. Major examples which resulted in American deaths were the World Trade Center and the Boston Marathon. The talk of cyber weapons and nuclear weapons just blows my mind. The world breathed a sigh of relief when Osama bin Laden was killed by our Navy Seals, yet we are constantly being made aware through the media that we are far from safe. Currently, a well-funded, rapidly growing radical, Islamic group, ISIS, is a worldwide threat. Even some young Americans, disillusioned with their life here in the US, are trying to hook up with the ISIS group.

School shootings have intensified since the Columbine school shooting in 1999 (15 years ago) in Colorado. Researchers claim that 17 school shootings since that time have common traits—"Copy Cat Phenomenon." I'm shocked by so much violence shown on the movie screens, and TV for entertainment. Perhaps our youth have become so desensitized to violence it seems normal—and they look for greater and greater thrills. Adrenaline addiction seems to have joined other addictions (especially prescription drugs) on the rise. Many thrill-seekers have already paid a hundred thousand dollars or more for a trip to the edge of space for the feeling of weightlessness and return to the earth, even with two disasters within a week in private commercial space travel. Excitement and thrills are of course part of a normal life, when they are balanced with rational thinking and wise risk assessment. I admit to being in awe of the courage and skill of Nik Wallenda (our local Sarasota celebrity) in his daredevil high-wire acts. I have learned that experiences which have pushed me out of my comfort zone can be very empowering, such as skydiving, and writing this book.

As I mentioned earlier, I wake up each morning looking for joy and peace. My blissful surroundings make the goal easy if I block out unhappy and fear-slanted news broadcasts. None of us can stop change—we can only adapt. Each generation adapts to their new challenges; some more successfully than others. I find myself no longer wanting to adapt. World news seems to go from astonishing to ridiculous. The same day that I applauded the news of the European spacecraft landing on a comet, the broadcasters reported that the "bubble butt" is in vogue for women and is big business for the cosmetic surgeons. (Booty-enhanced panties are also available if you don't want to go through the pain and expense of surgery.)

The changes I have experienced in the roles of women throughout these eight decades are amazing and mostly gratifying. I have felt pulled in so many directions as I tried to be the best I **could** be in one role—then the world changed and roles evolved. We all evolve in relation to our interests, personal strengths, environment and opportunities. For this very reason, Terri reminded me that parents can't take all the blame or the credit for how their children turn out.

Women in America have come a long way from being considered a man's possession or second-class citizens, unable to vote or even take out a bank loan without a male signature. Women have struggled with family, community, and societal expectations… who should we be, what should we be, and how should we be? Now women are major players in all aspects of society, even space travel, the military, and football. The following are examples of the inroads women have made in breaking the glass ceiling, i.e., overcoming the invisible but hard barriers to gender equality.

> The US will likely have a woman on the 2016 presidential ballot.
>
> Following the November 2014 midterm election, there are one hundred women in the US Senate.
>
> Becky Hammon, is the first full-time NBA assistant coach of the San Antonio Spurs.
>
> Two 13-year-old girls were in the 2014 Little League World Series; one pitched a shutout with a 68-mph fastball and was reported as being the best player on the field.
>
> There are over 50 active-duty women serving as generals or admirals.
>
> Mary Barra became the American auto industries' first female CEO.
>
> Locally, four out of five City Commissioners are female.

I wonder if each of these successful females actualized the life they wanted—or if it just happened. Sometimes we are successful by actualizing our goals; other times we seem to just be in the right place at the right time.

Sociologists and others are pondering what this change is doing to the institution of marriage—change is difficult. Both women and men are struggling with new cultural perceptions of femininity and masculinity. *Modern Family* reports that in 40% of families with children, the mothers make more money than the fathers, yet men still are not doing an equal share of work at home. It is difficult to believe that I have lived through the time when it was rare for mothers to work out of the home and now, 74% of the mothers work full time. Equal pay for equal work remains top on the list of women's issues. For example, in *Under Armour,* the movie industry was recently called a patriarchal culture as actresses make about half the salary as actors. It seems that women are needed, and even given great jobs, but are not adequately compensated.

The life I celebrate was made possible by a village of people. I may not have felt that at the time, but I was protected and lead. I'm grateful to God, my Guardian Angel (I feel it is my mother), teachers, friends, and the little town of Richmond, Indiana. Yes, the little town that once held such painful memories for me—now I have only gratitude.

While struggling through my journey, I questioned how much of my "scarlet letter" was a fact, and how much was my imagination. I contacted the only Richmond friend, Becky Lester Wuertemberger, with whom I have remained in contact, and a more recent friend, Jane Wyatt, whom I met here in Sarasota but she attended both my junior high and high schools. She remembered "the Whittymore sisters" though I didn't remember her. I shared with Becky and Jane my perception of Richmond's reaction to mother's suicide, and the shame and guilt I had harbored all these years. I asked for their honest feedback, to the best of their recollection, about the community's attitude about my family after Mother's death. Their input was an incredible blessing—seven decades later. It was an eye-opener and made me wish that I had made an effort to reclaim my life decades earlier. (See Appendix A for copies of their letters.) The negative conversations I had overheard from classmates back then did not represent Richmond. *Little Emily, it would be so heartwarming to think that our story might possibly help someone else.*

My life wasn't an accident. We have a choice in the direction we go—why did I make the choices that I made? Among other purposes well-served, this book is a way of sharing my blessings and staying connected to my soul mate. I believe when God blesses us, He wants us to share.

George may have been my knight, but God is the hero in my life; He has been my silent partner. Whenever I felt myself struggling with my writing, I prayed and remembered the powerful feeling of being in the presence of a stronger power when He told me I was to write a book. I discovered that if I was patient and **expected** my issues to be resolved… they were. I found myself writing with gratitude and authenticity. For someone who didn't enjoy writing, and closely guarded my private life… this was a major reversal. When I struggled with opening up and exposing my past, little Emily was my crutch. I wasn't opening myself up to criticism; she would not judge.

The great Indian leader, Mahatma Gandhi, reminds us that "…prayer is not asking. It is a longing of the soul. It is a daily admission of one's weakness… and so it is better in prayer to have a heart without words than words without a heart."

People and resources kept showing up which seemed so perfect for what my book-writing needed at that moment, I have to believe God helped me through every step of the way. Discovering *A Walk on the Beach* was an unexpected treat; Joan Anderson wrote about her dear friend and author, Joan Erikson. Early in this book, I referred to Eric and Joan Erikson's "Seven Life Stages" that had an impact on my early life. I was to learn that in their later years, they identified stages eight and nine; these creative writers are continuing to influence my life. In stage eight, I found this of interest: "Wisdom and integrity are the strengths of old age, and one should be generative—pass on what you know. In sharing there is real delight. People in every stage depend on other people. Out of connectivity real growth happens. If there is no reciprocity, nothing ever works… we were meant to experience and then to share it." Reading this, I thought, *maybe I do have a responsibility to distribute my book. If God wants me to do this, He will give me the courage.*

Throughout the years, reading and learning from books has drastically changed my life— but not as much as writing one. As an exercise for myself, I'm compiling a list of things I have learned through this experience (see Appendix B). Writing has been immensely helpful through the grieving process and at other times. The following is my letter to George on the third anniversary of his being with our heavenly Father:

My Dearest,

Even today, when your name comes up in conversation or I'm reminded if you—which is often—I see your face, and my eyes grow hot, my vision blurs and my heart aches. But I end up smiling and feeling grateful for the 57 wonderful years we had together. You gave me the unconditional love I needed to go on with my life. I can understand the following writing by Nisargadatta Mahar…

" Wisdom tells me I am nothing,

Love tells me I am everything.

And between the two

My life flows."

You continue to be with me as I enjoy many of the things we did together like walking on the beach and enjoying the magic of the sunsets; I feel your presence, your touch, your smell…it will have to be enough until I join you. Even yesterday, returning from my walk on the beach, as I came up the Sandpiper Boardwalk, I looked up at our condo (the top left corner) and remembered the many times we enjoyed returning to our condo, spreading a sheet on the floor by the sliding doors, and enjoying the warm sun on our bodies, and our private, intimate times. I'm smiling. There can be no sorrow at the end of such a beautiful journey—just gratitude.

I wish I knew how much you know of what is going on in my life. I found your notebook of poems that you had planned to have bound for me…so touching. Thank you, my loving soul mate. I plan to follow up with your wishes. I feel compelled to include one I especially treasure in this letter:

To You

(April 14, 1976)

You came into my life
As one on a wave.
One of several
Who dared come this way.
The experience in sharing
In professional views
Made me aware
Of the uniqueness of you.
Watching and reading you
Day after Day
Brought me to know
the quality of you.

Longing and looking was soon not enough,
It was replaced by the action encounter
of face to face.
A touch of your arm
Made me aware
That this was more
Than a casual affair.
It scared me at first
To think I could be
Touched by someone
I hardly knew.
But yet the feeling
Was so strong that
I chanced the meeting…
Knowing full well that
It would involve both you and me.
And now that I know
We share the joy of completeness
You are a strength to me
As I hope I am for thee.
So look up and smile
For you know I'll be there
With you no matter
When or where.
G

Today, November 19, 2014, in addition to being the third anniversary of your being with our heavenly Father, is International Men's Day. "It is an occasion," its organizers say, "for men to celebrate their achievements to community, family, marriage, and child care, while highlighting the discrimination against them." I celebrate you; you were the best.

I was so in awe that someone as special as you chose me to be your lifetime mate. As I look back, I often abdicated my own worth, empowering you as a key to my joy. That wasn't fair to you—nor to me. I've asked myself, was it my lack of self-worth or the era in which we lived?

Honey, you and I were so wrong in thinking that I was wise enough to work through my troubled past; it was a wise decision when I finally sought professional help. I would have been easier to live with had I done it earlier. I'm grateful for our love and strong chemistry that carried us through troubling times.

You probably know that my goal is to have Outhouse to Penthouse completed by Christmas with copies for the family. I have discovered my courage within and opened up and revealed my past—warts and all. As with you, I'm proud of our family, now three generations, and feel that you and I made mistakes, but we also did something right—especially, giving unconditional love.

Completing my book makes me feel empowered, setting a course and finally accomplishing what I set out to do. I have reclaimed my life, all of it, and have found the process liberating. A French proverb reminds us that "gratitude is a heart's memory." You were my biggest supporter as I wrote the early chapters; I've missed your help terribly.

Honey, while missing you, I am gradually becoming curator of my own contentment...I'm becoming okay with living alone. I no longer fear the future, or death. You were a strong role model for all your family. We knew you didn't want to leave us—there was so much you still wanted to accomplish—but you were a warrior in keeping your faith and understanding that it is not our way, but God's way. Your family has tried to complete your bucket list. I have found unused course outlines for courses you had hoped to teach. You so enjoyed developing new courses and programs.

I will take this time in my life to celebrate my past blessings, and with God's help continue to walk through any unresolved pain, accept my new normal (living without you), and identify all in my life that brings me joy (our family) , and be open to new opportunities. Do you think I can do all this?

Our family will celebrate another beach Christmas next month. You will be with us in our hearts as we share bountiful memories of you as a husband, father and grandfather. We will visit the navel orange tree planted in your honor at the rear of our condo, and feel your love surrounding us. (I go there often and talk to you as I am doing in this letter.)

There will only be three days that the family will all be here at the same time. Of course, they will want to be on the beach during the day. One evening, we will enjoy Marina Jack's sunset dinner cruise (we did that two years ago and it was a hit). This may turn out to be a new tradition. Beneva Christian church is bringing back their candlelight Christmas Eve Cantata. Tanya is doing an amazing job with the music and Jon backs her up with the sound and technology involved. This tradition, we will keep. We're dropping our traditional buying of gifts for everyone; instead the adults drew names. Of course, I will keep your tradition of the money envelopes on the tree. Only Nicole will have a stocking—our only kid (she doesn't consider herself one). What would Christmas be like without children? I'm ready for great-grandchildren!

I know Christmas gifts were such a big deal in the Oberle family, but we will focus on other ways of celebrating the birth of Jesus and our family time together. Finally, I expect to feel less sadness and guilt over mother's suicide, 69 Christmases ago. But the scene of my beautiful young mother lying lifeless on the floor beside her bed will never leave me.

Bryan isn't sure about his plans for Christmas. If he isn't here in person he will also be with us in our hearts and spirit. I have wonderful memories shelling and watching the sunsets with Bryan (remember how we always timed the sunsets?) Even with his fine education, certifications, and all the things he has going for him, he continues to be challenged in available job opportunities. This breaks my heart.

Jason and his significant other, Nikki, were here in October, and had an opportunity to spend time with the Indianapolis Oberles. We all decided that she would be a fine addition to the Oberle family. She will not join us at Christmas as she will be with her family in the East. They are both enjoying Austin, Texas; Jason is selling his property in Boston. He and Nikki are continuing to be blessed in their career opportunities in Austin. Jason often mentions how much he appreciated the networking help you gave him early in his career.

Doug has picked up your traditions. He starts my Christmas decorating with a beautiful poinsettia and accompanies me to the Havener's Christmas dinner in early December. It is an enormous blessing having Doug and Amy living across the street. Doug checks on me daily and Amy makes delicious soups and shares. She has a very caring heart. Remember, their emotional wedding just two months before you left us? As I watched Doug putting up Christmas lights at the Sandpiper, I know we were both thinking about the hours the two of you worked together when he was growing up, and after you retired—these are precious memories.

Our Terri tells me she will be walking without a limp on the beach at Christmas. You can imagine how much it hurt me seeing her limp with every step. As you, she inherited your mother's arthritis and in the last four months, she has had both hips replaced and one knee. She completed her consulting contract and will not take on another until after the holidays. Terri had been putting the surgery off until Nicole could drive. Remember, you proudly gave Nicole her first driving lessons?

John and Nicole managed well during Terri's surgeries; of course I wanted to be there to help, as mothers do. John stayed in the room with Terri each time she was in the hospital, until he was able to take her home. That relieved my mind considerably. Most hospitals seem to be understaffed during this down economy. Remember Terri saying, "Dad, I'm not going to jog, officiate, and all the other athletic things you did to damage your joints. I don't want all your surgeries [both knees—one twice, right hip and right shoulder]." We never know.

This will likely be the last Christmas we will have a "kid" until we have great-grandchildren. Nicole, (16) has discovered boys. To her parents delight, she is narrowing down college options. Volleyball continues to be a passion as is debate/drama competitions. She has been highly successful—even went to Nationals as a freshman. After touring a local TV station and interviewing both a male and female TV anchor person and is excited about majoring in broadcast journalism. The family is investigating universities with high rankings in this area of study. Of course her mother and brother will not let her forget OSU as an option. Some universities eliminate the out-of-state tuition if the student makes at least a 30 on their SAT scores; Nicole just recently took her SATs and scored a 30.

Can you imagine…BJ, with his church youth group, broke their annual "Pumpkin Patch" record by selling $50,000 worth of pumpkins! Excitedly, he said, "$20,000 will be used for mission work." He and Jane are both excellent role models for the youth and teenagers they work with. They celebrated their second wedding anniversary here in July.

Dave, Chris, their children, and grandchildren vacationed here in October. It is a great joy to spend time with that family. Dave, now the Oberle patriarch, is talking about an Oberle reunion during the Indianapolis 500 race the end of May, 2015. He phones me often, and keeps me updated on the other Oberles.

Thinking of this and other activities I want to do, I have scheduled back surgery. The less invasive treatments have not been successful in reducing my pain. I'm told that even surgery to put a rod in my lumbar spine will not promise that I will be pain free—I will visualize being lucky. Now, I think I'm emotionally strong enough to handle the trauma of a four-hour surgery and hopefully have a better quality of life.

Until I join you, my darling, I will continue enjoying our family, work at simplifying and redefining my life. I'm ready to invite new friends into my life for companionship who enjoy art, theater, and have other common interests.

Honey, I will continue to talk to you in writing as well as in conversation at your tree or wherever I am. You are my love and my soul mate.

Forever yours,

Marie

I'm learning that in the end, you have to be dependent on God and yourself and know that with God's help, you can handle things. A Japanese scholar, Raicho Hiratsuka, had these suggestions: "Stretch yourself out of your grasp. Transcend yourself again and again. We all go alone at some point. Let your life happen.

Novelist Stephen King has said, "I write to find out what I think." To me he means that until we set an experience down on paper, until we ponder the perfect words to describe it, we can't fully appreciate or understand it. In threading related experiences together, we are able to see a pattern in the quilt of our existence. "It's about creating a legacy that doesn't have dollar signs in front of it," he adds. "It has far greater residual value for family and friends."

Tom Clancy has another viewpoint. "Success is a finished book, a stack of pages, each of which is filled with words. If you reach that point, you have won a victory over yourself, no less impressive than sailing single-handed around the world."

I can't buy such a grand compliment—but I wonder about the Erikson's ninth Life Stage: transcen*dance*. "Joan Erikson states that "transcendence is really about transcen*dance*." Dancing had been a huge part of her life. I feel she continued to dance, in her mind, after the death of her Eric; she exercised her body and mind, working around and through the limitations brought on by age. She continued, "I used to think that when you get old you plateaued, somehow. But I've come to see how we are all capable of learning new tricks. As long as we are alive, we must keep transforming ourselves. It's rather curious, but no matter how old we are, we're always troubled by inexperience…always searching for direction."

I feel like she's talking about me. She makes me feel normal in my stage of life when she says, "Old age demands that we garner and lean on all our previous experiences." Writing my story has given my life confirmation, and helped me clarify what I believe.

"Look, there isn't anything I do that I don't enjoy. If I do it, then I enjoy it. But playful activities are the best because they are goalless, the result is unknown, they are full of fantasy, imagination, and random discovery. What can beat that?" added Joan Erikson. I take from this a change I need to make in my life. I no longer need to be goal-oriented…but let the rest of my life just happen. Live in the moment. I like this concept. I can't remember when I wasn't working toward a goal—usually goals. However, I don't want to give up my routine of daily exercise for my physical body, stimulation for my mind, and a random act of kindness—to me that is a meaningful day.

I thought of Erikson's ninth stage as I took seriously pastor Ronn's sermon on forgiveness. There were two situations in my past where I felt so much pain and humiliation, and I couldn't let them go. In times when they came into my mind, those terrible feelings returned. I remember saying I felt like I was like being raped in public, by the "good old boys." Women can be bright, have high morals and strong integrity, yet when men want to deny their true actions when found wrong, they are frequently successful by putting the woman down and stomping on her with bullying words, totally discounting her credibility and leaving her feeling humiliated or "raped."

I used pastor Ronn's recommendation and documented, as accurately as I could, the humiliation and pain I couldn't forgive. I prayed to be able to let go of any grudges from my past. I acknowledged that my predators had likely already forgotten the incident. The next morning while working at my desk, I came across the letters that detailed my pain and humiliation, and it was clear to me (this was another turning point) that there wasn't any reason to mail the letters. I was able to see that for them to remember it might cause them unnecessary pain.

Little Emily, I feel we're at another turning point—a doorway—a time of greater courage and power, as we come to the end of this amazing therapeutic journey. I vow to fully inhabit the life I have been given and be ready for the life that follows. I celebrate you—you have helped me say: this is what I went through; this is who I am. I now believe the value that Outhouse to Penthouse brings as a healing tool far outweighs the embarrassment it might bring. I needed to allow the person I had been to have a voice. I needed to give the guilt, shame and sadness the window to openness—to heal—to move from role-playing to authenticity.

God has lifted the grudges from my hiding place and reminded me that I am a composite of the good, the bad and ugly; but most of all, I like the person I have become. I pray that I will no longer go back to how I was when I was so deeply humiliated. Could it be that I am able to experience trance*dance* instead of being weighed down by an abundance of hurtful issues in my life? My spirit feels so much freer as I let go of layers of pain in my past. I'm pleased I had the experience of battling the forces of the "good old boy network" but I had enough—and achieved success in spite of everything. Now I feel at peace with the fact that by my nature, I'm more comfortable with my soft intuitive side and being of service to others.

My life proves that God can use our trials to work good, in spite of the pain they bring (Romans 8: 28). That is just one more way He can be honored.

Little Emily, It would be a double gift if some of what I have said resonates with readers, and helps them see they are not alone in their feelings of guilt and shame. Perhaps they will see that they too could become better architects of their own life, and in doing so, find self-acceptance earlier in life than I did. It has taken me a lifetime to feel "I am okay."

I like what W. H. Murray has to say (in his journal during his trek over the Himalayas) about commitment and risk; "The moment one definitely commits oneself, then Providence moves too. All sorts of things occur to help one that never otherwise would have occurred. A whole stream of events issues from the decision, which no one could have dreamed would have come their way." *This was my experience when I found the courage to tell my story.*

Great freedom comes with aging. It's easier to be positive. I'm finding a new kinship with myself; feeling that my body, soul and spirit are all connected. I care less about what people think— I question myself less and feel I've earned the right to be wrong. I've become kinder, less critical of myself and others…and have become my own friend. Our Father in heaven knows the best path, out of all possible paths, to bring us to completion (Psalms 142:3).

A Rabbi asked his students, "How do you know the first moment of dawn has arrived?" After a long silence, one student pipes up, "When you can tell the difference between a sheep and a dog." The Rabbi shakes his head no. Another student offers, "When you can tell the difference between a fig tree and an olive tree." Again, the Rabbi shakes his head no. The Rabbi circles their silence and walks between them, "You know the first moment of dawn has arrived when you look into the eyes of another human being and see yourself."

I can now look into your penetrating eyes little Emily, with a heart of understanding, compassion and love. I know now, who I am, and I am you. Finally, Emily and Marie are one—my life puzzle is almost complete. My life, more than 80 years of climbing hills, strolling and enjoying the valleys, and exploring the bends and forks in the road will lead me one day to God's penthouse. There my life puzzle will be completed. Until then, I will continue to repeat my morning affirmation, as I gaze at His magnificent sunrises.

"Today is a day the Lord has made;

It will be a day of completion,

Miracle shall follow miracle and

Wonders shall never cease." (Author unknown)

Thank you for this day, dear Lord, and for giving me the life that has resulted in my finding love, faith, joy and the pathway to ultimate peace.

p.s. And thank you God for making this book happen.

APPENDIX A
FAMILY TREE

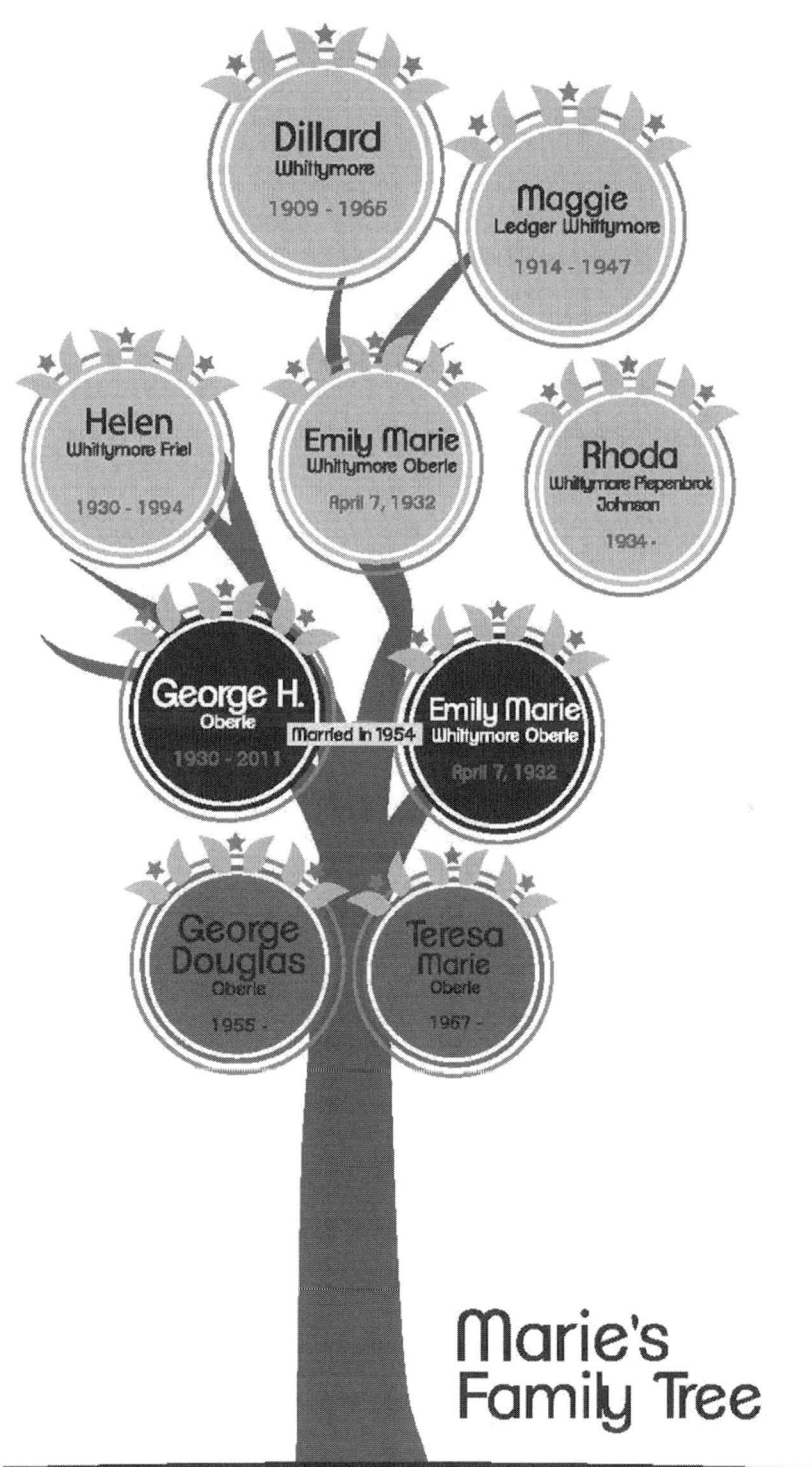

APPENDIX B
ODE TO DADDY "O"

By Teresa Marie Oberle Danner, aka Kitten

Life in the Oberle household was not as easy as you might think

Just keeping up with Dad's schedule could drive a person to drink.

He always had patience and handled things with such tact

Like the time I stalled the Mustang on the railroad track

Maybe pushing that car is what screwed up his back?

Or the time I ditched school; he kind of took it personally

I'm sure they heard him yell all the way to Missouri.

He was always looking for the "get rich quick" scheme

I think he learned a lot, but didn't earn a thing.

He says the best investments have been his kids and his wife

How about giving us all your money and you sit back and enjoy life?

This man is a builder, even without plans

You can tell that just by looking at his hands.

Any time I needed help, you know where I would go?

Straight to Mother, 'cause she handles the dough.

This man has a lot of talents, but he does have a fault or two

Like shooting up the flower bed when he saw a snake slither thru.

Or many a time he put a shovel into the ground

And disconnected the telephone of everyone around.

Another failure he's felt, no grandson named after him yet

However is now willing to settle for a granddaughter named Georgette.

He's dealt with baseball, football and basketball

I do believe he's done a little of it all.

But now I think the pride he takes is really in his lawn

He fertilizes and waters so you know what happens when he's gone.

It has to get attention as soon as he can get to it

Just think he could hire it done,

And get a chance to sit.

This man is very stubborn, as Mother and I can testify

We've worked many years, but we still don't see eye to eye.

There was a time he became as cold as ice

Like when we asked him to use something other than Old Spice.

Or to let his hair grow just a little for the shade

It's been thirty years, see the progress we've made?

This man is also a car buff from his earlier years

With the Indianapolis 500, and all of the cheers.

Now he has a Cadillac, and drives around in style.

I'm sorry to say it only gets one gallon per mile.

This man is such a good grandpa, he really loves his grandkids,

Bryan, Jason and BJ; you can tell they are all his.

My BJ was almost born at an OSU football game

But Mother said she had to do more shopping before he came.

Kathy is our only lasting outlaw, and she has hung in there with us

If she hadn't married Doug, you would have heard me cuss.

I grew up with two fathers, and Kathy took one away

I'll be grateful to Kathy til my dying day.

I call this man my daddy; you know I have just the one

Unless Mother didn't tell me that she went out and had some fun.

He has supported me all these years, and felt my misery

Isn't it time you found a single rich man and got rid of me?

Others call him Ref, Teacher, Grandpa, Husband and Dr. O

He's constantly in motion, his initials even spell "GO"

This man has taken his family from living in a dorm to living on a hill

But living is his life, I can never see him sit still.

Even as he retires, he is ready to take on more

Someone better call Miami and let them know what they're in for.

This man has had a lot of friends, and I've been introduced to a few

They have had pink hair, or disabilities, and even a tattoo.

But all of those friends that he has shared with Doug and me

Have seemed to become a part of our close knit family.

I know I was invited to be a roaster

But now I would like to become a toaster.

May you leave OSU with fond memories of the friends you'll keep

Forget the budget cuts and not be able to make ends meet.

Remember the streakers and the outdoor pool

And that being an Okie doesn't mean you're a fool.

I love you Daddy!!!

June 12, 1993

APPENDIX C
GEORGE'S MEMORIAL SERVICE

177

To present a broader, more accurate picture of this fun loving, caring, creative guy I met at Earlham College, I solicited input from family, friends, and colleagues. With their help, I will attempt to share with you **the many lives George has touched.**

Dr. Walter Cooper, Distinguished Service Professor, Univ. of Southern Mississippi, writes, "One of the first things that comes to mind about George, is how he valued you and family. By virtue of this as a core value that drives everything else George stands for, he developed the vast wealth of an endless network of friends and colleagues, which could be described as his 'extended family'. He was always ready and willing to help me, encourage me, and remind me of my infinite worth whether it in personal or professional endeavors." My thinking is that George attributes his devotion to his family as a legacy from his parents.

Yes, George and I are blessed with a close family consisting of two wonderful children: a son Doug (Amy), a daughter Terri (John), and four precious grandchildren: Bryan, Jason (Marcy), B.J., Nicole, and Brother David (Chris). Deceased are his parents: Margaret Crutchfield Oberle and George H. Oberle, sister Jackie Dorrell and brother Jerry.

George's Professional Experiences included: teaching, coaching, and educational administration in 12 different institutions, dozens of professional and honorary societies, leadership activities at the state, district, national and international levels.

George's professional related activities included: officiating basketball in 11 different conferences, officiating football in 4 conferences, research, publications, script writing, participant for radio and TV, conducting workshops, as well as speaking and consulting throughout the U.S.

Business and community leadership is important to mention. He developed 3 family related businesses, served on numerous community boards, coached Babe Ruth baseball, helped establish the Marian, Indiana Boys Club. In Sarasota he helped to establish the Sarasota Area Sports Commission, provided leadership at Beneva Christian Church, served on the Board of Directors for Siesta Key Association, Siesta Key Condominium Association, and the Anchorage Condominium Association. He left a positive impact on every community in which we lived.

Yes, George touched thousands of lives in his 44 years in a career he loved. His teaching, and educational experiences were at all levels of education, but most of his career was at the college or University levels. He was characterized as a "true developer" in his field. Dr. Merle Rousey, Dept. Chair, Earlham College from 1949-1958, writes, "It was my good fortune to have George as a professional student and an outstanding athlete with outstanding leadership

ability. He motivated others to contribute to significant program innovations. Later, he became my colleague, and preformed as an excellent coach and further proved professional excellence with his successes at Indiana State, Chicago State, Oklahoma State, and Barry Universities."

As an early developer of "Wellness facilities and programs" in the U.S., George has provided significant consultation for a variety of settings (both educational and business).

Students have used his teaching and administrative styles, to become leaders in their respective fields. He has mentored hundreds of graduate students that are now teaching throughout the world. They continue to call on him for advice and job recommendations. He continues to touch lives through his students.

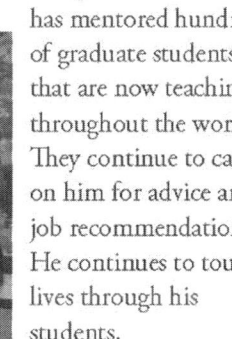

Professionally, George has been recognized for every teaching and administrative position he has held. In 2001, Indiana University, where George received his Doctorate, recognized his accomplishments by honoring him with the John Enright Distinguished Alumni Service Award. In 2002, Earlham College recognized him with its Outstanding Alumni Award. The American Alliance for Health, Physical Education, Recreation and Dance (a professional membership of 24,000) recognized George as one of the 12 most significant leaders in its growth, progress, and enhancement. His writings, research, tapes, and TV programs continue to touch lives.

In the area of sports, George was an All-State athlete while at Earlham College and a Hoosier College Baseball Coach of the year. Earlham also recognized George by his inclusion into Earlham's Athletic Hall of Fame.

For George, officiating basketball and football, was an enjoyable avocation. He was widely known for basketball officiating in the Big 10 and Big 8 conferences, as well as at the International level.

Two major highlights in George's officiating career were being selected as one of two Americans to officiate in the University World Games in Bucharest, Romania in 1981 and the **last** game of his career, with our son, Doug.

George was a strong advocate of the disabled. He worked in Indiana's first Special Olympic Games, which continues to this day. In 1987, he was appointed by President Reagan, and later reappointed by President George Bush to the National Council on Disability. He helped write and bring into law the American's with Disability Act.

Thomas Songster, Senior Vice President, Special Olympics International writes, "In George's work with Special Olympics and specifically in helping develop Unified Sports, his creative and professional style set the standard to make this program successful. The program now reaches more than 100,000 athletes around the world. I am sending these well deserved accolades from Turkey, where George's hand has reached students in more than 12 different universities." The Unified Sports Program is truly unique in that it combines the skills of the Special Needs Athlete with people without disabilities.

Our 2nd oldest grandson, Jason wrote, "Growing up I knew he was a great man, but never knew **how many lives he touched**, and how much he has accomplished. It is a great pleasure to have such a man as both a Grandpa, and a role model. I look up to him in many ways, and always find myself staring at the wall of plaques in his office thinking about the **many lives he has touched.** When Grandpa told me that one of his graduate students was a professor in my college, I made it a priority to talk to her about him. She smiled from ear to ear, and told me the positive impact he had on her life."

George Oberle: Husband, father, grandfather, educator, veteran, loyal friend and my husband and soul mate. He fulfilled each of these roles with strong faith, integrity, love and honor. Let us celebrate his **beautiful life** as he enters a new kind of life with his Creator.

Lovingly,

Marie Oberle

APPENDIX D
MARIE'S GEMS OF WISDOM

Wisdom I Acknowledged on My Journey to Discovering My Authentic Self:

Change begins when you practice ordinary courage.
Our imperfections are what connect us to one another.
We are more responsible for shaping our own lives than anyone else.
Everything is possible, and everything, even this day, is unknown until you live it.
We drain ourselves of inner fortitude by asking others to map our way.
To see a rainbow, you have to put up with a little rain.
Instead of living in the shadows of yesterday, walk in the light of today and the hope of tomorrow.
You remain young, only as long as you continue to improve yourself.
I believe that those that truly love us will never knowingly ask us to be other than who we are.
If marriage doesn't have the right chemistry, something is going to blow up.
Long term relationships ebb and flow—they require time to be separate and time for reconnection.
Strength is derived by working through our challenges or adversities with faith in God and in our self.
I believe when God blesses us, he wants us to share.
It is a waste of time to dwell on what your parents did to you; instead you should ask what you can do for yourself.
The day is to be experienced, not understood.
The only way to know what awaits us is to live it.
Your past doesn't have to predict the future.
It's okay to express your needs and have those needs met.
Life shrinks or expands in proportion to one's courage.
Optimism, like the happiness habit, can be learned.
I believe growth is the labor of a lifetime.
The most significant decision I can make on a day-to-day basis is my choice of attitude.
Life is 10% what happens to us, and 90% how we respond to it.
First, you make a habit—then, your habit makes you.
Genuine happiness can only be realized once we commit to making it a personal priority.
Learning to live in the present moment is part of the path of joy.
Inadvertently, we may become authors of our own misfortune with self-fulfilling prophecy.
It's never too late to have a happy childhood—but the second one is up to you and no one else.

© Marie Oberle, December, 2014

APPENDIX E
LETTERS FROM RICHMOND

Letter for Marie's book – Becky Lester Wuertemgerger

Dear Marie,

I want to answer your letter. I have read several sources that point out additional problems that survivors of loved ones who commit suicide must deal with—often on intense, and ongoing basis. These problems are included in numerous studies and papers. And actually, they are things that you mentioned in your letter. They are:

<u>Shame</u> –"lying about the cause of her death".

<u>Guilt</u> – couldn't prevent it, or somehow made problems unbearable, so "she couldn't go on with life."

<u>Why</u>? Obsessed with the question repeatedly; ongoing.

<u>Complicated grief</u> – Prolonged mourning, intense sadness, anger, and yearning, often for years— "Having spent so much time of my life trying to forget."

It would seem you are very familiar with the list. I think you can lay to rest any concerns you may have about your perceptions of the Whittymore girls. I have only heard <u>very</u> positive things about the three of you. In fact, I think you were probably the most respected and admired of the young women at Richmond Senior High School. To support my opinion, let me remind you of some of the laurels bestowed upon the three of you—remember, these were all honors <u>*voted*</u> on by your schoolmates:

Helen, you, and Rhoda were all Y – Teen group leaders. You and Rhoda were on the activities board. You were President of the Red Cross. Rhoda was Prom Queen and you were the Queen of Hearts. Again, all elected positions.

I don't know that we can ever forget the difficult or tragic parts of our lives. They are all chapters of our history. But they are finished chapters, and we do not change them. I think we can only include them in "The Table of Contents" and, as you say, "look upon them with more compassion and forgiveness."

You said, "I'm in search of joy, and finally peace." I suspect that you had a great many more friends in Richmond that you ever realized. I imagine that both "joy" and "peace" are somewhat intermittent, but I do think there is something present in every day to enjoy, and some days are absolutely delightful.

I'm so glad you wrote me. I hope you will keep me updated on the journey.

Becky Lester Wuertemgerger (4-25-2014)

Letter for Marie's book – Jane Schwemberger Wyatt

Dear Marie,

What I would like to share with your memoir readers is this:

When I was Growth Chairman at [Sarasota, FL] Beneva Christian Church, I often called visitors I had not met. I will never forget a call I made in 1998 to George and Marie Oberle. I told Marie that the only time I'd heard the name Oberle was in my hometown, Richmond, Indiana. She said George and she graduated from Earlham College. The Oberles I knew were not these Oberles.

Our conversation continued. To my amazement, I found that Marie and I had attended the same junior high school, Hibbard. I asked her maiden name… when she said Whittymore, I exclaimed, "Oh Marie! I used to watch you in assembly and want to be as pretty and special as you!" She must have been amazed…and amused.

That was the beginning of a close friendship. One evening in a restaurant, Marie looked across at me as the guys were deep into what happened in a game. She said, "You don't remember, do you?" Her eyes were bright with tears. She told me about her mother. I had a vague memory of it, but the three outstanding sisters had erased it until then. All I had remembered was how we all admired and loved them.

I finally began to convince her that the Whittymore girls were Richmond's pride and joy, and how thrilled I am to have her for my friend and mentor.

I truly believe God put us together and I am so thankful for this forever bond.

Jane Schwemberger Wyatt (5-19-14)

Little Emily, our journey continues…together.

Made in the USA
San Bernardino, CA
03 February 2015